Age Rage and

Stories of the Senescent Subject in Twentieth-Century French Writing

To Ed and Nette in
fond remembrance of our
time together in San Fran
... and congratulations on
becoming the 80th "library"!

Oliver.

FAUX TITRE

283

Etudes de langue et littérature françaises
publiées sous la direction de

Keith Busby, M.J. Freeman,
Sjef Houppermans et Paul Pelckmans

Age Rage and Going Gently

Stories of the Senescent Subject in Twentieth-Century French Writing

Oliver Davis

AMSTERDAM - NEW YORK, NY 2006

Cover illustration: 'The Regentesses of the Old Men's Home in Haarlem', Frans Hals (1664), courtesy of The Frans Hals Museum, Haarlem. Beauvoir saw Hals's painting as a model of balance in the representation of old age: 'il n'exalte ni ne décrie la vieilllesse' (*La Vieillesse*, p. 175). See this volume p. 37, n. 10.

Cover design: Pier Post

The paper on which this book is printed meets the requirements of 'ISO 9706: 1994, Information and documentation - Paper for documents - Requirements for permanence'.

Le papier sur lequel le présent ouvrage est imprimé remplit les prescriptions de 'ISO 9706: 1994, Information et documentation - Papier pour documents - Prescriptions pour la permanence'.

ISBN-10: 90-420-2026-1
ISBN-13: 978-90-420-2026-9
©Editions Rodopi B.V., Amsterdam - New York, NY 2006
Printed in The Netherlands

Contents

Acknowledgements

Thanks to Colin Davis for his inspiring and meticulous supervision of the thesis on which this book is based and to the Arts and Humanities Research Council for financially supporting that first stage of the work. Many thanks also to Christina Howells and Marianne Ahrne.

To Wesley Gryk.

Introduction

L'homme est un livre dont le titre
Est à-la-fois simple et riant
Et qui, de chapitre en chapitre,
Offre un détail intéressant;
Mais la table sage
La dernière page,
Que l'on consulte, hélas! trop tard
C'est le vieillard.[1]

    Among the First Republic's more neglected accomplishments was the inauguration of a festival in honour of old age, 'La Fête de la Vieillesse'.[2] This quaint piece of public poetry features in the official record of celebrations to mark the event in one *arrondissement*. The moral message and the metaphor are both somewhat trite. Life's journey is a book and the reader would do well to cast a respectful eye, at the outset, to 'la table sage': one should defer, that is, to the wise old man. Although this poetic fragment states that a respectful deference is owed to the elderly, on account of their wisdom (just as schoolchildren are reported to have paraded in the same festival carrying banners reading 'Respect à la vieillesse'), it nevertheless succeeds in suggesting a sense of the neglect from which they more usually suffer, this alleged sagacity notwithstanding: 'Que l'on consulte, hélas! trop tard'. This earnest exhortation to respect one's elders predates considerably the twentieth-century texts which form

---

[1] Verse 6 of an ode to old age, by one Citoyen Piis, as reportedly sung by a husband and wife duo during the celebrations marking 'La Fête de la Vieillesse' in the Fifth *Arrondissement* of Paris. See *Procès-verbal de la Fête de la vieillesse. 5ème Arrondissment* (Paris: Lemaire, An VI).

[2] On 24 June 1793, Hérault de Séchelles proposed that the Republic should honour old age as a new civic virtue. In Floreal II, Robespierre's ten-year plan included mention of a 'Fête de la Vieillesse', which was finally instituted on 26 October 1795. Symbolism demanded that it be the last festival in the year, on 27 August, and it continued to be celebrated throughout the Directory years. See Jean-Pierre Bois, *Histoire de la vieillesse* (Paris: P.U.F., 1994), p. 76. The only similar national festival still routinely celebrated, to my knowledge, is Japan's 'Respect for the Aged Day' (*Keiro no hi*).

my corpus here. Yet it neatly introduces my three main concerns: (i) the relationship between the written word and the human lifespan; (ii) the essential ambiguity of the ageing process, which may or may not bring wisdom or other gains; (iii) the corresponding ambivalence which characterizes human responses to that process, the choice in this case being between pious respect and dismissive neglect.

For all that growing old is, at least in principle, a universal human possibility – and one which the social and scientific achievements of the twentieth century have made available to more in the Western world than ever before – it has remained a minority interest in literary studies, especially by contrast with, for example, the related themes of death and illness and the contrasting theme of childhood.[3] This is not to say that, in its own right, it has attracted no attention whatsoever and I shall turn in a moment to the small body of existing work devoted to the subject. I shall argue that this work has been misguided in its reductive attempt to use literary texts as little more than storehouses of available images to be judged as to their 'positive' or 'negative' representation of the elderly. Such studies have looked mainly at the depiction of older characters in fiction and not, as I shall endeavour to do in the present work, at the ways in which non-fictional texts address themselves to the role played by the ageing process in subjective experience. My interest in the present study lies with the different creative possibilities and also the limitations of the written word, film and photography in modelling the role of ageing in subjectivity.

First, however, a general point. Age has never been more than a secondary or incidental concern in Western attempts to theorize human subjectivity. That the human subject ages has very seldom been thought to be a significant fact about that subject. It simply does not enter into any of the dominant philosophical, legal and ethical conceptions of human subjectivity. There can clearly be no disputing the fact that a distinction between childhood and adulthood forms part of these interrelated modes of theorizing the human subject and that such a distinction is, particularly in law, related to age. Yet adulthood,

---

[3] For example, Colin Davis, *Ethical Issues in Twentieth-Century French Fiction: Killing the Other* (Basingstoke: Macmillan, 2000), Philip Sandblom, *Creativity and Disease: How Illness Affects Literature, Art, and Music* (New York: Boyars, 1995), Margaret Waller, *The Male Malady: Fictions of Impotence in the French Romantic Novel* (New Brunswick: Rutgers University Press, 1993).

for the purpose of these theories of the human subject, is all of a piece: once an adult, becoming older is no longer a matter of any significance in itself.

This refusal to attribute intrinsic meaning to the ageing process is in marked contrast to, for example, death: the fact that human existence eventually comes to an end has always played a major part in the way that that existence is understood and represented. As Joseph Esposito has remarked, 'Philosophers have chosen to focus on the incomprehensibility of our death [...] rather than on the quiet process of dying that the aged experience, the closing up of the world, the eventual graying of sensation and desire in the very old'.[4] In the twentieth century, it is undoubtedly psychoanalysis that has been the most fertile source of new ways of theorizing the human subject, particularly in the latter half of that century and particularly in France. However, as I shall argue in Chapters Three and Four, psychoanalysis is itself premised upon a denial of significance to the ageing process. The readings of twentieth-century French texts presented in this book run against the grain of generalized neglect, or denial, of the ageing process that is a pervasive feature of the dominant conceptions of human subjectivity in Western culture.

Historical context

Although my focus here is the work of writers of the twentieth century, for reasons I shall explain in a moment, I am not suggesting that attempts to explore the relationship between language and the ageing process, in French, began in 1900. Montaigne, for one, discussed the meaning of old age at some length.[5] In the seventeenth century, French lexicographers were engaged in a long-running dispute about the meaning of the noun 'la vieillesse'. Richelet, in 1680, argued that old age began at forty; Furetière, in 1690,

---

[4] Joseph Esposito, *The Obsolete Self. Philosophical Dimensions of Aging* (Berkeley: University of California Press, 1987), p. 64. However, Esposito's specific concern about the neglect of ageing by moral philosophers has since begun to be addressed: see Norman Daniels, *Am I My Parents' Keeper? An Essay on Justice Between the Young and the Old* (New York: Oxford University Press, 1988).

[5] Montaigne, *Essais* (Paris: Garnier-Flammarion, 1969), I, ch. 57, 'De l'âge', 387-9.

distinguished between 'le déclin d'âge' at fifty and 'la vieillesse', which he thought commenced at sixty.[6] Both, however, felt that the mere stipulation of age in years (what gerontologists now usually refer to as 'chronological age'[7]) was inadequate without adducing further criteria based on character traits, yet neither could agree on exactly which traits were indicative of old age. Montaigne's work and this dispute between lexicographers are merely two important episodes from the history of literary and philosophical exploration, in French, of the meaning of old age and the relationship between it and language. Long before these relatively recent events, the first surviving written reference to old age occurs in a text from Ancient Egypt.[8] The reader is referred to the comprehensive survey by Simone de Beauvoir and the work of Georges Minois, which is more limited in scope, for an account of these and other significant moments in the rich pre-twentieth-century history of thinking and writing about old age.[9]

So why focus particularly on writing about old age in the twentieth century? In the twentieth century, old age ceases to be the sole preserve of literary and philosophical discourse. The long history of literary-philosophical engagement with old age, as detailed by Beauvoir and Minois, begins with that Ancient Egyptian inscription and embraces such landmarks as Cicero's *De Senectute*, Montaigne's chapter entitled 'De l'âge', Francis Bacon's *Of Youth and Age* and Victor Hugo's *L'Art d'être grand-père*, as well as a myriad of isolated references to old age in works where this is not the primary focus and of course countless elderly characters in plays, fiction and poetry. In the late nineteenth century, however, as I shall demonstrate in a moment, old age becomes the business of sociologists, psychologists, doctors, economists and demographers.[10] In this process of discursive colonization, literary and philosophical reflection on old age is pushed to the margins, dwarfed by the increasingly large body of medical and

---

[6] See Bois, *Histoire de la vieillesse* (Paris: PUF, 1994), pp. 49-51.
[7] See, for example, Cole, *The Journey of Life. A Cultural History of Aging in America* (Cambridge: Cambridge University Press, 1992), p. 3.
[8] Minois, *Histoire de la vieillesse en Occident de l'Antiquité à la Renaissance* (Paris: Fayard, 1987), p. 32.
[9] See Beauvoir, *La Vieillesse*, Ch. 3, pp. 97-229, and Minois, *Histoire de la vieillesse*.
[10] See also Bois, *Histoire de la vieillesse*, p. 112.

social-scientific[11] work on the subject. Thus it might be said that, in the twentieth century, literary discourse on old age such as I shall be considering here, by contrast with these new discursive approaches, can itself seem 'old' and even 'old-fashioned'. The differences between these two types of discourse are, moreover, extreme. Medical and social-scientific discourses seek to identify and address specific problems associated with the ageing process: they strive, in essence, to make ageing easier, whether for individuals or for societies confronting the problems associated with a 'greying' population. I would argue that literary-philosophical discourse, by contrast, is not primarily interested in ways of making ageing easier but is concerned, rather, with the question of the meaning of the process, in the first instance to the individual undergoing it. In the twentieth century, for the first time, interest in the meaning of the ageing process has been largely eclipsed by pragmatic and technical issues. As Thomas Cole puts it in his exemplary study:

> Since the early twentieth century, and especially after World War II, public discussion of aging has taken place largely within the frameworks of science and medicine. Biomedical and social scientists have effectively labelled aging as a problem that we can solve (or at least manage) given enough basic research and intervention.[12]

What Cole says here of 'public discussion' is probably true, in fact, of much private discussion and thinking too. The conflict between literary-philosophical and social-scientific approaches to old age, with their differing expectations and purposes, forms the backdrop to twentieth-century engagements with the topic. It is nowhere more visible than in Simone de Beauvoir's ground-breaking work, *La Vieillesse*, which I analyse in detail in Chapter One. Beauvoir endeavours in that work to present an exhaustive picture of old age, incorporating both literary-philosophical and social-scientific

---

[11] See Peter Stearns, *Old Age in European Society. The Case of France* (London: Croom Helm, 1977). Stearns situates the emergence of social-scientific interest in old age in the late nineteenth and early twentieth century, among economists: 'Social scientific, as opposed to medical, attention to the elderly is rather new. It was first developed by economists concerned with the funding implications of a society in which a growing minority will be retired, not only non-productive but an active drain on public resources' (Stearns, p. 7).
[12] Cole, *The Journey of Life*, pp. xxiv-xxv.

perspectives.[13] I shall argue in due course that many of the tensions
and paradoxes in this work, to which critics have tended to respond
with hostility or bewilderment, must be seen in the context of this
underlying conflict between two very different forms of discourse.

The argument just outlined should not be mistaken for, nor
become tinged with, nostalgia: there is no sense in regretting the
growth of social-scientific and the eclipse of literary-philosophical
attempts to engage with the ageing process. It is, however, important
to be aware of the marginal position of the latter discourse in the
socio-historical context of those texts I shall be analysing. Thomas
Cole's study of ageing in America (which also contains much to
interest the scholar working in a European context), *The Journey of
Life*, quoted above, does in places fall prey to such nostalgia.
Summarizing a transformation in attitudes to ageing that occurred
between the Reformation and the First World War, he writes: 'During
this long period, secular, scientific, and individualist tendencies
steadily eroded ancient and medieval understandings of aging as a
mysterious part of the eternal order of things'.[14] This seems to imply a
positive valorization of the ancient and medieval perspectives. This is
not an attitude shared by the present study, even though I shall, in
what follows, spend relatively little time on social-scientific discourse
and be mostly concerned with literary and philosophical approaches to
the topic.[15] In order to provide a sense of the wider cultural context,
however, I would at this point like to offer a brief analysis of the
social science that has come to be known as 'gerontology' and of its
medical counterpart.

---

[13] Beauvoir, *La Vieillesse*, p. 16.
[14] Cole, *The Journey of Life*, p. xx.
[15] And although Cole's description of the way in which old age was understood in the
ancient and medieval worlds may seem to imply that it was positively valorized there,
Georges Minois has noted that the culture of Ancient Greece was resolutely youth-
orientated and that medieval Christianity was much influenced by a common
association in the writings of the Church Fathers between old age and sinfulness. 'Le
vieil homme, c'est le pécheur qui doit se régénérer dans la pénitence; la jeunesse est
au contraire la fraîcheur de l'homme nouveau, sauvé par le Christ. Le péché, le mal
sont aussi hideux que les vieillards et, comme les vieillards, ils mènent vers la mort'
(Minois, p. 172). Minois notes that the link between old age and sin is made explicitly
in the work of John of Chrysostom and also of Augustine, the latter citing from Isaiah:
'While you grow older, I live' (Minois, p. 173).

Gerontology and Geriatrics

The term 'gerontology' was coined in 1904, by Elie Metchnikoff, who used it to denote what we would now understand as geriatric medicine, or geriatrics, rather than the branch of social science that has gone by the name 'gerontology' since its inception in the 1960s.[16] The term 'geriatrics' was coined in 1909, by E. L. Nascher, and its meaning remains unchanged. As Peter Stearns has demonstrated, however, geriatrics was born and indeed became well established in the preceding century.[17] He argues convincingly that France was in the forefront of attempts to develop this new specialization in elderly medicine: much of the work in this area emanated from the two largest hospitals designed to care for and house the elderly, the Salpêtrière (for women) and the Bicêtre (for men).

Charcot, before he became known for his work on hysteria, wrote a pioneering work on the subject: *Leçons cliniques sur les maladies des vieillards et les maladies chroniques*.[18] France led the way in this new field: from 1881, when it was translated into English, until 1914, when Nascher's *Geriatrics* appeared, Charcot's book was 'the major geriatric text in the United States'.[19] Yet as Peter Stearns also notes, nineteenth-century geriatric medicine 'was born at the research level, not abstracted from contact with real people but with little initial relevance to them'.[20] Stearns argues that the emphasis in this new branch of medical science lay chiefly upon analysing the process of decay rather than developing therapeutic strategies and accordingly that 'medical culture contributed to or at least paralleled a major stream of popular culture that associated old age with inevitable debility'.[21]

I shall return, in Chapter Four, to Charcot and his investigations at the Salpêtrière. After some fifty years of American

---

[16] See Cole, *The Journey of Life*, p. 195, and Beauvoir, *La Vieillesse*, pp. 28-9.
[17] See Stearns, *Old Age in European Society*, ch. 3, 'Geriatric Medicine', pp. 80-118.
[18] Charcot, *Leçons cliniques sur les maladies des vieillards et les maladies chroniques* (Paris: Delahaye, First Edition 1868).
[19] Cole, *The Journey of Life*, p. 195.
[20] Stearns, *Old Age in European Society*, p. 81.
[21] Ibid., p. 112.

dominance, in the 1950s and 1960s, France was once again at the forefront of geriatric medicine, thanks largely to the institute and journal founded by Bourlière, with its emphasis on psychiatric aspects of old age.[22]

Gerontology, the hybrid social science dedicated to the study of old age, combines elements principally from sociology and psychology. It emerged in the US in the 1950s and flourished in the decades that followed. It is perhaps questionable whether gerontology constitutes a single discipline, though there are many who seem to treat it as such. It is more accurately described, I would suggest, as an inherently interdisciplinary convergence around a single object of study. Those who describe themselves as gerontologists include, for example, psychologists studying changes in language use with age (length of sentences, complexity of syntax and so forth)[23] and sociologists interested in the relationship between ageing and masculinity.[24] Yet there are plenty who seem to view gerontology as a fully-fledged and coherent single 'discipline' in its own right.[25]

Thus gerontology is, if a discipline in its own right, then a very wide-ranging one. Those who describe themselves as gerontologists do, however, tend to share a little more than a common object of study: in addition, they invariably believe that society is inherently 'ageist'. A key moment in the development of gerontology was Robert Butler's promulgation, by way of an article written in 1969, of this concept of 'ageism', which he defined as follows:

> Ageism can be seen as a process of systematic stereotyping of and discrimination against people because they are older just as racism and sexism can accomplish this with skin color and gender. Old people are categorized as senile, rigid in thought and manner, old fashioned in morality and skills. Ageism allows the younger generations to see older people as

---

[22] Beauvoir, *La Vieillesse*, p. 30.

[23] Stuart-Hamilton, *The Psychology of Ageing: An Introduction* (London: Kingsley, 3rd Edition 2000), p. 127.

[24] For example, Jeff Hearn, 'Imaging of the Aging of Men', in *Images of Aging. Cultural Representations of Later Life*, ed. by Featherstone & Wernick (London: Routledge, 1995), pp. 97-115.

[25] For example, the vast majority of contributors to a collection edited by Steven Zarit, *Readings in Aging and Death: Contemporary Perspectives* (New York: Harper & Row, 1977). See, in particular, Zarit's short Introduction, 'Gerontology – Getting Better All the Time', pp. 11-12.

different from themselves. Thus they cease to identify with their elders as human beings.[26]

Ageism, or more particularly the struggle against its manifestations, could be described as the prevailing moral tone and methodological premise of the interdisciplinary hybrid that is gerontology. Ageism, according to Simon Biggs, 'is now established, amongst gerontologists at least, as a starting point for nearly all investigations of old age'.[27] Ageism, as conceived by gerontologists, is the product of all of the negative cultural representations of the elderly and of the ageing process. At around the same time as Simone de Beauvoir was articulating her view of the scandalous and fundamentally tragic character of the ageing process, in *La Vieillesse*, gerontologists in the US were waging war on the ageism they perceived was afflicting their society. The following comment of Steven Zarit's is suggestive of the zeal of this particular crusade:

> Despite the predominantly negative feelings people have about old age, gerontology is an optimistic discipline. It separates myths of aging from what actually occurs as we grow older [...] The most pervasive myth about aging is that it is a constant downhill course.[28]

Thus gerontology is cast as a demystifying and objective science, one which seeks both to dispel pervasive misconceptions about the nature of the ageing process and to propagate positive images of old age.

The enthusiasm for 'positive ageing' spread well beyond the confines of specialist research institutes. Writers of self-help literature, including Alex Comfort and also many less distinguished communicators, popularized a vision that was, as Thomas Cole has argued, essentially a prescriptive mirror opposite of ageism: the

---

[26] Robert Butler, 'Ageism: another form of bigotry', *Gerontologist* 9:243 (1969), p. 5.
[27] Simon Biggs, *Understanding Ageing. Images, Attitudes and Professional Practice* (Buckingham: Open University Press, 1993), p. 86. The idea that gerontology is premised on the notion that we live in an 'ageist' society will be confirmed by a perusal of the following two key texts in the field: Simon Biggs, *Confronting Ageing* (London: Central Council for Education and Training in Social Work, 1989), and Anthea Tinker, *Elderly People in Modern Society* (London: Longman, 3rd Edition 1992).
[28] Zarit, *Readings in Aging and Death*, p. 11.

elderly were encouraged to be active, sexual, productive and self-reliant.[29]

A key figure in the anti-ageism movement is the psychoanalyst Erik Erikson. In *Childhood and Society*, as I demonstrate in Chapter Four, he develops Jung's notion of a 'morning' and 'afternoon' of life, each with their own appropriate tasks and attitudes, into a 'life course' of eight distinct stages.[30] His scheme is prescriptive and undoubtedly reassuring, working to rid the experience of growing older of ambivalence and ambiguity. Rather than a brute process of disengagement and decline, ageing becomes a meaningful progression through a hierarchy of stages, each closer to perfection than the last. As with all exponents of positive ageing, Erikson's is an exhortation to look on the bright side, a plea for simple optimism rather than a serious attempt to render the chaotic diversity of human responses to a complex process.

Champions of 'positive ageing' have tended to draw an analogy with, and strength from, both feminism and anti-racism. This is a connection made explicitly in the excerpt from Robert Butler's article on ageism that I cited above. It is worth noting, however, that there is one important difference between anti-ageism and these two other liberation movements. As a general rule, the young become the old, the supposed oppressors *become* the oppressed, the other, but this is not true, at least not as a general rule, in the case of the other two liberation movements.[31] Thus for all that *La Vieillesse*, as I shall demonstrate in Chapter One, borrows many of its analytical structures and argumentative strategies from *Le Deuxième Sexe* and, as such, is in many ways a formal analogy of its more celebrated precursor, it continually comes up against this one crucial difference. In *Le*

---

[29] Cole, *The Journey of Life*, p. 211. See Alex Comfort, *A Good Age* (New York: Crown, 1976).

[30] Erik Erikson, *Childhood and Society* (New York: Norton, 1950), pp. 219-31.

[31] This view is echoed by Mike Featherstone and Andrew Wernick: 'While gender and race continue to be constituted as relatively unambiguous social categories which entail discrimination and power deficits for the outsider group, this division is by no means as clear cut with reference to the elderly and their relation to the young and middle-aged. Unlike the other social oppositions, youth and old age, and indeed all positions in the life course, are transitional statuses within a universal process. Unlike the other oppositions, provided we live long enough we will experience a movement into the opposite status'. See Featherstone & Wernick, 'Introduction' to *Images of Aging*, pp. 1-15, p. 8.

Deuxième Sexe, Beauvoir analyses the conflicting images of women propagated by patriarchal societies and implies all along that such images, or myths, are more false than true.[32] Yet in *La Vieillesse*, by contrast with the American proponents of 'positive ageing' (who reacted with great hostility to this work), Beauvoir seems to believe that there is some truth to many of the pervasive myths about ageing that she analyses. She posits the essentially tragic and scandalous character of the ageing process: her work combines a political zeal for reform of the real conditions experienced by elderly members of society with an undisguised philosophical pessimism about the experience of growing old.

I shall develop these arguments in relation to *La Vieillesse* in Chapter One. Here I want merely to signal what I would suggest is a key contextual difference, a division between two very different approaches to the non-medical study of old age. First, the gerontological view, primarily social-scientific, which originated in the US and which is bound up both with a belief in the inherently ageist character of Western societies and with the conviction that the discipline is able to challenge that state of affairs by debunking the various stereotypes of old age. And second, a more sceptical approach, one which is more pessimistic about the potential for changing the nature of our experience of ageing, which is literary-philosophical rather than social-scientific in orientation and which tends in tone towards the bleak. The present study is much closer to the second approach than the first: it is primarily literary, though engages necessarily but tangentially with the social-scientific discourse forming part of the cultural context. It is informed by the belief that a search for the significance of old age cannot proceed indiscriminately to discard as worthless various cultural stereotypes designated as unduly 'negative' at the outset. This alignment can also be justified by the fact that the first approach – which begins with the premise of ageism and the duty to fight it with positive thinking – has its roots in a specifically US cultural and historical context and cannot therefore simply be transplanted to the very different milieu of

---

[32] Beauvoir's readers disagree about precisely where she stands on this point, though few would seriously argue that she suggests that patriarchal myths of femininity are more true than false. See Linda Zerilli, '"I am a woman": female voice and ambiguity in *The Second Sex*', *Women in Politics*, 11:1 (1991), 93-108.

twentieth-century France.[33] In addition to this issue of cultural specificity, there is another reason to pause for thought, as I shall now indicate, before joining the anti-ageist crusade.

There is cause to be sceptical about the attempt by gerontologists to divert attention from any representation of old age and the ageing process that is deemed to be insufficiently 'positive'. In their Introduction to *Images of Aging*, Mike Featherstone and Andrew Wernick scrutinize the enthusiasm for 'positive' images of old age that has long been a major component in the war on ageism led by the gerontologists. They note that mid- to late twentieth-century consumer culture is, in fact, saturated with precisely the sort of 'positive' images of old age of which gerontologists invariably bemoan the lack:

> For the middle classes at least, positive aging is alive and well. Of course positive aging does not provide the solutions to the problems of deep old age and death: its message is essentially one of denial, keep smiling and carry on consuming.[34]

This point is developed in Chapter Two of the same work:

> It is noticeable how closely some of the central issues and crusades which [gerontologists] have developed parallel the assumptions about aging which are found in the popular media and the discourse of marketing people who have identified a new market in selling the consumer goods, technologies and paraphenalia for active, positive old age.[35]

Thus they argue that gerontology's enthusiasm for positive images of old age is inextricably bound up with (and, they seem to imply, is tainted by) the imperatives of a consumerist culture.[36] This may come as little surprise in view of the cultural and historical circumstances in

---

[33] Beauvoir herself signals the chasm dividing, to generalize, American and French attitudes to ageing and death at the beginning of her Introduction to *La Vieillesse*, p. 7.

[34] Featherstone & Wernick, 'Introduction', *Images of Aging*, p. 10.

[35] Featherstone & Hepworth, 'Images of Positive Aging', *Images of Aging*, ch. 2, p. 30.

[36] Herbert Blau makes a similar point: 'as with everything else in American life which emerges from neglect in persuasive numbers, the elderly have become sellable prospects in the marketplace of amelioration'. See 'The Makeup of Memory in the Winter of our Discontent', in *Memory and Desire*, ed. by Schwartz & Woodward (Bloomington: Indiana University Press, 1986), ch. 1, p. 26.

which the new discipline emerged: specifically, in the first flush of modern, mediatized, American consumerism in the 1950s and '60s. The present study accordingly strives to mark a certain distance from the simple-minded optimism characteristic of some gerontological research.

Ageing and Old Age in Literature

By contrast with the number of doctors and social scientists, relatively few literary critics have engaged at any length with the topic of ageing. This section analyses selected examples of those who have, before going on to outline my argument in this book against this background.

The study of old age in literature is a relatively recent phenomenon. It can be said to have begun with Harvey Lehman's *Age and Achievement*.[37] This rather eccentric statistical study is not confined to literature alone: Lehman also investigates the work of scientists, doctors, philosophers, musicians and other creative artists. The hypothesis, as he states it in the Preface, is straightforward: 'to set forth the relationship between chronological age and outstanding performances'.[38] The study that follows is largely a statistical survey of the relation between what he terms 'productivity' and the chronological age of various authors. He argues that authors write differently as they get older, that is in different styles and genres and with differing degrees of what he terms 'success'. Yet he never resolves (nor does he really try very hard to resolve) the inherent difficulties in defining 'success' and 'outstanding performance' in the context of literary production. Nor indeed is it clear that chronological age – age in years – has any other advantage than that it is easily quantifiable. Although the relevant chapters[39] are, at best, rather crass exercises in the sociology of literature, his work has nevertheless been influential on later critics, not least because it was among the first to raise the question of the relationship between age and literature.

---

[37] Harvey Lehman, *Age and Achievement* (Princeton: Princeton University Press, 1953).
[38] Ibid., p. vii.
[39] Ibid., chs. 6-8.

Lehman's many graphs and tables soon metamorphosed into the concept of 'late style', which has remained influential ever since, even though it is clearly the product of an almost bygone era of biographical criticism.[40] It should be noted, however, that while the notion of 'late style' is obviously related to ageing, and specifically to that of the author, those who follow in Lehman's footsteps are not concerned with the ageing process insofar as it is represented *in* texts. Instead, they seek to identify certain themes and stylistic features which they hold to be related to the age of the author. Yet whether or not these are in fact related to the age of the author in question, and the way in which they are so related, will always in such studies be a matter of considerable speculation.

If work on 'late style' is primarily author-focussed, the other leading approach to the study of ageing in literature concentrates mainly on the way in which fictional characters are represented. A particularly fine example of this approach is Janice Sokoloff's *The Margin That Remains*.[41] She studies a range a characters of different ages, from different periods of English literature from the eighteenth to the twentieth century. Challenging the findings of psychoanalyst Erik Erikson, mentioned in the previous section, she concludes:

> On the basis of the representations of the life courses of characters in these six novels, it is misleading to assign particular qualities to particular stages of life; and most especially the quality of 'integrity' to adulthood. The development of human character in life as in fiction is not necessarily linear [...].[42]

---

[40] For more on the development of 'late style' criticism, see Andrew Achenbaum's Introduction to *Perceptions of Aging in Literature: A Cross-Cultural Study*, ed. by Bagnell & Spencer Soper (New York: Greenwood, 1989), p. xiii. Studies representative of the 'late style' approach include Wyatt-Brown & Rossen (eds.), *Aging and Gender in Literature* (Chalottesville: University Press of Virginia, 1993); Freeman, J. T., *Aging, its History and Literature* (New York: Humane Sciences Press, 1979); Porter & Porter, *Aging in Literature* (Troy, Michigan: International Book Publishers, 1984); Woodward, K., *At Last the Real Distinguished Thing: the Late Poems of Eliot, Pound, Stevens, and Williams* (Columbus, Ohio: Ohio State University Press, 1980) and Ladimer, Bethany, *Colette, Beauvoir, and Duras. Age and Women Writers* (University Press of Florida, 1999).

[41] Janice Sokoloff, *The Margin That Remains: A Study of Aging in Literature* (New York: Peter Lang, 1987).

[42] Sokoloff, p. 129.

Sokoloff argues that models of ageing, particularly of 'successful' ageing, proposed by gerontologists are misleading because they suggest too neat a progression between categories that are themselves too simplistic: she suggests that literary representation – and specifically that of particular characters – demonstrates that matters are in fact more complex. I shall return in a moment to this issue of complexity or, as I see it, ambivalence and ambiguity in literary representations of old age. It will be noted that Sokoloff's approach ranks the theories of social scientists alongside the 'evidence' to be found in literary texts and that the latter is held to refute the former. There is reason to dispute the legitimacy of such an approach: can these two very different kinds of evidence really be played off against one another in this way? My concern here, however, is more to put forward Sokoloff's study as exemplary of a character-based approach to the study of ageing in literature. This is an approach which has the advantage over Lehman's attention to 'late style' that it is directed at ageing in so far as this occurs in the text rather than as it affects the author. Yet it remains problematic in that it treats characters as though they were real people, whose qualities might well have been described in another way: it is overwhelmingly content-based and seldom attends to the way in which this content is articulated.

Most work on ageing in literature can be placed in either of the above two categories, depending on whether it focuses on the age of the author or that of particular characters. There is a parallel between this divergence of approaches to ageing in literature and the two main distinguishable strands in feminist literary criticism: images of women and women's writing (writing about women and writing by women). The former starts with the content, the latter with the author. The 'late style' approach has the advantage of engaging in detail with the way in which the text says what it says, as opposed to the character-based approach which focuses mainly on the represented content. Yet in the former case, the relation to age is extra-textual, it being the age of the author, and invariably highly speculative; in the latter, we do at least come to grips with the representation of ageing insofar as it occurs in the text. It should by now be clear that there would be some merit in a study which combined the best features of these two respective approaches: attention to form and to ageing insofar as it is figured in the texts themselves. This book strives to effect such a blend; I shall explain exactly how when I proceed to outline my argument, below. Before I do, however, I would like to comment briefly on one important existing work that looks at ageing largely in a French literary context.

Kathleen Woodward's *Aging and Its Discontents* is a wide-ranging study of ageing in literature.[43] Woodward examines representations of ageing in texts which include, most notably, Proust's *Le Temps retrouvé* and Beckett's *Malone meurt*. She describes her approach as 'psychoanalytic' and qualifies this with the following intention:

> to present psychoanalytic interpretations of aging, with the emphasis on old age, through readings of literary and psychoanalytic texts [...] I read the literary texts and the psychoanalytic texts in a reciprocal fashion, asking what the two together can suggest to us about aging.

Most of the chapters pair a single and basic category in psychoanalysis (narcissism, introjection, or mourning, for example) with a fictional scene or scenes drawn from literature.[44]

Yet Woodward's easy recourse to psychoanalysis is more than a little surprising. For however influential it may have become in contemporary literary studies, psychoanalysis is, at first sight, a peculiar ally in a study of ageing. As I shall argue in Chapter Four, psychoanalysis has for a long time been fundamentally indifferent to the ageing process; indeed it could be argued that psychoanalysis is premised upon a denial of the reality of human ageing. This is an issue which Woodward never really addresses. Instead, as the above quotation suggests, she proceeds to 'pair' sketchily expounded psychoanalytic concepts with episodes from literature involving old age. Thus the closing scene of *Le Temps retrouvé* is paired with Lacan's Mirror Stage and passages from *Malone meurt* with Winnicott's theory of the transitional object. The inherent risk in such a strategy is that the connection will prove arbitrary, contrived or overly associative. In the above two cases, the way in which Woodward describes her reading strategy is telling, suggesting indeed

---

[43] Woodward, *Aging and Its Discontents. Freud and Other Fictions* (Bloomington: Indiana University Press, 1991). Not all of the texts she analyses are French but most are.

[44] Ibid., p. 8.

that there is little more than a whimsical association to justify these pairings of scenes from literature with psychoanalytic concepts:

> it is the peculiar emphasis in Samuel Beckett's *Malone Dies* on tangible objects, which seem to disappear one by one, *that led me to wonder if it might not be useful* to think about transitional objects of old age in addition to transitional objects of infancy, as theorized by D.W. Winnicott.[45]

> it was the closing party scene in *The Past Recaptured* which, *with Lacan's mirror stage of infancy in mind, suggested to me* the idea of a mirror stage of old age.[46]

In both instances, the italicized passages point to the primarily associative character of the pairings in question. It is, moreover, very difficult to know what to make of Woodward's resulting composites: given that Winnicott's and Lacan's respective theories are intrinsically bound up with the state of early infancy, how can they possibly be transplanted in this way, on the strength of a mere association, to an entirely different stage in life? From a literary point of view, moreover, there are other problems which recall those already identified, above, in author- and character-based approaches to the question. For Woodward derives the specifically age-related component in these pairings from selected literary scenes and the analytical or interpretative categories from psychoanalytic theory (and it must need be this way around in view of the inherent indifference of psychoanalysis to the ageing process). The result is, on one hand, another content-focussed reading of the literary texts in question and, on the other hand, a reading of the psychoanalytic material that is highly selective in its strategic decision to ignore what follows from these being models of processes that take place in early infancy, models which, even if repeated later, always refer back to this formative stage.[47]

Thus my concerns about Woodward's study of ageing are twofold: it is limited by its adoption of an overwhelmingly content-

---

[45] Woodward, *Aging and Its Discontents*, p. 9. My italics.

[46] Ibid., p. 9. My italics.

[47] I have analyzed in detail Woodward's reading of *Le Temps retrouvé* elsewhere. See my 'The Ageing Process in *A la recherche du temps perdu*' (unpublished master's thesis, The University of Oxford, K2832, 2001), in particular pp. 32-4.

based approach to the literary texts and by its unduly selective readings of the psychoanalytic material.[48]

Having reviewed critically selected examples of the existing scholarship on ageing in literature and surveyed the historical context, I now turn to the question of defining ageing, before going on to justify my choice of material and then to outline my own argument. What exactly is to count as 'ageing' and 'old age'? For gerontologists, economists and legislators, it is no simple matter to pinpoint when old age begins. Whatever the criteria they use, however careful or crudely chronological they are, there will always seem to be something rather arbitrary about the chosen definition.[49] Rejecting chronological age – age in years – as too crude, gerontologists have evolved complex distinctions between, for example, an individual's 'social', 'biological' and 'psychological' ages.[50] And even if 'old age', the state, were to be satisfactorily located, what exactly is to count as 'ageing', the process?

On this point of definition, I would suggest that matters are rather more straightforward where literary texts are concerned. It is not my place to lay down the law about when old age begins, ruling out certain cases and accepting others. I shall, instead, be guided by Peter Stearns's advice to 'let aging begin when people think it begins'.[51] Thus wherever there is talk of ageing or old age in a given text, openly or implicitly, this is potentially relevant material for the

---

[48] The reader is also referred to the excellent and wide-ranging recent collection of essays edited by Alain Montandon, *Ecrire le vieillir* (Clermont-Ferrand: Presses Universitaires Blaise Pascal, 2005). Many of these combine aspects of both approaches outlined above, though none in quite the way I go on to do here. They include essays by Mariane Bury on Maupassant; Luc Fraisse on *Le Temps retrouvé*; Francine Dugast-Portes on Colette; Claude Foucart on Thomas Mann and Marcel Jouhandeau; Marie-Odile André on Roger Martin du Gard. This recent resurgence of interest in ageing in literarature is greatly to be welcomed.

[49] A case in point is Beauvoir, who addresses the matter of definition in *La Vieillesse* in a footnote to her Preamble: 'C'est généralement à 65 ans que les sociétés industrielles d'aujourd'hui mettent les travailleurs à la retraite. J'appellerai vieux, vieillards, âgés, les gens de 65 ans et au-delà.' (n. 1, p. 19). To some this may seem crude, to others the sign of a refreshingly no-nonsense approach. It is interesting, however, that this vexed question of definition should have been relegated to a footnote by Beauvoir rather than discussed at any length in the main body of the text.

[50] See Introduction to *Connecting Gender and Ageing: a Sociological Approach*, ed. by S. Arber & J. Ginn (Buckingham: Open University Press, 1995).

[51] Stearns, *Old Age in European Society*, pp. 16–17.

purposes of this study. Because I am studying discourse (and primarily literary discourse) about ageing, rather than ageing individuals, it is appropriate that the criteria of relevance be primarily discursive rather than, say, biological or chronological. The second, related, question (what counts as 'ageing'?) may also be resolved with some ease. Ageing, for the purposes of this study, will be taken to mean 'becoming old': ageing is simply the process which leads to old age. Throughout, I endeavour to work with the concepts of ageing and old age available in the texts themselves rather than taking an independent view as to what can legitimately be classed as ageing.

Whereas most of the existing work on ageing in literature has concentrated on fiction (and mainly novels), I shall be focussing here on texts that are theoretical, autobiographical and biographical. This not only redresses an imbalance in the existing scholarship but would seem to be an appropriate point of departure for an inquiry into the role of ageing in subjectivity.

Even Beauvoir's *La Vieillesse* – an essay on the history, sociology and philosophical significance of old age – is explicitly presented as the view of one who has herself reached this stage in life[52] and it contains, moreover, numerous autobiographical anecdotes. My reading of this text, in Chapter One, is concerned mainly with Beauvoir's attempts to frame the subject's experience of ageing in terms of ambivalence and schizoid splitting. I do not dwell on the detail of her survey of the situation of old people in France at the time (c.1970), this having been largely superseded, though I endeavour to take due account of the role that sociological and political aspects play in the text as a whole. *La Vieillesse*, as I shall demonstrate, despite being a substantial work by a major writer, has been seriously neglected both by scholars of Beauvoir's work and by researchers pursuing the question of old age in literature and other fields. I endeavour to subject Beauvoir's essay to the sustained critical scrutiny it deserves and also to use its formulation of the fundamentally ambivalent or schizoid experience of old age as a point of departure for my exploration of other works in the chapters that follow.

André Gide's *Journal* and *Ainsi soit-il* are the joint focus of Chapter Two. Prompted by Beauvoir's somewhat reductive readings of these texts in *La Vieillesse*, I endeavour to reassess the role that

---

[52] See Beauvoir, *La Vieillesse*, p. 7.

ageing plays in Gide's life-long project of written self-fashioning. I explore the range of different textual models of the ageing process deployed in this work, a range considerably wider than that indicated by Beauvoir. It is in the nature of diaries to have time, as it were, inscribed in their very form. I explore this dimension of the *Journal*. Although Gide's *oeuvre* as a whole has inspired responses from a great many critics, his *Journal* has rarely been considered worthy of study in its own right and has usually been treated simply as a storehouse of biographical and other information useful in the elucidation of his other works.

In Chapter Three I turn to the work of one of Beauvoir's most devoted readers and admirers, Violette Leduc. I examine Leduc's autobiographical trilogy (of which, indeed, Beauvoir edited and published the third volume after Leduc's death). I read this alongside a selection of Freud's writings, first because both psychoanalysis and Leduc's work seem to be fixated on the formative influence of childhood suffering and to deny meaning to the ageing process. Second, Leduc's autobiography is also, particularly in its second volume, an account of her mental illness and the failure of psychoanalysis to provide effective treatment, a failure which proves to be intimately related to the question of its non-recognition of the ageing process. Leduc's *oeuvre* has begun in recent years to attract a modest amount of critical attention, particularly from scholars interested in the way it tackles issues of gender.[53] The autobiographical trilogy, however, and its second and third volumes in particular, has been neglected in relation to the other texts (novels and *récits*).[54]

Chapter Four undertakes a critical discussion of theoretical and clinical work by psychoanalysts on ageing and subjectivity, in France, the UK and the US, in the years after Leduc's experience of

---

[53] See Isabelle de Courtivron, *Violette Leduc* (Boston: Twayne Publishers, 1985); Pièr Girard, *Oedipe masqué. Une lecture psychanalytique de L'Affamée de Violette Leduc* (Paris: des femmes, 1986); Alex Hughes, *Violette Leduc: Mothers, Lovers, and Language* (London: Modern Humanities Research Association, 1994), and *Heterographies: Sexual Difference in French Autobiography* (Oxford: Berg, 1999), ch. 1.

[54] Susan Marson's helpful study of the relations between narrative time and narrated time seldom touches on the embodied time of the ageing process. See Marson, *Le Temps de l'autobiographie: Violette Leduc ou la mort avant la lettre* (Paris: Presses Universitaires de France, 1998).

its failure. My discussion aims to establish connections between work done in France and research by analysts from very different institutional and theoretical backgrounds in the UK and US.

Beauvoir's autobiography, in particular *La Force des choses*, and her biographical texts *Une Mort très douce* and *La Cérémonie des adieux*, together with a documentary film on which she collaborated and in which she features prominently, *PROMENADE AU PAYS DE LA VIEILLESSE*, form the focus of attention in Chapter Five. The later volumes of Beauvoir's autobiography have attracted scant critical interest in their own right, from any perspective.[55] The two biographical texts are rich in relevant material and allow a comparison to be drawn with Beauvoir's stance in *La Vieillesse*. The film can reasonably be described as a 'lost' work, one rediscovered in the course of research for this book. The collaborative nature of this project is particularly noteworthy: in *La Vieillesse*, Beauvoir theorizes that ageing, for the subject, is essentially a process of 'othering', of becoming 'other'. And by working on the film she collaborated – worked with others – to project an image of this process.

An ethics of care for the ageing other is also implicit in Guibert's *Suzanne et Louise*, the intergenerational 'roman-photo' examined in Chapter Six. It is suggested, however, that the nature of this care is ambivalent for it also allows the photographer-novelist to forge a negative self-definition in relation to his elderly subjects, to avoid the experience of his own ageing by concentrating on theirs: next to them, he is certainly not old. It is suggested in the conclusion, by analogy with Heidegger's argument about the subject's thinking of another person's death, that Guibert's concern for his great-aunts' ageing is inauthentic, a screen for meditating on the prospect of his own encounter with the process. Although many of Guibert's other texts have been studied extensively and reprinted on numerous occasions, *Suzanne et Louise* had long remained out of print and been almost entirely neglected by scholars of his work.[56]

A common theme in this discussion of my choice of material is that of neglect. Even in the case of major, established, writers such

---

[55] One of the main exceptions being Ursula Tidd's important study, the relevant parts of which are addressed in Chapter Five, below, *Simone de Beauvoir: Gender and Testimony* (Cambridge: Cambridge University Press, 1999).

[56] It was finally republished, in a facsimile edition, in October 2005 by Gallimard. See Chapter Six, below.

as Beauvoir, it transpires that their work on old age (*La Vieillesse* and, in particular, *PROMENADE*) has largely escaped notice. I chart this neglect in so far as it has affected specific works in the relevant chapters and return, in my Conclusion, to reflect on this phenomenon.

There are inevitably other twentieth-century French texts which may be thought to be relevant to my topic that do not form part of my corpus: in particular, the work of Proust and Colette. The significance of matters temporal in *A la recherche du temps perdu* will hardly be disputed. I have discussed ageing in this novel at length elsewhere.[57] Colette explores the theme of ageing extensively, in particular in *La Vagabonde, Chéri, La Fin de Chéri* and *Képi*: older women in these novels are invariably paired with younger men. Colette's account of ageing is undoubtedly more positive than those I shall be considering; it has proved, moreover, a rich source of material for critics concerned specifically with the question of gender and ageing. Questions of gender and ageing feature in this book in the context of discussions of Beauvoir (in Chapters One and Five) and Guibert (Chapter Six). Colette's work in general and its treatment of ageing in particular has already succeeded in attracting considerable critical interest.[58] The aim here is to look at a wider range of texts engaging with the topic of ageing, many of which have hitherto failed to attract the attention they deserve.

What little work has been done on the meaning of ageing in culture has hitherto been led by social scientists (sociologists, psychologists and gerontologists). Most are united in the belief that Western societies are inherently 'ageist' and that their work as researchers must undermine the pervasive 'negative stereotypes' of older people which, collectively, are thought to constitute the social evil of ageism.

---

[57] See my 'The Ageing Process in *A la recherche du temps perdu*' (unpublished master's thesis, University of Oxford, no. K2832, 2001).
[58] See Diana Holmes, 'Colette, Beauvoir and the Change of Life', *French Studies* LIII:4, October 1999, 430-443. Note that Holmes's discussion of Beauvoir in this article is limited by an unwillingness to engage with *La Vieillesse*, to which she merely alludes in passing. See also Ryan Song, 'Comparative Figures of Ageing in the Memoirs of Colette and Beauvoir: Corporeality, Infirmity, Identity', in *Corporeal Practices. (Re)figuring the Body in French Studies*, ed. by Prest & Thompson (Oxford: Lang, 2000) and Bethany Ladimer, *Colette, Beauvoir, and Duras. Age and Women Writers* (University Press of Florida, 1999).

While acknowledging that this approach may have a certain pragmatic value, I argue that such gerontological preconceptions amount to little more than a cheery attempt to suppress the negative. Gerontologists seldom engage with philosophical and literary material but, when they do, their approach is invariably reductive. I endeavour to show that the writing of age, if read with due care, affords a unique insight into the inherent ambiguity of the human lifespan, which may be seen in terms both of growth and decline, and into the extremes of ambivalence which characterize human responses to the ageing process.

The few existing studies of ageing in literary texts may, in their approach, be divided into two main categories: (i) the 'late style' approach, which isolates various stylistic features and hypothesises about their relation to the age of the writer; and (ii) the character-based approach, which examines the representation of elderly or ageing characters. The former harks back to the era of biographical criticism while the latter is insufficiently attentive to the formal features of the text by comparison with its represented content. I attempt to draw on and integrate the better parts of both approaches by combining an attention to formal aspects with an analysis of ageing insofar as it is represented in the text, rather than in the person of the author.

The approach is interdisciplinary (involving philosophy, literary studies and psychoanalysis), multigeneric and involves three distinct media (looking at a treatise, a diary, two authors' autobiographies, theoretical papers, a film and a 'photo-novel'). In its approach, the present work draws methodological inspiration from Simone de Beauvoir's unjustly neglected work, *La Vieillesse*, of which the first chapter is an in-depth analysis and a reappraisal.

Chapter One

Gerontology against ontology in Beauvoir's *La Vieillesse*

Few of those who know her work well would deny that Simone de Beauvoir made a major contribution to both feminism and gerontology, whether or not they agree with her conclusions in either field. Yet while the significance of her principal contribution to feminism, *Le Deuxième Sexe*, has been debated extensively throughout the half-century since its publication, her later work on the situation of older people in society, entitled *La Vieillesse*, has seldom even been mentioned, let alone explored in its own right, either by Beauvoir specialists or by gerontologists.[1] An explanation for this

---

[1] *La Vieillesse* is seldom accorded more than a passing mention, even in book-length studies of Beauvoir's work. For example, Toril Moi, who briefly discusses the representation of old age in Beauvoir's autobiographical writing in her *Simone de Beauvoir: the Making of an Intellectual Woman* (Oxford: Blackwell, 1994), pp. 236-43, makes no attempt to examine this in the context of *La Vieillesse*, a work alluded to on only three occasions in the entire study. By contrast, two substantial chapters are devoted to *Le Deuxième Sexe*. In the important collection of essays edited by Elizabeth Fallaize, *Simone de Beauvoir: a Critical Reader* (London: Routledge, 1998), *La Vieillesse* is mentioned in two contributions: a piece by Elaine Marks dealing mainly with old age in the autobiographical writing and the editor's Introduction. Five chapters, however, are devoted to *Le Deuxième Sexe*. Elisabeth Badinter has remarked that *La Cérémonie des Adieux* was "son *vrai* livre sur la vieillesse", thereby, by implication, writing off *La Vieillesse*. (At a symposium on Beauvoir at the Bibliothèque Nationale, 28 February 2001.) Diana Holmes, in an article which discusses at length Beauvoir's representation of old age, manages largely to ignore *La Vieillesse*, alluding to it in a single sentence ('Colette, Beauvoir and the Change of Life', *French Studies* LIII:4, Oct. 1999, 430-43, p. 437). One recent exception to this tendency towards neglect is Penelope Deutscher's chapter in *The Cambridge Companion to Simone de Beauvoir*, ed. by Claudia Card (Cambridge: Cambridge University Press, 2003), ch. 14, 'Beauvoir's *Old Age*', pp. 286-304. Deutscher reads *La Vieillesse* as Beauvoir's response to certain assumptions in early Sartrean ontology of the subject: 'Sartre's subject is embodied, sometimes sick and fatigued, but patently a young adult body. Beauvoir's response is that an excessive weighting of ontological freedom generalizes and neutralizes those lived and embodied differences that should also hold our theoretical attention' (Deutscher, p. 302).

apparent lack of interest will emerge in the course of this chapter. First, however, I shall introduce the work in question, before moving on to examine its structural tensions and historical context, its central philosophical thesis, its treatment of gender and, finally, its performative dimension. My discussion of this text will serve to introduce themes pursued in later chapters.

First published in France in 1970, *La Vieillesse* was translated into English by Patrick O'Brian and published in Britain and the United States two years later. In Britain the translated work was entitled, quite correctly, *Old Age*. In the US, however, publishers felt that this title was not sufficiently optimistic and decided instead to call the book *The Coming of Age*.[2] Not only does this attempt at market-manipulation confuse matters by introducing other connotations – to 'come of age' refers, of course, to an entirely different period of life – it also betrays the spirit of a work, which, as I shall endeavour to show, rejects euphemism and offers a thoughtful critique of precisely this sort of marketable optimism.

La Vieillesse was reviewed favourably in France on publication, in marked contrast to *Le Deuxième Sexe*.[3] However, unlike almost all of Beauvoir's other works, her treatise on old age is no longer in print in France. Moreover, by contrast with *The Second Sex* and most of Beauvoir's mature work, it is also no longer in print in either its British or American versions. Yet this is no trivial pamphlet: *La Vieillesse* is a remarkable work of synthesis and argument, which runs to some six hundred pages in the original; Beauvoir herself seems to have thought that *La Vieillesse* was at least as significant a work as *Le Deuxième Sexe* and indeed described the two essays as 'symétrique' in *Tout Compte fait*.[4] It will become clear that the relation between the two works is rather more complicated than their author suggests here, yet I shall take seriously Beauvoir's sense that both are substantially interrelated.

---

[2] Deirdre Bair, *Simone de Beauvoir: A Biography* (London: Vintage, 1990), p. 674, n. 24.
[3] Bair notes that 'when *La Vieillesse* (*Old Age*) was published in France in January 1970, reviewers hailed it with remarkable unanimity of praise'. Bair, p. 539.
[4] Beauvoir, *Tout Compte fait* (Paris: Gallimard, 1972), p. 183.

Structural tensions and historical context

This section gives a structural overview of *La Vieillesse* and argues that many of the tensions identified therein may be explained in terms of the work's historical and discursive context. *La Vieillesse* bears a close resemblance to *Le Deuxième Sexe* in crude structural terms. Both works are divided into two parts: the 'view from the outside' followed by the 'view from the inside'. In the Introduction to *Le Deuxième Sexe*, the aims of the first part are described thus: 'discuter les points de vue pris sur la femme', by biology, psychoanalysis and historical materialism (the subsection entitled 'Destin'); to consider 'comment la "réalité féminine" s'est constituée' ('Histoire') and finally, to ask 'pourquoi la femme a été définie comme l'Autre' ('Mythes').[5] The second part is said here to describe 'du point de vue des femmes le monde tel qu'il leur est proposé'. In the Preamble to *La Vieillesse*, Beauvoir announces what appears to be an almost identical approach:

> Pour autrui, le vieillard est l'objet d'un savoir; pour soi, il a de son état une expérience vécue. Dans la première partie de ce livre, j'adopterai le premier point de vue. J'examinerai ce que la biologie, l'anthropologie, l'histoire, la sociologie contemporaine nous enseignent sur la vieillesse. Dans la seconde, je m'efforcerai de décrire la manière dont l'homme âgé intériorise son rapport à son corps, au temps, à autrui.[6]

Yet these two approaches, which may appear in these introductory remarks to correspond almost exactly, turn out to imply rather different ways of treating the various cultural discourses they go on to consider. For in *Le Deuxième Sexe*, it is not the case that Beauvoir refers to various cultural discourses in order to inventory neutrally how they position women, only then to look at how women position themselves in the second part. Rather, the discourses themselves are subjected to a rigorous questioning and internal subversion, even as they are permitted to dispense their supposed 'knowledge'.[7] By

---

[5] Beauvoir, *Le Deuxième Sexe* (Paris: Gallimard, 1949), I, p. 32.

[6] Beauvoir, *La Vieillesse*, p. 16.

[7] This subversion from within principally takes the form of a discursive strategy of amplification and defamiliarization. See Linda Zerilli in '"I am a woman": female voice and ambiguity in *The Second Sex*', *Women in Politics*, 11:1 (1991), 93-108.

contrast, Beauvoir's attitude to the various cultural discourses in Part
One of *La Vieillesse* is considerably less critical and more deferential:
medical science and sociology, in particular, are thought of as capable
of contributing to the solution rather than as being part of the problem,
as complicit in oppression. This difference in approach is just
discernible in Beauvoir's introductory remarks setting out the similar-
seeming structure of the two works: there proves in fact to be a great
deal of difference between her plan in *Le Deuxième Sexe* to *discuss*
'les points de vue pris sur la femme' and, in *La Vieillesse*, her aim to
examine 'ce que la biologie, l'anthropologie, l'histoire, la sociologie
contemporaine nous *enseignent* sur la vieillesse'. The use of
enseigner, which I have emphasised here, is important: medical
science and anthropology, in particular, are set up from the start of the
later work as having something to teach us about old age, as being
capable of contributing to 'our' understanding of old age and thereby
to a more tolerant treatment of older people. The elevation of
sociological and medical discourse in the first half of *La Vieillesse* is
often at the expense of literature, which is treated primarily as a
storehouse of the various 'mythes' and 'clichés', the imprisoning
stereotypes of old age.[8]

Whereas the divisions between chapters in the first part of *La
Vieillesse* correspond neatly to divisions between academic
disciplines, chapters in the second part are less clearly distinguishable
by topic and indeed have vaguer titles. They cover areas such as self-
image, the perception of time and the experience of sexuality and
activity in later life. The final chapter, 'Quelques exemples de
vieillesses', is a compendium of gleanings from biographies of Great
Men, mostly writers. Whereas statistical data and patient analysis
characterize the written texture of the first part, the second is marked
by a preponderance of literary material, mixed with anecdote,
philosophical reflection and impassioned argument. Thus the

---

[8] This new deference to medical knowledge calls for some explanation, particularly in
view of Beauvoir's hostility to it in *Le Deuxième Sexe* (as institutional support for
patriarchal misconstruction and mistreatment of the female body) and in her preface
to *Djamila Boupacha* (Paris: Gallimard, 1962), where she describes the complicity of
the medical establishment in colonial Algeria with state-sponsored torture. It is a shift
which perhaps reflects the increased dependence of elderly people on medical
expertise, a greater desperation and a greater vulnerability at the hands of
unscrupulous practitioners.

difference in analytical perspective from the first part to the second also corresponds to a difference in the kind of writing and the material under consideration: broadly speaking, this may be characterized in terms of a split between the discourse of the social sciences on one hand and literary-philosophical discourse on the other; or, put differently, a split between gerontology and ontology. Beauvoir's book juxtaposes a wide variety of radically different ways of looking at old age, perspectives which have seldom – before or for that matter since – been embraced, together, between the covers of a single work on the subject. Beauvoir's treatise is a confluence of different perspectives and testimonies, a polyvocal and often apparently self-contestatory compendium of different approaches.

The sense that *La Vieillesse* is a work divided against itself, which I have characterized in terms of a clash between gerontology and ontology, can be related to the fact that Beauvoir's work stands at an historical threshold: as I noted in my Introduction, discourse on old age of a medical, social-scientific or economic persuasion is a relatively recent phenomenon and its emergence in the late nineteenth century marked a break with a long tradition of humanist literary-philosophical discourse on senescence, a tradition which stretches back at least as far as Aristotle, if not to Ancient Egypt.[9] This tradition has tended to highlight the sense in which old age reduces the human subject, erasing both achievements and differences. Thus for a writer such as Montaigne, whose reflections on old age Beauvoir admires in her study, to think lucidly about getting older is a matter of casting a cold eye on all human endeavour, a question of recognizing its vanity, in the strict sense.[10] Beauvoir's study owes much to this humanist tradition of bleak meditation on the significance of human decline. It also shares, in its second part, aspects of the mode of analysis typical

---

[9] According to Georges Minois, the first ever surviving example of writing about old age, by a nameless scribe in Ancient Egypt, was bleakly meditative. See Georges Minois, *Histoire de la vieillesse en Occident de l'Antiquité à la Renaissance* (Paris: Fayard, 1987), p. 32.

[10] Commenting on Montaigne's discussion of old age, Beauvoir admires 'le regard direct et exigeant qu'il dirige sur une réalité qu'on s'efforce généralement de masquer' (*La Vieillesse*, p. 170). Beauvoir's book also aspires to this unflinching gaze and testifies to the difficulties involved in achieving it. As she says of Frans Hals's painting, 'The Regentesses' (see cover), so too of her own work: 'il n'exalte ni ne décrie la vieillesse: il cherche à saisir la vérité des visages qu'il représente' (*La Vieillesse*, p. 175).

of this tradition: in particular, a predominance of anecdotal references
to the lives of prominent individuals – men, to be precise (Goethe,
Whitman, Tolstoy, Hugo...).[11] Yet although Beauvoir's study to some
extent places itself within this tradition, it is important to note that it is
far more contestatory and polyvocal than works by other
representatives of that same tradition in the twentieth century such as
Italo Svevo, Jean Améry and Marcel Jouhandeau, which all lack the
'gerontological' counterpoint present in Beauvoir's book.[12] As writing
and as historical documents, these examples of the ontological
tradition are far less complex and interesting than Beauvoir's *La
Vieillesse.*

As I noted in my Introduction, the social science of
gerontology, in so far as it is a specialized discipline, a professional
enterprise with its own institutional context and shared assumptions, is
a recent phenomenon. A central assumption of gerontology is that we
live in an 'ageist' society and that one of the aims of the discipline is
to change this state of affairs for the better.[13] It is also generally
assumed in gerontology that the most effective way to combat ageism
is to analyse stereotypes of decline and disengagement, dismiss them
as valueless and replace them with 'positive' images of old age.
Beauvoir's study does the analysis – pointing out the limitations of
certain stereotypes of older people – but stops short of dismissing
them as altogether valueless and replacing them with more 'positive'
images. In fact, her work is implicitly critical of the assumptions

---

[11] This tradition of writing which sees the decline of old age as a sign of the vanity of
human endeavour is clearly male-dominated. That Beauvoir should have placed
herself in such a tradition may, at first glance, seem somewhat surprising, though
should be compared with the way in which her sense, as an author, of the French
literary tradition in which she situated herself was also very much that of a succession
of Great Men. Toril Moi has analysed this paradoxical attitude of Beauvoir's from a
sociological perspective in her *Simone de Beauvoir: The Making of an Intellectual
Woman* (Oxford: Blackwell, 1994), ch. 2.
[12] Italo Svevo, *As A Man Grows Older* (London: Putnam, 2nd Edition 1949), translated
by Beryl de Zoete (*Senlilità*), Jean Améry, *Du Vieillissement. Révolte et résignation*
(Paris: Payot, 1991), translated by Annick Yaiche (*Über das Altern*, Stuttgart, Klett,
1968), Marcel Jouhandeau, *Réflexions sur la vieillesse et la mort* (Paris: Grasset,
1956).
[13] Mike Featherstone & Mike Hepworth, 'Images of Positive Aging', in Featherstone
& Wernick (eds.), *Images of Aging. Cultural Representations of Later Life* (London:
Routledge, 1995), ch. 2, 29-47.

underlying much gerontological research. For the ontological strand in Beauvoir's treatise suggests that there is a limit to how optimistic a picture of old age it is honest to portray; there is, she thinks, something inevitably alienating about growing older which no amount of positive thinking can overcome.[14] Her study is implicitly sceptical about this particular side to gerontology. Such scepticism about the ambitions of a recently-emerged field of study does not, however, diminish Beauvoir's own insistence in *La Vieillesse* on the need for radical political change in order to improve the socio-economic situation of older people.[15]

Beauvoir read much of the best gerontological research of her day before writing *La Vieillesse* and this is clearly reflected in the finished work, particularly in the first half. Beauvoir's study manages, however, to escape the narrow confines of one professional specialism and to question its central assumptions by engaging with the age-old tradition of philosophical writing on senescence and its significance for the individual and for our understanding of the human subject. Beauvoir's work stands, then, at an historical and disciplinary threshold, engaging with and embodying both contemporary gerontology with its predominately social-scientific methodology and right-thinking political objectives but also the universalizing, 'ontological', tradition of literary-philosophical thinking on the nature of old age.

The ambivalence of Beauvoir's study with respect to these two very different approaches to her subject – the ontological and the gerontological – may explain why some readers of the work have found it to be self-contradictory and also, perhaps, why it has been neglected by scholars working within the confines of a single discipline. This is an essay in which emancipatory anti-ageist gestures – 'Cessons de tricher [...] ce vieil homme, cette vieille femme, reconnaissons-nous en eux'[16] – coexist alongside an ontologically-grounded pessimism which suggests that such recognition is impossible, that we are bound to reject the idea of ourselves as old,

---

[14] Or, as Jean Grimshaw puts it, 'We should not suppose that we can simply learn to "accept" the shock of aging bodies and faces and changes in life patterns by some kind of "power of positive thinking", feminist or otherwise'. Grimshaw, 'Aging, Embodiment and Identity', *Women's Philosophy Review* 29 (2002), 64-83, p. 82.
[15] See, in particular, her Conclusion.
[16] Beauvoir, *La Vieillesse*, p. 11.

whether in the present or in the future. She stresses the necessity of radical social and political change before the condition of older people can be ameliorated – 'Changer la vie' – at the same time as she ridicules smaller-scale, gradualist, solutions.[17] Stereotypes which Beauvoir analyses and criticizes in the first part of the treatise, stereotypes which aim to represent the older person as Other, are invariably reasserted in the second part, which I examine in the next section, the ontological part in which Beauvoir argues that ageing is about becoming this Other even as we fail to recognize ourselves in it. These tensions, which correspond to the different perspectives and assumptions rubbing up against one another in Beauvoir's work, remain unresolved.

Beauvoir's ontological thesis: contradiction, otherness and Cartesianism

Having discussed in general terms the place of gerontology in *La Vieillesse*, I shall now examine more closely its philosophical counterpoint. This is most in evidence in the second part of Beauvoir's book, particularly in Chapter Five. Just as, in *Le Deuxième Sexe*, the position of women is described by Beauvoir as that of the Other ('Il est le sujet, il est l'Absolu: elle est l'Autre'[18]), in *La Vieillesse*, it is older people who occupy the position of the Other in relation to their younger counterparts: 'les mythes et les clichés mis en circulation par la pensée bourgeoise s'attachent à montrer dans le vieillard un *autre*'.[19] Yet whereas in *Le Deuxième Sexe* the positions of Subject and Other are relatively stable over time, in *La Vieillesse* they are decidedly unstable: this Other is what the Subject, every

---

[17] 'Changer la vie' is the last sentence of Beauvoir's Conclusion to *La Vieillesse* (p. 570. Konrad Bieber speculates that the source of this final sentence may have been the title of a volume of reminiscences by Jean Guéhenno but fails to mention that it is, in the first instance, a quotation from Rimbaud which subsequently became a barricade slogan during *Mai '68*. Beauvoir's Conclusion is a call for the complete reorganization of society along Marxist lines as the only way of changing the situation of older people in society, some two years after the events of 1968. See Konrad Bieber, *Simone de Beauvoir* (Boston: Twayne, 1979), p. 187 n. 15.
[18] Beauvoir, *Le Deuxième Sexe*, I, p. 15.
[19] Beauvoir, *La Vieillesse*, p. 9.

subject, gradually but inexorably becomes in the course of a lifespan. That this cannot be said of the relationship between the male Subject and the female Other, at least as this is presented in *Le Deuxième Sexe*, is one crucial difference between the two works. In *La Vieillesse*, the subject (and, as I shall argue in the next section, particularly the male subject) is *othered*, against not only his will but also his desire, over time.

I shall, in this section, rehearse and analyse Beauvoir's account of this process of 'othering' with age. She begins by claiming that the plain truth that they too, one day, will be old is something which younger people simply refuse to accept:

> Devant l'image que les vieilles gens nous proposent de notre avenir, nous demeurons incrédules; une voix nous murmure absurdement que *ça* ne nous arrivera pas: ce ne sera plus nous quand *ça* arrivera. Avant qu'elle ne fonde sur nous, la vieillesse est une chose qui ne concerne que les autres.[20]

The younger person, impervious to good sense, thinks that old age is something that only happens to others. Instead of arguing that this refusal is something which weakens as the subject ages and gradually becomes the Other that he or she once feared to be, Beauvoir contends instead that the initial, youthful, rejection of old age endures into old age itself. Thus: 'La vieillesse est particulièrement difficile à assumer parce que nous l'avions toujours considérée comme une espèce étrangère: suis-je donc devenue une autre alors que je demeure moi-même?'.[21] Beauvoir is adamant in *La Vieillesse* that human beings cannot (that is, are constitutionally or ontically unable to) meet the fact of their old age with calm acceptance: the subject, instead of reconciling himself with this Other as he becomes it, will vehemently resist this recognition: 'en nous, c'est l'autre qui est vieux'.[22] Nor is the rejection of old age considered to be merely one of several possible responses. Beauvoir suggests, rather, that this state necessarily involves 'une contradiction indépassable':

> Nous achoppons à une sorte de scandale intellectuel: nous devons assumer une réalité qui est indubitablement nous-même encore qu'elle nous atteigne

---

[20] Beauvoir, *La Vieillesse*, p. 11.

[21] Ibid., p. 301.

[22] Ibid., p. 306.

du dehors et qu'elle nous demeure insaisissable. Il y a une contradiction indépassable entre l'évidence intime qui nous garantit notre permanence et la certitude objective de notre métamorphose. Nous ne pouvons qu'osciller de l'une à l'autre, sans jamais les tenir fermement ensemble.[23]

The best that can be hoped for, then, is a highly unstable dialectic in which the subject's inner conviction of enduring self-sameness is confronted by and resists the inevitability of change, which is experienced as coming from without. In spite of her Preamble in which, as I noted, Beauvoir demanded that 'we' stop cheating – 'Cessons de tricher [...] ce vieil homme, cette vieille femme, reconnaissons-nous en eux'[24] – she suggests here, in Chapter Five, that such recognition is impossible in any enduring or stable form. Indeed, not only does Beauvoir argue here that old age is necessarily scandalous and contradictory but, throughout the work, both sides of the dialectic which makes it so are intensified such that the text repeatedly and violently restages the clash of these opposites. This reenactment typically takes the form of a sudden reaffirmation of the alienating inevitability of the body's decline in the midst of a passage which had previously been concerned with the elderly subject's freedom to decide how to live out their old age: 'Cette détérioration est fatale, nul n'y échappe'[25]; 'Cependant, quel que soit le contexte, les données biologiques demeurent. Pour chaque individu la vieillesse entraîne une dégradation qu'il redoute'.[26] These passages restage, textually, a clash between the elderly subject's ageless self-perception and the fact of old age, a confrontation which Beauvoir suggests is an everyday occurrence in the lives of older people, a feature of their interactions with others: indeed his being old is revealed to the subject principally in the reactions of others. In this interplay lies 'la complexe vérité de la vieillesse':

Elle est un rapport dialectique entre mon être pour autrui, tel qu'il se définit objectivement, et la conscience que je prends de moi-même à travers lui. En moi, c'est l'autre qui est âgé, c'est-à-dire celui que je suis pour les autres: et cet autre, c'est moi. [...] Notre expérience personnelle ne nous indique pas le nombre de nos années. Aucune impression cénesthésique ne

[23] Beauvoir, *La Vieillesse*, p. 309.
[24] Ibid., p. 11.
[25] Ibid., p. 321.
[26] Ibid., p. 47.

nous révèle les involutions de la sénescence [...] La vieillesse apparaît plus clairement aux autres qu'au sujet lui-même.[27]

Yet although we may agree that 'notre expérience personnelle ne nous indique pas le nombre de nos années', in the strict sense that it fails to present us with a figure for the number of years elapsed, is it really true to say that older people are constitutionally unable to apprehend their age without this first being revealed to them in the behaviour of others? How does this 'contradiction indépassable' actually function?[28] I shall now turn to examine its Cartesian mechanism.

Beauvoir's view, in the Preamble to *La Vieillesse*, of old age as 'le domaine du psychosomatique', is developed early on, in the first chapter, 'Vieillesse et biologie'. The psychosomatic character of old age finds exemplary expression in those compensatory mechanisms

---

[27] Beauvoir, *La Vieillesse*, p. 302.

[28] I am not arguing here that Beauvoir's view of old age as necessarily contradictory is right. Indeed, that old age need not be experienced as a scandal and a contradiction is what many of the writings of Gide and Jouhandeau on the subject, to which Beauvoir herself alludes, suggest. Rather than engaging seriously with their work, however, Beauvoir tends either to oversimplify it (in Gide's case, as I shall argue in Chapter Two, below) or to ridicule it as an example of bourgeois self-delusion. Referring to Jouhandeau's *Réflexions sur la vieillesse et la mort*, she protests that, 'Ces fadaises spiritualistes sont indécentes si on considère la condition réelle de l'immense majorité des vieillards' (*La Vieillesse*, p. 335). Yet Jouhandeau never purported to be offering an account of a universal, cross-class, experience of old age. As the title of his *Réflexions* suggests, they are offered not as a manifesto for political change but rather as meditative writings. Jouhandeau is dismissed with such vehemence because he suggests that old age need not be experienced as scandalous, it need not be lived as 'une contradiction indépassable', and also because he suggests that the subject is capable of assuming his old age himself, without the mediation of an other. The treatment of Gide and Jouhandeau in *La Vieillesse* should be contrasted to the place of honour accorded to Proust in this work: for, in *Le Temps retrouvé*, as Beauvoir notes, the narrator's decrepitude is revealed to him in the speech and conduct of others towards him. Along with Montaigne, Proust is one of few authors in *La Vieillesse* to escape a general belittlement of literature at the expense of sociological and medical discourse. Ursula Tidd has commented of Beauvoir that, 'in her memoirs and *La Vieillesse* she [...] represents our relationship to time as inscribed through the body, as a relationship which we experience through the body, in an almost Kafkaesque way' (*Gender and Testimony*, Cambridge: C.U.P., 2000, p. 74). I would add that a no less appropriate literary precursor, and one to whom Beauvoir repeatedly refers in *La Vieillesse*, is Proust. The Proustian paradigm would seem to suit Beauvoir's purpose almost exactly: the narrator rejects the idea that he is this old man which others see him as.

developed by individuals growing older in order to offset the reality of
their bodily decline:

> Quand il y a maladie, stress, deuil, échec grave, ce ne sont pas les organes
> qui brusquement se détiorent: la construction qui en dissimulait les
> insuffisances s'effondre. Le sujet avait en réalité subi dans son corps
> l'involution sénile mais il avait réussi à la compenser par des automatismes
> ou des conduites réfléchies.[29]

As Beauvoir describes them, these compensatory patterns are neither
entirely corporeal nor entirely mental, but both. When they collapse,
the bodily consequences can be dramatic: the subject 'devient soudain
incapable de recourir à ces défenses et sa vieillesse latente se révèle.
Cette chute morale se répercute sur les organes et elle peut entraîner la
mort'.[30] Lived experience for the elderly is construed here as the
complex interimplication of bodily decline and psychosomatic
compensation. The interrelationship of body and mind in such
experience is exemplified both in the successful development and
functioning of these compensatory structures and in the repercussively
devastating effects of their collapse.

Yet this model of 'psychosomatic' imbrication, said to
characterize old age, is hardly reflected in the analytical structure of
the work as a whole. For, on the following page, the task of an
analysis which properly links psychology and biology, psyche and
soma, is deferred: 'Lorsque, plus loin, j'étudierai la psychologie des
vieillards, ce sera dans une perspective totalitaire, en la liant à un
contexte biologique, existentiel, social'.[31] The remains of the first
chapter present the findings of medical specialists on the decline of
the ageing body but without regard for the psychology of subjective
experience. In structural terms I would argue that this is a profoundly
Cartesian move, though one partially concealed by a promise to fill in
the gaps and make the proper connections later on. This 'plus loin' is
presumably meant to be the second part of the essay and, in particular,
Chapter Five, subtitled 'Expérience vécue du corps'[32], which must

---

[29] Beauvoir, *La Vieillesse*, p. 38.
[30] Ibid., p. 38.
[31] Ibid., p. 39.
[32] Ibid., pp. 301-82.

surely suggest that the intervening chapters (around half the entire study) do not even try to function 'psychosomatically'.[33]

The discussion in Beauvoir's Chapter Five, however, hardly fulfils the expectations raised in the Preamble. This is not an integrated analysis which confirms and mirrors the supposedly special psychosomatic character of old age, but rather – at the opposite extreme – one which describes and restages the clash between the subject's inner 'évidence intime' of his permanence and the outer 'certitude objective de [sa] métamorphose', the traces of which are written on the body for others to read. Even the language of this chapter reflects the Cartesian division between mind and body: Beauvoir writes, for example, that 'des signes nous viennent du corps'[34] – which implies that this 'nous' is to some degree separate or, at least, separable from the body which encases it, and of old age that 'elle nous atteigne du dehors', suggesting that the subject is enclosed in, and other than, its body. So, far from being the anticipated rejoinder to Cartesian mind/body dualism, old age, in its clash between inner, subjective, certainty and outer bodily metamorphosis would appear to be a quintessentially and painfully 'Cartesian' period.

Is it possible to reconcile Beauvoir's insistence on the specially psychosomatic character of old age with her demonstration that old age is a painfully Cartesian predicament? Perhaps, for what Beauvoir's account implies is that old age is at once the moment at

---

[33] Nor is this the only deferral in the work. In the Preamble, Beauvoir argued that 'Il ne suffit [...] pas de décrire d'une manière analytique les divers aspects de la vieillesse: chacun réagit sur tous les autres et est affecté par eux; c'est dans le mouvement indéfini de cette circularité qu'il faut la saisir' (*La Vieillesse*, p.16). Again, she is implying that old age is a special condition which requires a correspondingly special mode of analysis. However, in her prefatory remarks to the second part of the work, which immediately precede Chapter Five, it would appear that the task of a properly integrated analysis has been deferred: 'C'est dans la perspective d'une synthèse finale *qu'il faut lire* ces chapitres' (*La Vieillesse*, pp. 299-300, emphasis added). Rather than offering a unified analysis, as promised, she notes that in this section she will proceed 'successivement' through each of 'les facteurs qui définissent la condition de vieillard'. The portion I have emphasised suggests that this deferral not only postpones the task of an integrated analysis until later in the text, but actually seeks wholly to transfer this obligation from the text and its author to the reader.

[34] Beauvoir, *La Vieillesse*, p. 302.

which the subject's Cartesian pretensions are at their most extreme ("I am not this withered shell") *and* the period in which, typically, this would-be disembodied 'I' is most strikingly affected by the vicissitudes of the body, the time at which the fact that subjectivity is embodied can least be ignored. This coheres with Beauvoir's insistence on the intellectually scandalous character of old age, for it would accordingly be the time when the Cartesian attitude is both the most ardently desired and yet the least plausible option available to the subject. This unfortunate combination adds a mind/body axis to the schizoid splitting which, as I have shown, Beauvoir argues is a defining feature of our experience of old age. Even though Beauvoir is no Cartesian, she suggests that the desire to disown the body – the Cartesian temptation – becomes increasingly strong with age.[35]

It should be clear how Beauvoir's position, as I have interpreted it, differs from that of those 'moralistes'[36] she criticizes in *La Vieillesse*, who argue that old age brings a blessed liberation of the self from the body. She suggests instead that although the separation of self from body is not something which old age could in any sense really achieve, it is – in spite of this – a state to which the elderly subject pretends, which he earnestly desires. To desire this separation is not liberating, she argues, but rather a case of anguished (if

---

[35] Ryan Song has given a somewhat sketchy account of the role of Cartesianism in *La Vieillesse*. She claims that, 'The body in Colette and Beauvoir, contrary to the Cartesian dualism which dominated most of Western metaphysics from the Renaissance to Modernity, can be consulted as a reliable source of self-knowledge. And, old age serves as a privileged site of such consultation'. See Song, 'Comparative Figures of Ageing in the Memoirs of Colette and Beauvoir', in *Corporeal Practices. (Re)figuring the Body in French Studies*, ed. by Prest & Thompson (Oxford: Lang, 2000), pp. 79-89, p. 80. Yet old age, for Beauvoir, is precisely when the Cartesian delusion of the self's independence from the failing body is most intense. There is no evidence in *La Vieillesse* for Beauvoir's espousal of the sort of reading of self-knowledge off the body which Song describes. Song argues later that 'Beauvoir reverses the negation which Cartesian rationalism attempts to deal to the status of the body by making the body, with its real and/or potential infirmities, the defining influence in psychic experience' (p. 84). Yet close attention to Beauvoir's abovementioned discussion of the complex psychosomatic structures which compensate for bodily or mental failure suggests that Beauvoir privileges neither body nor mind. In any case, the supposed 'reversal' which Song describes would, in fact, remain eminently Cartesian in its reliance on the notion of a non-minded body exerting 'influence' over 'psychic experience'.

[36] See, in particular, Beauvoir, *La Vieillesse*, pp. 335-6.

inevitable) denial, one intermittently undercut by a body which, at this point in life in particular, just will not be ignored. Her second line of attack, which we shall encounter in a moment, is to show that – contrary to popular opinion – sexuality does not fade with age but rather continues to make its presence felt, albeit in different ways. The desire dignified by these 'moralistes' not to coincide with the body, a desire characteristic of old age, is seen by Beauvoir as just one side of a dialectic. She endeavours to restore the second term by juxtaposing the Cartesian pretension to disembodiment with the reality of the quintessentially psychosomatic character of old age. Thus the desire for separation from the body's needs is no liberation, but rather, because it cannot be realized, a source of pain and frustration.[37]

How original is Beauvoir's portrait of old age in terms of alienation and Cartesian contradiction? Although she vehemently attacks Marcel Jouhandeau's *Réflexions sur la vieillesse et la mort*, there are certain similarities between his account and this chapter of *La Vieillesse*. For example, Jouhandeau writes that 'le moment est peut-être venu pour moi d'être autre, non un autre'[38] and 'à mesure que l'on vieillit, on devient plus étranger à soi'.[39] Yet the tone and manner of Jouhandeau's account could hardly be more different from *La Vieillesse*: as his title suggests, these are more a series of etiolated musings, very much in the tradition of literary-philosophical meditation on old age and quite at odds with (and seemingly unaware of) the new-found, politicized, seriousness of twentieth-century gerontological accounts. Beauvoir's text, as I have argued, combines elements of both approaches.

A greater influence on Beauvoir's study than Jouhandeau must, I would suggest, have been André Gorz, who published a two-part essay entitled 'Le Vieillissement' in *Les Temps modernes* in the

---

[37] Ryan Song argues, by contrast, that Beauvoir is suggesting that ageing 'should be graciously accepted as an expected and proper part of existence' (Song, p. 84). Yet Chapter Five of *La Vieillesse*, in particular, is adamant that such acceptance is not only impossible but the very desire for it is a form of denial. Old age is *scandalous* for Beauvoir in *La Vieillesse*, the site of irresolvable contradictions and not something which could ever be 'accepted'.

[38] Marcel Jouhandeau, *Réflexions sur la vieillesse et la mort* (Paris: Grasset, 1956), p. 15.

[39] Ibid., p. 90.

early 1960s.[40] Although Beauvoir mentions, in a footnote to *La Force des choses*, that she had read Gorz's essay, curiously she makes no reference to it in *La Vieillesse*.[41] Central to Gorz's argument in 'Le Vieillissement' is that ageing entails alienation. His essay combines narrative and analysis, much of the narrative being written in the third person, even when it concerns himself; this is a device which reflects the alienation he suggests is characteristic of old age. Several passages bear a strikingly close resemblance to arguments advanced in Beauvoir's study and which I have just examined:

> L'âge avait fondu sur lui, il le rencontrait *dehors* comme un ensemble d'interdits, de limites, d'obstacles indépassables [...] il n'y avait d'âge nulle part en lui, pas plus qu'il n'y avait en lui d'évidence qu'un jour il dût mourir. L'un et l'autre, le vieillissement et le fait qu'il fût mortel, étaient des réalités à la fois omniprésentes, venant à lui des quatre coins du champ social, et parfaitement opaques à l'intelligence: scandaleuses.[42]

> Ce que j'entends montrer, c'est que l'âge [...] nous vient originellement des autres, que nous n'avons pas d'âge pour nous-mêmes, mais seulement en tant qu'Autres.[43]

Moreover, Gorz's essay is one of very few works on old age which, like *La Vieillesse*, combines a political point about the way in which capitalist societies dispose of members of their workforce once they have been 'used up' with a philosophical analysis of the universal human possibility of getting older and being old. It seems probable, then, that Gorz's short essay influenced Beauvoir's later and considerably more developed work.

Old age, according to Beauvoir in *La Vieillesse*, is thus a time of painful contradictions, irresolvable schizoid splitting. There is no such thing, she suggests, as calm acceptance of growing old: calm is not acceptance but denial. Yet if this philosophical account of old age is universalist in the sense that it allows of no exceptions, and in that it deals with *the* body, what room does this allow for the gendered specificity of older men's and older women's experience?

---

[40] André Gorz, 'Le Vieillissement', *Les Temps modernes*, no. 187 (December 1961), 638-65, and no. 188 (January 1962), 829-52.

[41] See Beauvoir, *La Force des choses* (Paris: Gallimard, 1963), II, p. 445.

[42] Gorz, *Les Temps modernes*, no. 187, p. 639.

[43] Ibid., p. 641.

Gender

One might have expected that the author of the *Le Deuxième Sexe* would be particularly interested, in *La Vieillesse*, in the situation of older women. Indeed one might have expected that Beauvoir would expand and problematize the brief and rather negative portrayal of the older woman which forms Chapter Nine of the second part of her earlier work. Yet this is not so and Beauvoir does not even refer to the analysis she provided some twenty years earlier. *La Vieillesse* is overwhelmingly concerned with the situation of older men. Apart from a striking four-page discussion of the sexuality of older women – which happens to be preceded by some thirty pages on the sexuality of their male counterparts[44] – there are very few gender-specific references in the work. Bethany Ladimer has argued that 'women are virtually absent' from both the anthropological and the historical chapters and that, 'only one woman, Lou Andreas Salomé, is studied in the entire text, whereas there must be at least thirty case histories of well-known aged men'. Even in this instance, as Ladimer goes on to observe, 'there is absolutely no explicit mention of any aspects of Salomé's experience that might have been affected by her gender'.[45] Ladimer is right about the case histories, most of which fall within the second half of the book. Yet although there is little attention to the specificity of older women's experience, I shall argue in this section that it would be wrong to think, as Ladimer appears to do, that the end result of this imbalance is a 'privileging' of the older *man*'s experience.

Elaine Marks has argued that similarities between society's treatment of women and old people are usefully brought to the fore by Beauvoir's characterization of both as 'Other', such as in the following passage from *La Vieillesse*:

> Le vieillard chez les primitifs est vraiment l'*Autre*, avec l'ambivalence qu'entraîne ce terme. Autre, la femme est traitée dans les mythes masculins à la fois comme une idole et comme un paillasson. Ainsi – pour d'autres raisons, d'une autre façon – le vieillard dans ces sociétés est-il un sous-

---

[44] Older women: Beauvoir, *La Vieillesse*, pp. 367-71; older men: ibid., pp. 336-66.
[45] Ladimer, *Colette, Beauvoir, and Duras. Age and Women Writers* (University of Florida Press, 1999), pp. 120-1

homme et un surhomme. Impotent, inutile, il est aussi l'intercesseur, le
magicien, le prêtre; en deçà ou au-delà de la condition humaine, et souvent
les deux ensemble.[46]

Beauvoir is clearly alluding here to her analysis in *Le Deuxième Sexe*,
though the somewhat evasive parenthesis ('pour d'autres raisons,
d'une autre façon') suggests she recognizes that any parallel between
the situation of women and older people is far from straightforward.
This notwithstanding, Elaine Marks argues that 'what seems most
interesting in her analyses are the ways in which sexism and ageism
are intertwined'. Marks adds that 'the disgust and fear provoked by
the female body in Western discourses are related to similar effects
provoked by old bodies'.[47] The argument that patriarchy involves
ageism is certainly an interesting one, yet one of the most conspicuous
and surprising facts about *La Vieillesse* is precisely that, vague
allusions aside, Beauvoir does not actually pursue such an argument
there: contrary to Marks's claim, one thing that Beauvoir does not do
in *La Vieillesse* is discuss the relationship between sexism and ageism,
nor does she attempt to link the representation of the female body in
patriarchy to that of the old body, except in the most allusive, tentative
and uncertain of ways, as in the above quotation.[48] Of course, readers
of both works are free to make links of their own between the two
varieties of oppression, yet it is nevertheless striking and significant
that there is no attempt to develop such connections explicitly in *La
Vieillesse*. In fact, the various symmetries between the two works and
the respective forms of oppression they analyse go hand in hand with
an elision of the older woman in *La Vieillesse*.

The elision of older women in *La Vieillesse* has to be seen in
its historical and literary-historical context. As I argued above,
Beauvoir's study owes much to a humanist tradition of bleak
meditation on the significance of human decline. It also shares, in its
second part, aspects of the mode of analysis typical of this tradition: in

---

[46] Beauvoir, *La Vieillesse*, p. 94.

[47] Elaine Marks, 'Transgressing the (In)cont(in)ent Boundaries: The Body in Decline',
Yale French Studies, no.72 (New Haven & London: Yale University Press, 1986), p.
194.

[48] Moreover, although she alludes in passing to a 'tradition misogyne' in literature (*La
Vieillesse*, p. 181), Beauvoir makes no attempt to analyse the possible connections
between ageism and sexism.

particular, as I have already noted, a predominance of anecdotal references to the lives of Great Men. Yet it is only relatively recently – in the late nineteenth and the twentieth centuries, in fact – that there has been a significantly greater proportion of older women than older men in Western society. Only relatively recently, too, have women been widely recognized as producers of cultural artefacts. Throughout much of the history of Western culture, old age has been a predominantly male experience, in quantitative terms, the dangers of multiple childbirth having been largely responsible for relatively few women reaching this stage in life.[49] That Beauvoir's treatise to some extent places itself within a male-dominated tradition and refers surprisingly little to the experience of older women reflects not only Beauvoir's own attitude to her models and precursors, but also the fact that her work stands historically at a moment of transition: a long-standing tradition of humanist meditation on old age, which had arisen in social conditions that allowed many more men than women to reach this stage, and many more men to write openly about having reached it, was gradually being forced to redefine itself in the context of the relatively recent phenomenon of there being many more older women in the world than older men. Yet even taking this historical context into account, I would suggest that there is still something surprising about the elision of the older woman in *La Vieillesse* which demands further investigation.

Beauvoir had addressed the situation of the older woman, albeit briefly, in *Le Deuxième Sexe*.[50] I want to highlight two points in her earlier account and compare them with her discussion in *La Vieillesse*. In *Le Deuxième Sexe*, Beauvoir suggests that female ageing is patriarchally constructed in terms of a succession of crises, corporeal and mental.[51] This she contrasts with the way in which the patriarchal imaginary envisages male ageing – as a process of smooth

---

[49] Minois, *Histoire de la vieillesse*, p. 122. See also Stuart-Hamilton, *The Psychology of Ageing: An Introduction* (London: Kingsley, 3rd Edition 2000), p. 18.

[50] Beauvoir, *Le Deuxième Sexe*, II, ch. 9: 'De la maturité à la vieillesse'.

[51] In *Le Deuxième Sexe*, women's sexual development is construed in terms of a succession of violent crises: 'la crise de l'adolescence' (II, p. 140), 'la crise de la puberté' (II, p. 63), birth – 'cette crise' (I, p. 68). These transitions are marked by violence: 'C'est par un rapt réel ou simulé que la femme était jadis arrachée à son univers enfantin et jetée dans sa vie d'épouse; c'est une violence qui la change de fille en femme.' (II, p. 148).

development: 'Tandis que celui-ci vieillit continûment, la femme est brusquement dépouillée de sa féminité'.[52] She then moves on to characterize the subjective experience of the older woman in terms of a feeling of depersonalization:

> Un des traits les plus accusés chez la femme vieillissante, c'est un sentiment de dépersonnalisation qui lui fait perdre tous repères objectifs [...] ce n'est pas *moi* cette vieille femme dont le miroir renvoie le reflet. La femme qui "ne s'est jamais sentie aussi jeune" et qui jamais ne s'est vue aussi âgée ne parvient pas à concilier ces deux aspects d'elle-même.[53]

Beauvoir is suggesting here that ageing, for women, necessarily involves alienation, a defensive splitting of the self into the ageless inner *me* and the ravaged outer shell.

Thus, in *Le Deuxième Sexe*, Beauvoir claims that men age – from infancy to old age – smoothly ('continûment'), by contrast with the succession of violent traumas which, she thinks, characterizes women's ageing. Yet in *La Vieillesse*, as I demonstrated in the preceding section, Beauvoir argues that ageing brings crisis and contradiction to the lives of men and women alike. This modifies her earlier view, for now it is not only women for whom ageing is a series of traumas to be assimilated, but men as well.[54] In particular, Beauvoir's attention to the abovementioned range of compensatory psychosomatic structures (those which may be abruptly removed by shock, stress and failure, with concomitant physical decline) represents an attempt to reintroduce crisis into the account of the male lifespan. Thus what was presented initially, in *Le Deuxième Sexe*, as an analysis specific to women's ageing, has become, in *La Vieillesse*, a universal characteristic of a supposedly genderless process. Similarly in the second case I described, where Beauvoir suggests in *Le Deuxième Sexe* that the older woman's subjective experience is one of depersonalization: an ageless self becomes defensively dissociated, she thinks, from its outer body-image. Yet in *La Vieillesse*, as I showed in the previous section, Beauvoir argues that such

---

[52] *Le Deuxième Sexe*, II, p. 456.

[53] Beauvoir, *Le Deuxième Sexe*, II, p. 462.

[54] Kathleen Woodward argues that 'Beauvoir seems to have been temperamentally repelled by changes in the body', 'Simone de Beauvoir: Aging and its Discontents', in Benstock (ed.), *The Private Self. Theory and Practice of Women's Autobiographical Writings* (London: Routledge, 1988), pp. 90-113, p. 96.

depersonalization is not just a feature of the older woman's experience but is a universal characteristic, affecting older men and older women alike. Alienation and schizoid splitting are now said to be characteristic of a universal human experience of old age.

In addition to this universalist account of elderly experience in both sexes, *La Vieillesse* also emphasises, in the section on the sexuality of the older man, what might be termed a crisis of masculinity in later life. It is generally agreed that *Le Deuxième Sexe* at least describes (and may also endorse) a view of the female body as 'une chose opaque aliénée',[55] an opposition between the female body as opaque prison and the male body as the transparently efficient instrument of projects:

> L'homme oublie superbement que son anatomie comporte aussi des hormones, des testicules. Il saisit son corps comme une relation directe et normale avec le monde qu'il croit appréhender dans son objectivité, tandis qu'il considère le corps de la femme comme alourdi par tout ce qui le spécifie: un obstacle, une prison.[56]

In *La Vieillesse*, however, the male body, with age, ceases to be this transparent instrument and becomes an imprisoning obstacle: 'il existe cruellement comme frustration et souffrance';[57] 'le corps, d'instrument, devient obstacle'.[58] So *La Vieillesse* demonstrates that men too are destined, with age, to corporeal alienation. Toril Moi has argued that there is a sense in which male (hetero)sexual desire is, paradoxically, accorded a privileged position in the earlier work, leading to a general 'overvaluation of masculinity'.[59] I would suggest,

---

[55] Beauvoir, *Le Deuxième Sexe*, I, p. 67.

[56] Ibid., p. 15. Note that although it seems clear from the way in which this remark is framed that in this case Beauvoir is describing how *men* construe the female body (or, as we might prefer to say, how the female body is construed under patriarchy) and is not herself endorsing this commonplace, elsewhere the framing is absent and the distinction between description and promotion very much harder to decide. See, for example, the following remarks: 'Son destin physiologique [celui de la femme] est très complexe; elle-même le subit comme une histoire étrangère; son corps n'est pas pour elle une claire expression d'elle-même; elle s'y sent aliénée' (ibid., p. 400). Do comments such as these imply that the narrative of the female body is contingently an alien one, because patriarchy has made it so, or is it, in some sense, necessarily so?

[57] Beauvoir, *La Vieillesse*, p. 293.

[58] Ibid., p. 336.

[59] Moi, *Simone de Beauvoir: An Intellectual Biography*, p. 160.

however, that it is here that *La Vieillesse* proves to be far more than a second-hand *Second Sex*, for it may be used as a corrective to this 'overvaluation of masculinity', with its exposure of the vanity of the patriarchal male self-image.

Thus old age shakes men out of their quiet self-satisfaction, their presumed social and corporeal superiority, shattering the supposedly seamless unity of the male lifespan. The male adult rejects the old man he will become: 'Il hait dans le vieillard sa future condition'.[60] Echoing a refrain from *Le Deuxième Sexe*, Beauvoir writes:

> Le petit garçon trouve dans son pénis un *alter ego*: c'est dans son pénis que toute sa vie l'homme se reconnaît et qu'il se sent en danger. Le traumatisme narcissiste qu'il redoute, c'est la défaillance de son sexe: l'impossibilité de parvenir à l'érection, de s'y maintenir, de satisfaire sa partenaire.[61]

The fear of this 'traumatisme narcissiste', the enduring but usually repressed underside of the adult patriarch's phallic self-esteem, becomes more intense, and even the paralyzing norm, in the sexuality of the elderly man. Beauvoir suggests that elderly men are more inclined to masturbate and to seek out prostitutes than their younger counterparts.[62] Indeed, her general vision of elderly male sexuality is a catalogue of what, in conventional terms, are defeats and embarrassingly deviant compromises:

> Il prend plaisir à des lectures érotiques, à des oeuvres d'art libertines, à des gauloiseries verbales, à fréquenter des jeunes femmes, à des contacts furtifs; il se livre au fétichisme, au sado-masochisme, à des perversions diverses et, surtout après 80 ans, au voyeurisme.[63]

---

[60] Beauvoir, *La Vieillesse*, p. 117.

[61] Ibid., p. 341.

[62] Beauvoir insists that the sexual behaviour of the elderly man varies with social class, though for reasons which seem facile: working-class men are more likely to remain sexually active on a regular basis because 'Les ouvriers, les paysans ont des désirs plus directs, moins asservis aux mythes érotiques que les bourgeois' (*La Vieillesse*, p. 343). This is Beauvoir's own bourgeois 'mythe érotique', recalling Zola's fascination with working-class sexuality as supposedly untrammelled and even bestial in, for example, the country fair scene in *Germinal*.

[63] Beauvoir, *La Vieillesse*, p. 343.

It is difficult not to discern in these pages a certain delight at the idea of old age being a time in which male sexual desire is caught up in much of what patriarchal society itself sees as deviant. This is the time of schizoid splitting and self-contradiction, the moment at which the male subject becomes Other, the moment at which a lifetime of repressed psychosexual complexes, rather than dissipating, seize control, finally deflating phallic self-esteem: 'Chez ceux qui étaient déchirés par des conflits qu'ils surmontaient tant bien que mal, l'âge exaspère les antagonismes'.[64]

So although we may initially be surprised by the lack of interest in the experience of older women in *La Vieillesse*, this elision does not amount to a 'privileging' of older men, since the material about them is largely negative. The universalist account of the elderly experience of both sexes in *La Vieillesse* constitutes a generalization of the account of the older woman in *Le Deuxième Sexe*. Although this involves a regrettable loss of specificity, it nonetheless restores a measure of balance in the aftermath of the distorted opposition, which Beauvoir implied in *Le Deuxième Sexe*, between the female lifespan as a series of crises and male ageing as smooth development.[65]

The performative dimension, or 'senescent textuality'

It should be clear by this point that *La Vieillesse* is itself a text rich in contradictions and unresolved ambiguities. In a certain sense, then, it performs its own description of the contradictory character of old age. In this section, I pursue further the performative dimension to *La Vieillesse*. In addition to contradiction, old age is also thought by Beauvoir to be characterized by repetitiveness. It transpires that the

---

[64] Beauvoir, *La Vieillesse*, p. 382.
[65] Diana Holmes has argued that 'when Beauvoir writes of the physical process of ageing she reproduces, apparently uncritically, the view that the ageing female body – far more than the male – constitutes a blatant signifier of mortality, a redundant, even repulsive object that (as she had feared) inspires horror when recognized as one's own reflection and inevitably ceases to inspire sexual desire' (Holmes, p. 435). This is true of Beauvoir's account in both *Le Deuxième Sexe* and *La Force des choses* but is misleading about *La Vieillesse*, where, as I have argued, she goes to great lengths to reintroduce crisis, repulsion and non-recognition into her account of elderly *male* experience.

text is itself, on several different levels, a repetitive performance. Whereas it can be argued that the textual 'repetitions' in *Le Deuxième Sexe* function to ironic (and political) effect[66], much of the repetition in *La Vieillesse*, by contrast, would appear to be accidental and occasionally even compulsive. First there is the repetition of text from elsewhere: long passages from works of geriatric medicine[67] are reproduced with little analysis or comment, as are whole lists of raw statistical data.[68] The fate of works of literature and (auto)biography is generally more extreme still: rather than engaging in dialogue with them, Beauvoir's text simply throws down excerpts to illustrate points that have, essentially, already been made. Literary and (auto)biographical material is very seldom used to advance the argument, is allowed next to no voice of its own: its is overwhelmingly a subservient and supporting role. This is in marked contrast to the polyphonic or multivocal character of *Le Deuxième Sexe*, in which individual testimony, such as that of poet Cécile Sauvage, moves the argument forward. The engagement of this earlier work with its cited material is often very sophisticated and far more than simple repetition. For example, a number of accounts which featured in Stekel's notorious *La Femme frigide* are reproduced, yet Beauvoir's text frees these women's voices from the pathologizing context of Stekel's study and, crucially, restores a certain agency by reinscribing them within an existentialist framework. Instead of casting 'frigidity' as a complaint which afflicts women, as Stekel did, Beauvoir's existentialist feminism restores a sense of women's agency

---

[66] The issue of repetition in *Le Deuxième Sexe* has admittedly proved contentious. One charge against Beauvoir with respect to her view of the female body in this work is, in Toril Moi's words, that she becomes 'thoroughly ensnared in the very patriarchal categories she sets out to describe' (Moi, *Simone de Beauvoir*, p. 173). Writing in Beauvoir's defence, in a comparison between her and Kristeva's views of maternity, Linda Zerilli argues: 'Beauvoir's dramatization of the maternal body in process [...] is not a rearticulation of masculinist values nor an embracement of the subject of modernity; it is a sophisticated and underappreciated feminist discursive strategy of defamiliarization: a highly charged, always provocative, and at times enraging restaging of the traditional drama of maternity' (Zerilli, p. 112). I agree with Zerilli.

[67] See, for example, the account of mental illnesses common in the elderly, pp. 518-30.

[68] See, for example, the table headed 'Quelques budgets' on p. 256 and the 'Tableau des ressources des personnes âgées', pp. 248-53.

to these case histories: 'La frigidité même nous est déjà apparue comme un châtiment que la femme impose autant à soi qu'à son partenaire [...] elle s'interdit le plaisir'.[69] As Judith Butler has argued, one of the redeeming uses of the existentialist framework in this earlier work is to show that oppression, 'despite the appearance and weight of inevitability, is essentially contingent'.[70] Thus, in conjunction with her detailed analysis of the way in which oppression is materially entrenched in patriarchal society, Beauvoir's commitment to (and advancement of) a certain form of existentialism in *Le Deuxième Sexe* infuses her account with emancipatory potential. My main point here, however, is that the use of literary material in *La Vieillesse* is, by contrast, largely repetitious in that it is mere citation.

Only rarely does Beauvoir list her biographical sources in *La Vieillesse*. Yet from their frequent reappearances, the attentive reader soon realizes that the *dramatis personae* of this study are, in fact, few in number. Dozens of anecdotes from the lives of the following, in particular, are spread throughout the text from Chapter Three to the end: Whitman, Goethe, Tolstoy, Hemingway, Victor Hugo, Gide, Jouhandeau, Schopenhauer, Clemenceau, Rodin, Paul Claudel, Swift and Chateaubriand. References to the lives of these individuals (though not to the mere handful of biographies from which these anecdotes are presumably drawn) occur over and over again: the impression created is one of constricting repetitiveness.[71]

Yet arguably more striking even than this strong readerly sense of repetitiveness are the examples of word-for-word repetitions. Thus Freud loses the same grandson twice (without any indication in the second instance that this information has already been communicated, or in the first that it will be repeated).[72] Images are twice defined in extremely similar terms[73] and the same line of Victor Hugo's is quoted and analysed twice.[74]

---

[69] Beauvoir, *Le Deuxième Sexe*, II, p. 187.

[70] Judith Butler, in *Simone de Beauvoir: Witness to a Century*, ed. by Hélène Wenzel, p. 35.

[71] In particular: Goethe (pp. 329-30; 349-50; 495), Tolstoy (pp. 330-2; 335; 351; 376-82; 405; 462-4; 470, 495-6), Victor Hugo (pp. 218-20; 335; 351-5; 373-6; 422; 467; 531-7), Swift (pp. 202-3; 391; 477) and Chateaubriand (pp. 322; 348-9; 552-64).

[72] Beauvoir, *La Vieillesse*, pp. 499, 546.

[73] Beauvoir, *La Vieillesse*, pp. 309, 386.

[74] Ibid., pp. 220, 535.

The presence of all these repetitions – of structure, sources, characters, anecdotes, forms of expression and quotations – in *La Vieillesse* is more than a sign of editorial laxity, though it may also be this. For, as I mentioned, one of the characteristics of old age which Beauvoir emphasises is indeed the tendency to repeat: in her survey of anthropological material, Beauvoir concludes that old people in what she calls (with the scare-quotes) 'primitive' society are those who help to perpetuate its very fabric by passing on technical and ritual knowledge[75]. They are agents of repetition. Similarly, in modern Western society she suggests that the elderly tend to function as agents of political repetition because they vote for conservative politicians.[76] Finally:

> Les personnes âgées ont beaucoup de mal à s'adapter aux situations neuves; elles réorganisent aisément des choses connues mais résistent aux changements. Acquérir ce qu'on appelle un *set* – c'est-à-dire une attitude, une orientation d'esprit – leur demande un gros effort: elles sont esclaves des habitudes prises antérieurement, elles manquent de souplesse. Une fois le *set* adopté, elles le lâchent difficilement. Même en face de problèmes auxquels il ne convient absolument plus, elles s'y cramponnent. Leurs possibilités d'apprentissage se trouvent donc très réduites.[77]

Beauvoir returns to this point much later, citing the tendency to repeat as the conclusion of a number of surveys on older men in the workplace: 'ils tendent à persévérer dans leurs fautes et ils sont paralysés par les montages acquis […] adopter de nouvelles attitudes – de nouveaux *sets* – leur est difficile'. On the production-line, however, this can be an asset: 'ce qui joue en leur faveur, c'est la répétition: en usine ils recommencent à longueur de journée les gestes appris et ils finissent par les exécuter automatiquement'.[78] In Beauvoir's eyes, this makes the abrupt cessation of these repeated activities, at retirement, all the more of a shock.

Generalizing, Beauvoir observes of 'le vieillard' that, 'il prend l'habitude d'avoir des habitudes'.[79] For one who works with ideas, Beauvoir suggests that the tendency to repeat which comes with old

[75] Beauvoir, *La Vieillesse*, p. 99.
[76] Ibid., p. 295.
[77] Ibid., pp. 40-41.
[78] Ibid., p. 247.
[79] Ibid., p. 492.

age, may have positive benefits – those usually referred to vaguely as
'experience':

> en effet quelque chose demeure: une aptitude à réapprendre ce qu'on a su,
> des méthodes de travail, des résistances à l'erreur, des garde-fous. Dans
> plusieurs domaines - philosophie, idéologie, politique - l'homme âgé est
> capable de visions synthétiques interdites aux jeunes.[80]

Yet as these examples of areas of work suggest, this kind of
experience is the preserve of the middle classes and, in particular, the
intellectual. The tone of this admission is striking: experience, even
intellectual experience, is not an accumulated stack of knowledge but
rather a set of skills – acquired gradually and by dint of much
repetition – permitting some limited recovery of all that has been lost
elsewhere and providing some small immunity to error. The gains of
experience, which repetition teaches, are then meagre indeed: scant
consolation, yet perhaps the only consolation, for all that has been
taken away from the subject. It is as though the strong humanist
subject who calls for revolution in this very work is simultaneously
undermined from within, replaced, in post-structuralist fashion, with a
nexus of aptitudes and discursive possibilities allowing for the
slenderest margin of liberty and resistance.

*

Old age, for Beauvoir, implies increasing automatism. *La
Vieillesse* reflects this, it being in a sense the mechanical replication of
certain tried and tested 'méthodes de travail', in accordance with the
familiar 'recipe' stipulating that knowledge from different discourses
be excavated in libraries, gathered, summarized, re-presented and
connected, in pursuit of one of those 'visions synthétiques interdites
aux jeunes'. Faithful to its own senescent logic of repetition, *La
Vieillesse* seems on one level to be less the trace of a forward-looking,
humanist, project and much more the playing-out of various
discursive possibilities and acquired aptitudes: a text which is itself an

---

[80] Beauvoir, *La Vieillesse*, p. 403. This tentative suggestion of Beauvoir's, that
'experience' is both an intelligible notion and perhaps not all bad, should be
contrasted with the views expressed by Roquentin on this matter in Sartre's *La
Nausée* (Paris: Gallimard, 1938), p. 103.

'automatic' production, bearing witness to as well as describing the growing automatism of old age.

That *La Vieillesse* has been neglected by students of Beauvoir's work is not just to be explained by the fact that it has long been out of print. As I hope to have shown, it represents a formidable challenge to any would-be interpreter. Although Beauvoir described it as the 'symmetrical' companion to *Le Deuxième Sexe*, many of the conceptual and structural similarities paradoxically contribute to a work which seems indifferent to many of the key conclusions of its more celebrated precursor, perhaps most notably by showing remarkably little interest in the situation of older women. Yet, as I argued, this lack of interest cannot be interpreted as a 'privileging' of elderly male experience, at least not in terms of value. I argued that Beauvoir's account of elderly experience in Chapter Five of *La Vieillesse* is derived from a straightforward universalization of her earlier findings with respect to the older woman in *Le Deuxième Sexe*. Although this involves a loss of specificity, when considered in conjunction with the emphasis on the crisis-ridden character of elderly male development, the new account does to some extent correct an imbalance in Beauvoir's earlier treatise.

The textual tensions in *La Vieillesse* can to some extent be accounted for in terms of its historical context. Beauvoir is both attempting to write a twentieth-century, social-scientific (gerontological), account of the socio-economic realities of life as an elderly person in an ageist society and, at the same time, to contribute to an age-old tradition of bleak meditiation on the philosophical significance of senescence.

Yet although this is a work that is, in many other ways, contradictory and ambivalent, it is safe to conclude that Beauvoir, for all her commitment to improving the socio-economic lot of the elderly, was convinced that there is something inevitably, 'ontically', alien about old age (and inevitably alienating about the ageing process). Although *La Vieillesse* constitutes an extended attempt to understand and empathise with the situation of the elderly, it also endeavours to articulate why all such attempts must inevitably fail; Beauvoir's philosophical interest here lies in the limits of empathy and the meaning of human decline. Gerontologists and other readers of this text have tended to dismiss these findings, in the crudest way possible, making them out to be distorted and overgeneralized autobiography, considerations relevant mainly to the particular circumstances of Beauvoir's own life. Toril Moi, whose 'intellectual biography' of Beauvoir seldom even refers to Beauvoir's six-hundred page study of old age, does not hesitate to dismiss her engagement with this topic in *La Force des choses* as disguised evidence of 'depression'.[81] Kathleen Woodward, similarly, suggests that 'old age served her as a metaphor for disease, depression and death'.[82] These interpretations seem to me to oversimplify Beauvoir's engagement with old age, reducing its significance and, in Woodward's case, failing to recognize that Beauvoir's study offers a critique of the gerontological assumption, which to a great extent underpins Woodward's own work on ageing in literature, that 'positive thinking' about old age is always both possible and desirable.

Beauvoir's study is not without its limitations. Yet it remains a rich document from a period of transition in which the tensions between an age-old tradition of bleak, 'ontological', writing on the subject comes into conflict with the relatively recently-emerged discipline of gerontology. In particular, it may lead us to question – as others have recently begun to do[83] – the gerontological assumption that the most effective way to combat societal ageism is to flood the cultural sphere with unreservedly 'positive' images of older people. Above all, it offers a lesson in accepting a degree of unresolved ambivalence in what we are prepared to hear and write about old age.

By virtue of its reflexive and performative dimension – the way in which both contradiction and repetitive automatism are enacted in the fabric of the text itself, both of which are said by Beauvoir to be characteristic of old age – *La Vieillesse* consistutes the first of my examples of 'senescent textuality'.

---

[81] Moi, *Simone de Beauvoir: An Intellectual Biography*, p. 242.
[82] Woodward, 'Simone de Beauvoir: Aging and its Discontents', p. 93.
[83] For example, Featherstone & Wernick, 'Introduction'.

Chapter Two

André Gide's split senescent subject

Gide's transition from bright young thing to grand old man of the French cultural establishment was – characteristically – public, painful and textual. This chapter analyses Gide's many experiments, in his *Journal*, with different textual models for the ageing process. These are far more diverse and complex than Beauvoir suggests in her rather cursory reading of Gide's work in *La Vieillesse*. She oversimplifies Gide's engagement with the ageing process by drawing attention only to those passages that support her own view of that process, one which I examined in the previous chapter.[1] She notes primarily that his *Journal* provides many illustrations of the painful divide between a subject's youthful self-image and the objective reality of his or her being old.

While I do not dispute the presence of such examples. I shall attempt to demonstrate that there is a great deal more to Gide's engagement with the ageing process than this. Gide's work in fact contains a number of competing textual models of that process. Some involve a pedagogical relationship with another person, while many may be termed 'autopedagogical' (that is, they are concerned with self-fashioning and imply an 'educative' relation to the self). Others are based on physical processes in the natural world, on analogies with travel, or with political and historical change. A few are crude – the older pederast preying vampirically upon the youth of his student/victim – but most are intricate and multifaceted, balanced on the knife-edge of ambivalence. Indeed I shall argue that Gide's diary is characterized by an underlying ambivalence towards the ageing process: while on occasions he will suggest that the accurate and clear-sighted representation of this process might be among the greatest ambitions of diary-writing, elsewhere there is evidence of the most elaborate equivocation and denial, as though the proper role of the diary were in fact to shore up its author's youthful self-image.

---

[1] Beauvoir, *La Vieillesse* (Paris: Gallimard, 1970), p. 314.

Ambivalence is not the only feature of Gide's treatment of ageing that is shared with *La Vieillesse*. Gide's diary-writing is also the second of my examples of what I have called 'senescent textuality'. I shall examine, in particular, the tension between Gide's aspiration in the *Journal* towards an *art de bien vieillir* and the reality of *ressassement* and desirelessness in his writing of old age, one described and also performed both here and in his unjustly neglected short appendix to the diary, *Ainsi soit-il ou Les Jeux sont faits*.

The representation of decline: aspiration and equivocation

In the *Journal*, it often seems as though the representation of his own decline into old age were foremost among the aspirations of Gide's diary-writing:

> La constatation de la progressive déchéance de l'âge exige la sincérité la plus difficile, peut-être, à obtenir de soi-même. Un journal qui tiendrait compte de cela serait d'un bien grand intérêt. Du reste je ne crois pas à la fatalité de cette déchéance, et n'était quelque affaiblissement de mes sens (la vue surtout), je ne me sentirais guère atteint par l'âge; si je ne le voyais dans la glace et si je ne me le redisais sans cesse, rien en moi ne me ferait souvenir que je suis entré depuis trois jours dans ma cinquante-neuvième année. Mais peut-être est-ce un des privilèges de la vieillesse, de ne pas trop s'apercevoir elle-même de ce qui crève les yeux de tous.[2]

Yet the conditionals in the second sentence allow for a degree of uncertainty about the relationship between the 'journal' in question here and Gide's *Journal*. The familiar Gidean rhetoric of sincerity is lent a new twist by the legal and political overtones of 'constatation' and 'déchéance' respectively: it is a matter of officially registering that, in old age, the sovereign has been deposed, a reign has come to an end – and thereby, in a sense, enacting this deposition – as much as one of merely recording or transcribing decline. The suggestion is that writing about ageing and old age has not merely a descriptive role but a more intimate connection with its subject-matter. The idea that discourse about old age enacts as well as describes is picked up later in the passage: 'si je ne me le redisais sans cesse', he notes, there

---

[2] Gide, *Journal* (Paris: Gallimard/Pléiade), vol. II, ed. by Martine Sagaert (1997), p. 61 (25 November 1927).

would be nothing to remind him of this process. And since many of Gide's 'conversations' with himself seem to take place in his diary, this must, to some extent, apply to writing too. In the case of senescence, it is not just that words present a mirror-image of a process but – as in the case of the mirror in the passage above – the image itself makes an impact and plays an active part in subjective experience.

Writing makes ageing a reality for the subject, just as mirrors do; in both cases, the suggestion is that this subject would otherwise continue to live in the blithe ignorance of assumed youthfulness. The kind of 'sincérité' in question is a determination to forego the dubious 'privilège' of old age – which amounts to blindness, or even denial – by using self-writing as a means to self-realization, a way of recognizing that one is an ageing subject. Gide suggests, however, that such self-realization can at best be intermittent: he seems to be in agreement with Beauvoir (see Chapter One, above) that the objective reality of being old is not immediately accessible to the subject's consciousness and is not available at all in any stable or enduring form. In a similar vein to Beauvoir, who suggested that this lack of immediacy in recognition persists into old age, a seventy-one year-old Gide notes: 'Pas de jour, pas d'heure où je ne me redise mon âge. Je n'ai pas dit: où je ne le sente'.[3] In the following passage, the difficulty involved is redescribed in overtly textual and pedagogical terms:

> Si je ne me redisais sans cesse mon âge, certes je ne le sentirais guère. Et même me répétant, comme une leçon qu'on a du mal à apprendre *par cœur*: j'ai soixante-cinq ans passés, je parviens mal à m'en convaincre et ne me persuade que de ceci: que l'espace est étroit où mes désirs et ma joie, mes vertus et ma volonté, peuvent encore espérer de s'étendre. Ils n'ont jamais été plus exigeants.[4]

---

[3] Gide, *Journal*, II, p. 698 (31 May 1940). See also ibid., p. 75 (29 February 1928): 'Malgré ce rhume abrutissant, je ne me sens pas beaucoup vieillir, et même me suis rarement senti l'esprit plus dispos, tout l'être plus gonflé d'aspirations, de désirs. Mais je suppute sans cesse mon âge et me redis que le terrain tout brusquement peut manquer à mes pieds. J'obtiens de moi de n'en pas éprouver trop de tristesse' and *Journal*, I, p. 1047 (18 November 1917): 'Si je pouvais ignorer, oublier mon âge, combien je m'en apercevrais peu! Je devrais ne me le redire que pour me pousser au travail'.

[4] Gide, *Journal*, II, p. 488 (23 Mar 1935). Gide returns to the idea of learning his age 'by heart' in his entry for 29 September 1940: 'Si je ne connaissais mon âge "par

Old age is a text, 'une leçon', an educational and perhaps even a holy text, destined to be recited yet also destined to retain a degree of externality, to remain alien, to the diligent and the devout alike. In his seventies, Gide set about learning lists of Latin vocabulary and lengthy passages of Virgil by heart.[5] This gradual colonization of his time and mind by the dead language of an old master – and, as in Dante's case, mentor – can be viewed as an analogy, or way of *acting out*, the process described in the passage above: he is learning by heart, taking to heart, the lesson of death's slow and inexorable victory. And this process is a linguistic one: the 'letter' of death is invited in and gradually takes over. As in psychoanalytic acting-out, however, the meaning of the process remains inaccessible to consciousness: Gide becomes thoroughly steeped in the 'leçon' of senescence, but this immersion is not knowledge.[6] In the passage above, the attempt to learn the text of senescence yields only the banal realization of the limited scope available for the satisfaction of imperious desires. In the later pages of the *Journal*, however, and particularly in *Ainsi soit-il*, it is the threat of desirelessness ('inappétence' or 'anorexie', as Gide calls it) which typically brings him back to the 'leçon' of choice, Virgil:

> Cette inappétence est intellectuelle autant que physique. J'ai grand mal à m'intéresser à ce que je lis. Au bout de vingt pages, le nouveau livre me tombe des mains; et je reviens à Virgile, qui ne m'offre plus précisément de surprise, mais du moins un constant ravissement.[7]

---

coeur" et ne me le redisais sans cesse, je m'en apercevrais à peine et ce ne serait pas pour en souffrir' (ibid., p. 735).
[5] First mentioned on 25 June 1944 (*Journal*, II, p. 993). Gide had long been a reader of Virgil but this is the first time that Virgil is put to this particular use. In that Gide had always borrowed compulsively from Classical authors, Virgil in particular, this could be seen as the final and most intense form of a protracted kind of deathly embrace.
[6] Freud asserts: 'the patient does not *remember* anything of what he has forgotten and repressed, but *acts* it out. He reproduces it not as a memory but as an action; he *repeats* it, without, of course, knowing that he is repeating it'. Freud, 'Remembering, Repeating and Working-Through', in SE 12, pp. 145-156, p. 150.
[7] Gide, *Ainsi soit-il ou Les jeux sont faits* (Paris: Gallimard, 1952), p. 24.

In this 'constant *ravissement*' there is perhaps more constancy than rapture. Only the repetition of the familiar brings pleasure in this state of desirelessness: force of habit brings Gide back to Virgil. The chief virtue of this author's work lies in providing Gide with a reassuring form of stable pleasure. Moreover, the pleasure in question must in part be one of returning to the classrooms of his youth and to a mode of learning – recitation – that had a considerably more important role in education at the end of the nineteenth century than it did in the France of the 1950s. Thus the notion of learning the '*leçon*' of old age by heart is paradoxical or equivocal because this very mode of learning implies a return to his youth by way of the pedagogical method of a bygone era: the aspiration to learn old age 'by heart' is tinged for a moment with equivocation, in this implicit return to the classrooms of his youth.

Many entries in the *Journal* seek to ascribe a range of self-improving moral purposes to the very activity of diary-writing: in particular, the idea that by recording how his time is used, the diarist will come to use it more profitably.[8] In this process of written self-examination, it becomes especially important to identify correctly the nature and causes of inactivity or wasted time. One particular conflict relevant here is the relationship between the presentation of tiredness and that of old age: 'À partir de trente-cinq ans, la tentation vous vient facilement de mettre au compte de l'âge le moindre effet de la fatigue, et d'aider même à sa durée en ne la considérant pas d'abord comme un malaise passager.'[9] This is cast as a moral temptation, for if lassitude is ascribed to old age and is accordingly deemed inevitable, then the impulse to struggle against it is weakened and the work-ethic crumbles. This imposes a duty of rigour on the diarist, for the diagnosis of age-related infirmity is not, he fears, simply a neutral observation but an utterance capable of actively undermining his resolve in the future. The difference between the moral significance attached to tiredness and that imputed to old age is suggested in the following passage: 'J'écris ceci maintenant que je me fais vieux, et ce

---

[8] Gide discusses the self-improving moral potential of diary-writing in an entry from the Autumn of 1894, only to dismiss the idea as 'Très mauvaise et pas à garder. Va contre ma pensée' (I, pp. 185-6). He retained the idea, however, and several other entries reiterate it. See, for example, his entry for 16 December 1921 (I, p. 1148).

[9] Gide, *Journal*, I, p. 440 (Hendaye, 1905).

soir que je me sens fatigué.'[10] Gide's use of *se faire vieux* is of particular interest: though not a neologism, it is nonetheless a rare expression. Strictly, *se faire vieux* means simply *devenir vieux* (i.e. *vieillir*) and thus denotes an involuntary process. Yet this unusual expression also recalls a second category of similar-seeming constructions, all of which do imply an intentional aspect: *se faire humble, se faire communiste* and so on.[11] I would accordingly suggest that the use of *se faire vieux* in place of the eminently more customary and concise equivalents, *vieillir* and *devenir vieux*, implies an attempt to introduce an element of volition into the ageing process, by way of association or linguistic cross-contamination with similar structures. Moreover, the binary structure of the sentence quoted foregrounds a contrast between the passivity of *se sentir* ('fatigué') and the active, and I have suggested intentional, quality of *se faire* ('vieux'). Gide allows himself simply to feel tired – a comparatively harmless (because transitory) affliction. There is a sense that the relationship between the diary and its writer's experience of senescence is intimate and therefore fraught with danger, as though there were a risk of his writing himself into old age.

Gide tends either to invest the ageing process with an element of volition, or else only to allow senescence into the text alongside a range of other, covering, options. The following passage is an example of this second approach:

> Est-ce vieillesse, accumulation de fatigue, ou disposition maladive? Véritable orgie de néant à quoi m'invitait la froideur et laideur du temps, mon incuriosité totale à l'égard d'Alger, et une complète absence de tous désirs.[12]

---

[10] Gide, *Journal*, II, p. 85 (1 July 1928).

[11] *Le Robert* (1985) distinguishes between two relevant categories of the construction *se faire* + adjective: (i) e.g. *se faire rare*, where *se faire* means *devenir* or *commencer à être*; (ii) e.g. *se faire humble*, where *se faire* means *se rendre* or *devenir volontairement*. (Note that Littré (1889) is in agreement on this point.) Strictly, Gide's 'je me fais vieux' falls into the former category. My argument, however, is that this unusual expression (chosen in preference to *vieillir*) leans towards the second category and thus acquires an overtone of volition. Thus I shall treat Gide's use of *se faire vieux* as implying an attempt to introduce volition into the subject's experience of the ageing process. If this argument is not accepted, then it must at least be agreed that the preference for *se faire vieux* over the shorter and more usual *vieillir* draws attention to the process by making it lexically laborious.

[12] Gide, *Journal*, II, p. 111 (16 January 1929).

In fact, as Gide approaches old age, he becomes markedly more reluctant in his *Journal* to attribute the way he feels to being old.[13] Compare the above passage, written when he was fifty-nine, to the following, written at thirty-six:

> C'est effrayant ce que j'ai vieilli ces derniers temps. Certainement quelque chose en moi ne va plus. On ne peut ni vieillir plus vite, ni s'en apercevoir davantage. Je ne puis encore prendre cela au sérieux; je crois à une fatigue passagère. Déjà j'éprouvais cette affreuse vieillissure l'an passé à même époque.[14]

Both passages entertain the idea of old age as the root cause of his malaise, yet the second far more emphatically, indeed ostentatiously, than the first. It is as though the older he becomes, the more seriously damaging the effect of admitting irreversible decline is felt to be. Gide's neologism in the second passage, 'vieillissure', implies both a process of wearing-down ('vieillesse' and 'usure') and a certain familiarity, as though he were giving senescence a pet name. This may be thought to suggest an affectation of decrepitude on Gide's part and to recall the Romantic trope of old age commencing in the poet's early twenties and indicating a premature world-weariness. Gide is sometimes, though seldom, inclined in this direction: he remarks in a bitter moment of lucidity (indeed of depressive 'hyper-lucidity'[15]), on one occasion, that 'ce que j'appelle "fatigue", c'est la vieillesse, dont rien ne peut reposer, que la mort'.[16]

Yet such extreme, unequivocal, and arguably self-indulgent references to old age are rare in the diary. Tiredness is almost always Gide's preferred alternative self-diagnosis, presented more compellingly alongside old age and often a range of other possible explanations. Nonetheless, it appears that some early readers of his published diary expressed surprise at his being prepared to admit to

---

[13] This is no longer the case in *Ainsi soit-il*, however, where 'inappétence', 'anorexie' and the 'absence de tous désirs' are attributed directly to old age.

[14] Gide, *Journal*, II, p. 535 (16 May 1906).

[15] The term is Kristeva's. The depressed person is 'hyperlucide' because he or she will 'see through' meaning: 'Une séquence signifiante, forcément arbitraire, lui apparaîtra lourdement, violemment, arbitraire: il la trouvera absurde, elle n'aura pas de sens'. See *Soleil noir. Dépression et mélancolie* (Paris: Gallimard, 1987), p. 62.

[16] Gide, *Journal*, II, p. 113 (29 January 1929).

the age-related diminution of his creative faculties. In the following
passage, Gide comments on their consternation:

> Mais, pour moi, précisément, cette constatation n'a rien d'horrible; il me
> paraît tout naturel de vieillir et je ne m'en sens pas plus honteux que je ne le
> serai de disparaître. Je crois qu'il y a dans la sincérité d'un aveu plus
> d'éloquence et d'enseignement que dans les plus savantes feintes de
> l'éloquence [...] Au reste, je reconnais que ces aveux de défaillances, je ne
> les ferais peut-être pas si volontiers, si j'étais bien convaincu que ces
> défaillances dussent être définitives. Mais ce qui me rassure un peu et me
> les fait considérer comme n'étant pas nécessairement l'effet de la vieillesse,
> c'est que, de tout temps, j'en ai connu de semblables et parfois de très
> prolongées.[17]

Once again, Gide refers here to the 'constatation' of decline, recalling
his earlier comment that senescence requires of the diarist 'la sincérité
la plus difficile'. Yet this rhetoric of sincerity, as is often the case in
Gide's   diary,   is   accompanied   by   some   devious   rhetorical
manoeuvering, indeed precisely the sort of 'savantes feintes' deemed
inferior in this very same passage, where sincerity is held to contain
'plus d'éloquence [...] que les plus savantes feintes de l'éloquence'.
For   despite   appearing   initially   to   assume   fully   his   published
'constatation' of senescent decline, Gide goes on to suggest that the
failings described, those which caused consternation among his
readers, may not in fact have been due to old age at all. This passage
effectively sees Gide both extolling the virtue of plain-speaking about
old age and, at the same time, offering an exemplary case of the most
'savante' equivocation. And Gide goes on to distance himself even
further from the initital 'constatation' by suggesting a wider moral and
pedagogical role for his diary: 'Je crois que le simple aveu que j'en ai
fait [de ces défaillances] au moment même où j'en souffrais ne sera
pas sans apporter quelque secours à ceux qui se découragent trop
vite'.[18] Yet in this masterful demonstration of rhetorical ingenuity, it is
no longer at all clear what exactly he had been admitting in an 'aveu'
that was supposedly 'simple': by the end of this passage, it is certainly
no longer a question of acknowledging age-related infirmities in the
belief that it is 'tout naturel de vieillir', but rather an altogether more

---

[17] Gide, *Journal*, II, pp. 494-5 (29 May 1935).
[18] Ibid., p. 495 (29 May 1935).

vaguely-defined set of 'défaillances', ones which may in fact bear no relation to the ageing process.

This tendency towards equivocation is, on other occasions, more blatant than devious:

> Tout ici baigne dans un azur splendide, comme au temps de mes *Nourritures*. Si je ne me redisais sans cesse (et pourquoi?) que je suis vieux, à peine sentirais-je mon âge. Peut-être la curiosité m'entraîne-t-elle un peu moins et les aurores me paraissent-elles moins surprenantes. [...] Le monde garde son attrait, mais ces droits sur tout que je m'accordais naguère, je me les reconnais moins volontiers, à présent que je sais si peu nombreux ceux avec qui je les partage. Du reste ceci n'est pas question d'âge.[19]

Here a lengthy exploration of the impact of old age is cut short and indeed revoked in the curt final sentence. Here, as elsewhere in Gide's diary, 'mes *Nourritures*' functions as an age-related index of a certain way of relating to the world (cf. 'La pensée de Marc me maintient dans un état constant de lyrisme que je ne connaissais plus depuis mes *Nourritures*'), one associated with youth.[20] The work is invariably cited as evidence in an argument for his having changed with age, in relation to it, and usually in the context of his having come to entertain a less open relation to the world. After so lengthy a consideration of specifically age-related changes, the closing denial is not only utterly unconvincing but really too simplistic, too petulant, to constitute a proper engagement with the preceding investigations. In fact it is almost childish, a kind of regressive refusal to engage with the reality of senescence in all its compexity. In the following passage, by contrast, there is equivocation of a very much more sophisticated, as it were adult, kind:

> Mon âme est demeurée jeune à ce point qu'il me semble sans cesse que, le septuagénaire que je suis indubitablement, c'est un rôle que j'assume; et les infirmités, les défaillances qui me rappellent mon âge, viennent à la manière du souffleur, me le remettre en mémoire lorsque je serais enclin à m'en écarter. Alors, comme un bon acteur que je veux être, je rentre dans mon personnage et me pique de le bien jouer. Mais il me serait beaucoup plus naturel de m'abandonner au printemps qui vient; simplement je sens que je n'ai plus le costume qu'il faut pour cela.[21]

---

[19] Gide, *Journal*, II, p. 472 (18 August 1934).
[20] Gide, *Journal*, I, pp. 1050-1 (15 December 1917).
[21] Gide, *Journal*, II, p. 753 (6 March 1941).

The trope of old age as an act is far from unique to Gide; what is interesting in this passage is the way in which this trope is itself 'acted out', rendering the relation between actor and role both complex and shifting. The role of the seventy year-old is one mastered only intermittently, the distance between actor and role having to be closed periodically by the intervention of a 'souffleur'. Contrary to Beauvoir's reading, the passage also opens a distance between Gide and the metaphor of old age as a stage role: 'comme un bon acteur *que je veux être*' implies that Gide is not, then, entirely this actor.[22] So if old age is a role to be acted out, then this very acting-out is itself a role or posture. Thus one figure is nested inside another, in a microscopic *mise-en-abyme* which effectively interposes two layers of textual interpretation between Gide and old age.

The closing sentence of the above passage is also relevant to my argument with regard to the place of volition in Gide's engagement with old age: the implication throughout this passage is that he chooses to embody the 'personnage' of the seventy year-old, priding himself on giving a good performance, maintaining the kind of professional relationship which an actor enjoys with a prompter. Thus age-related decline is once more portrayed as a purposeful, deliberate, activity, that is one over which the subject has a large measure of control. Yet, in the last sentence, this familiar position is partially revoked: the 'naturel' is now beyond his reach, lacking as he does this particular costume. This last sentence forces a rereading of the entire passage and a reassessment of the claim that old age is a volitional activity: the actor, if actor he be, is not entirely free in his choice of roles but constrained, as it were, by a diminishing wardrobe. Above all, he is not free not to act, for such 'naturel' is precisely one of the roles for which he is no longer equipped.

The passage just examined provides a particularly rich example of the way in which Gide's *Journal*, in spite of its author's aspiration to plain-speaking in this matter, responds equivocally to the ageing process. It also serves to introduce the theme of my next section, namely the way in which the *Journal* experiments with different textual tropes or models for the ageing process (in the above,

---

[22] See Beauvoir, *La Vieillesse*, pp. 314-5.

that of the actor and role), developing, complicating and, in the end, invariably limiting or rejecting them.

Modelling the Ageing Process

(i) The dominant model: pedagogy and 'autopedagogy'

Gide's early diary entries are very much concerned with the idea of self-fashioning. As a young man, the dominant conception of his own development advanced in the diary may be termed 'autopedagogical' – one of self-teaching – and involves the careful selection and combination of various 'influences' in a deliberate attempt to shape a certain personality.[23] Such influences include reading matter, friends, environment, music, moral principles and working practices:

> Il faudrait limiter et définir ma personnalité *telle que je la voudrais* plus tard pour marcher vers un idéal *choisi* et *voulu*, et ne pas laisser cette personnalité se former seule au gré des circonstances. Il faut arriver à se faire *tel que l'on se veut*. *Choisissons* donc les influences. Que tout me soit une éducation.[24]

If the determination to sustain a sense of volition is a key feature of Gide's representation of his advance into old age, as I argued in the previous section, then this may be seen as a stubborn vestige of the very pronounced emphasis here and throughout the early part of the diary on willed control over his own development: the above passage is saturated with words denoting or implying volition, which I have italicized. As is often the case with such stipulations – consider numerous manuals of musical technique from the medieval and early modern periods – the suspicion may arise that they were intended to modify practices or patterns of behaviour which were actually quite at odds with those they advocate, though this is not the point at issue here. There can, however, be no question that we are dealing with a certain self-image, one to which the idea of volition and progress is

---

[23] See Philippe Lejeune, *Le Pacte autobiographique* (Paris: Seuil, 1975), pp. 165-72.
[24] Gide, *Journal*, I, p. 35 (14 October 1888).

central. This gradual elaboration of self-image is supposedly the project of a lifetime, indeed is life-as-project:

> La vie d'un homme est son image. A l'heure de mourir, nous nous refléterons dans le passé, et, penchés sur le miroir de nos actes, nos âmes reconnaîtront *ce que nous sommes*. Toute notre vie s'emploie à tracer de nous-mêmes un ineffaçable portrait. Le terrible, c'est qu'on ne le sait pas; on ne songe pas à se faire beau.[25]

Here the autopedagogical project of self-fashioning acquires an aesthetic aspect which makes explicit its narcissistic bearing: this is not just about learning, but also about self-prettification – how that learning is regarded, by oneself and others – how the subject will look. The published *Journal* forms part of this self-image, this 'ineffaçable portrait', and within it the importance accorded to the subject's control over his own development with age is great indeed, especially in the early part. The degree of control at issue here is suggested in the following passage:

> Je voudrais, à vingt-trois ans, à l'âge où la passion se déchaîne, la dompter par un labeur forcené et grisant. Je voudrais, tandis que les autres courraient les bals, les fêtes et les débauches faciles, trouver une volupté farouche à vivre d'une vie monastique, seul, absolument seul, ou entouré de quelques blancs chartreux, de quelques ascètes, retiré dans une agreste chartreuse, en pleine montagne, dans un pays sublime et sévère.[26]

In this vision of ascetic withdrawal, the fantasy of self-willed solitude is given such free rein that a qualifying repression follows immediately ('[...] seul, absolument seul, *ou* [...]', my italics): the autopedagogical pretension to fierce mastery, the taming of youthful exuberance by way of 'un labeur forcené' itself shows signs of being a fantasy running riot, out of control. The illusion of an isolated and self-developing consciousness executing perfectly a life-plan devised in advance is undermined even as it is expressed. Moreover, the sexual overtones which hard work acquires in the passage ('grisant', 'volupté farouche'), as well as the ice-and-fire scenario as a whole, suggest that this may be more about deriving a heightened form of pleasure from the 'enthousiasme' with which youth is usually

---

[25] Gide, *Journal*, I, p. 149 (3 January 1892).
[26] Ibid., p. 46 (24 February 1889).

associated. Simply being young is not enough: what is required is a reflective, technical, art of being young and the *Journal* is itself very much implicated in the elaboration of such an art. Even as a young man, then, it could be said that Gide has a cult of youth, in the sense not only of idealizing youth as a privileged phase but also of approaching youthfulness as something that must be cultivated, raised with skill into a value, reflected upon and lived artfully.

Yet to conceive of ageing in terms of controlled self-fashioning, as the younger Gide does – to imagine that he is wholly in control of his development over time – is surely to prepare the way for a rude awakening. Entertaining a cult of youth seems destined to leave the ageing individual bereft and exiled. Gide's *Journal*, moreover, evinces and contributes to the elaboration of an attachment to being young, and especially to the *idea* of being young, which is as extreme as any I shall consider in this book. His diary traces a number of ways in which he sought to negotiate the problematic transition from the state of being a young man with an ideal of ageing in terms of projective self-fashioning to that of an older man who remained attached to Youth, as a value in itself. In broad terms, Gide's way of negotiating this transition involves moving from his initial, autopedagogical, attitude into pederastic pedagogy.

Gide is infamous as an advocate and practitioner of pederasty; this is one feature of his life and work that has always attracted critical interest.[27] My intention is not to rerun the various discussions here but rather to situate this aspect of Gide's life and work more clearly in the context of his engagement with the ageing process in the *Journal*. In particular, what happens to the fantasy of controlled ageing when transferred to a pedagogical and pederastic context? While the autopedagogue can easily entertain fantasies of complete self-control, of directing his own development through the years, can the pederastic pedagogue really think it possible to select every 'influence' which contributes to the shaping of another individual?

The following passage, which is a creed of sorts, provides an indication of how the question of control is affected by the transition from autopedagogy to pederastic pedagogy:

---

[27] Most notably in Naomi Segal, *André Gide: Pederasty and Pedagogy* (Oxford: Oxford University Press, 1998), to which the present discussion is greatly indebted.

On a dit que je cours après ma jeunesse. Il est vrai. Et pas seulement après la mienne. Plus encore que la beauté, la jeunesse m'attire, et d'un irrésistible attrait. Je crois que la vérité est en elle; je crois qu'elle a toujours raison contre nous. Je crois que, loin de chercher à l'instruire, c'est d'elle que nous, les aînés, devons chercher l'instruction. Et je sais bien que la jeunesse est capable d'erreurs; je sais que notre rôle à nous est de la prévenir de notre mieux; mais je crois que souvent, en voulant préserver la jeunesse, on l'empêche. Je crois que chaque génération nouvelle arrive chargée d'un message et qu'elle le doit délivrer; notre rôle est d'aider à cette délivrance. Je crois que ce que l'on appelle "expérience" n'est souvent que de la fatigue inavouée, de la résignation, du déboire. Je crois vraie, tragiquement vraie, cette phrase d'Alfred de Vigny, souvent citée, qui paraît simple seulement lorsqu'on la cite sans la comprendre: "Une belle vie, c'est une pensée de jeunesse réalisée dans l'âge mûr."[28]

This creed – 'je crois' features some seven times and 'je sais', twice – is typical in its attempt to unite pederasty and pedagogy. The first sentence alludes to a specific complaint which reflected a general feeling among some of his readers that Gide's work was inflected by a sense of his lost youth, an attempt to recover in text what he had lost in life. In spite of the elevated, pedagogical, tone of the passage, it begins with a comic, lightly veiled, allusion to pederasty ('et pas seulement la mienne' – running after youths as well as Youth). Indeed the passage as a whole is an intricate attempt to interweave sexual desire and pedagogical seriousness: the 'irrésistible attrait' of youth serves as a prelude to truth and the whole discussion of who should learn what from whom. The fervour built from the repetition of 'je crois' and the expansive movement of the passage serves to bind the pederastic to the pedagogical. The pederastic pedagogue is cast as a Socratic midwife to the truth born of Youth: 'notre rôle est d'aider à cette délivrance'.

In the transition from self-fashioning to pederastic pedagogy, there is accordingly a degree of abandonment, a renunciation of the aspiration to complete control: whereas the young man is expected to be rigorously self-disciplined, it is for the older man not only to assist him – as the midwife – but also to give way before him (youth 'a toujours raison contre nous'). In fact, despite the Socratic allusion, this passage complicates considerably the traditional Platonic view of the pederastic relationship: for here the young man is both irresistibly

---

[28] Gide, *Journal*, I, pp. 1150-1 (26 December 1921).

attractive *and* in possession of a truth which the older generation lacks. Youth is dominant both sexually and intellectually. Similarly, the scepticism about '"expérience"' does, in its general bearing, run counter to the Platonic vision of the pederastic relationship: the older man's gift is supposed to be wisdom, this being all he has to offer in exchange for the sexual obligingness of the younger partner. Yet here the role of the older man is to give way entirely to Youth and its message, assisting him if possible but, above all, aspiring to learn. In this sense what we have here is a new kind of pederastic pedagogy: one in which the younger partner has all the work to do and, seemingly, little to gain in return. It is a model in which the sexual-intellectual exchange mechanism at the heart of Platonic pederasty no longer functions. Indeed, it is a model in which the older partner is represented as being very much more dependent upon his younger counterpart than in the supposed Classical precedent.

Gidean pederastic pedagogy is, among other things, a defence against the narcissistic trauma threatened by the ageing process. For, as I have argued, if the young Gide has a strong attachment to the idea of being young, for its own sake, then this does not simply disappear as he ceases, with age, to coincide with this idea. Rather, younger partners allow a transformation to occur: the instinct for self-fashioning and the emphasis on self-control are converted into a more discrete form of educational manipulation of which midwifery is the model. For there is much more than sex and wisdom at stake in Gidean pederasty: it is a way of negotiating the ageing process which allows the attachment to youth not to be given up but rather transformed. It enables a redistribution of psychic attachments in response to this process. This helps to explain why, as I noted above, the older partner in Gidean pederasty is represented as being far more dependent upon his younger counterpart than in its Platonic precursor. For the younger individual is effectively incorporated into the pederast in order to conceal the narcissistic wounds inflicted by the many psychic, somatic and social losses which come with age. The younger partner functions as a prosthetic substitute, a necessary part of a psychic economy which continues to operate in accordance with an ideal of youthfulness. This account of Gidean pederasty is borne out most clearly in such passages of the *Journal* as the following, which deal with the absence – temporary or permanent, real or imagined – of the younger lover:

Certains pourrissent, et d'autres s'ossifient; tous vieillissent. [...] Avec M.
[Marc] toute ma jeunesse est partie; je somnole en attendant son retour et
perds mon temps comme s'il m'en restait beaucoup à perdre. Je dors trop,
fume trop, digère mal et m'aperçois à peine du printemps. L'être
s'abandonne quand il n'a plus à songer qu'à lui-même; je ne m'efforce que
par amour, c'est-à-dire que pour autrui.[29]

It is *Gide*'s youth that is absent in Marc's absence: gone too is a sense
of temporal discipline, the controlled use of time which was, as I
noted, so important an element in his own youthful project of self-
fashioning.[30] Marc has become an essential part of Gide's psychic and
somatic constitution and the bodily disturbances which his absence
occasions are particularly striking. The somewhat platitudinous tone
of the concluding sentence may mislead, yet this is no plea for
disinterested altruism but rather an admission that the younger other is
an indispensible element in the life of an ageing individual, one
without whom even the basic functions of human existence can hardly
be performed. This then is what might be called the prosthetic role of
the younger lover in Gidean pederastic pedagogy. The younger
partner takes on all that the older, alone, can no longer do ('lorsque je
voyage, c'est avec un compagnon jeune; je vis alors par
procuration'[31]), sometimes including even the very business of living.
Such a vicarious existence allows the older Gide to remain attached to
the passions of his youth – in this case travelling – and thus avoid the
necessity of a traumatic renunciation.

(ii) Other models of the ageing process

Although the autopedagogical and pedagogical-pederastic
models which I analysed in the preceding subsection are dominant in
the *Journal*, they coexist alongside and sometimes interact with a

---

[29] Gide, *Journal*, II, p. 30 (5 May 1927). Gide is in Switzerland. See Alan Sheridan,
André Gide. A Life in the Present (London: Hamish Hamilton, 1998), p. 416.
[30] See also the entry for 4 May 1918: 'Me passer de M. ne me paraît déjà plus
possible. Toute ma jeunesse, c'est lui' (*Journal*, I, p.1065) and 13 October 1929:
'Tout me fatigue et m'ennuie. Avec ce petit m'a quitté ce qui me restait de jeunesse'
(*Journal*, II, p. 152). The emphasis in both is again on *Gide*'s youth.
[31] Gide, *Ainsi soit-il*, p. 25.

number of other textual models of the ageing process. I shall examine a selection of these in the present subsection, noting any relationship with the dominant conceptions already outlined.

Particular places – and their familiarity or lack of it – are frequently used as spatial markers of temporal change. The experience of travel does in general enjoy an intimate relationship, for Gide, with his experience of the ageing process. Large sections of his *Journal* proper and many of the short texts republished alongside it in the new Pléiade edition are travelogues that forge a close association between the movement through space that is travel and the traveller's movement through time that is senescence. This link is brought to the fore in his epigraph to 'Le Renoncement au voyage', a text which returns repeatedly to this theme: 'J'avais l'âge où la vie commence à prendre un goût plus douteux sur les lèvres; où l'on sent chaque instant tomber d'un peu moins haut déjà dans le passé.'[32] Age is beginning to change both the quality of a life and the experience of time. There is a sense of the sudden death of the present moment which the syntax performs: the lack of the syntactically necessary comma between 'haut' and 'déjà' precipitates the reader onwards with uneasy haste.

In the work that follows, this sense of age-related existential disappointment is successively positioned and repositioned in relation to the scenery and objects of North Africa. Of Algiers, Gide writes: 'Mais les hôtes, hélas! sont changés; tout m'y paraît moins neuf; j'y suis moins jeune.'[33] Observed changes to the environment seem to reflect back the image of the subject's senescence; the compressed 'j'y suis moins jeune' brings together the subject, the place and the recognition of age. The text seems to insist on the bond between the changed city and the ageing traveller. And as if the growing sense of a present 'déjà dans le passé' were not sinister enough, dreams conspire to do away with the future:

---

[32] Republished in *Journal*, I, p. 365. *Le Renoncement au voyage*, Gide's account of his travels in North Africa in 1903-4, was written in 1904 and published in 1905 in the *Mercure de France*. In the following year, the work was amalgamated with some of Gide's earlier travel writings and republished as *Amyntas*. (See Sheridan, *André Gide*, p. 207.) The editors of the new Pléiade edition of Gide's diary have chosen to include many of Gide's shorter autobiographical texts, in the appropriate chronological positions.

[33] Gide, 'Le Renoncement au voyage', *Journal*, I, p. 367.

> J'ai rêvé que je revenais ici – dans une vingtaine d'années. Je passais et
> n'étais plus reconnu par personne; les enfants inconnus ne me souriaient
> pas; et je n'osais pas demander ce qu'étaient devenus ceux de jadis, que
> j'avais peur de reconnaître dans ces hommes courbés, fatigués par la vie.[34]

In view of the importance of the 'prosthetic' youth in pederastic-
pedagogical negotiations of the ageing process, there is something
particularly terrifying about the vision of children for whom growing
up involves becoming 'courbés, fatigués par la vie'. For this dream
represents the antithesis of Gidean pederasty, as I have described it:
these are children who objectify and accordingly intensify the
pederast's sense of his own senescence. The dream is interesting, too,
for its intimation of a sense of colonial guilt largely unknown to the
waking Gide of this period: these are children whose passage from
youth into old age will be rapid – 'courbés' and 'fatigués' not just by
'la vie' in some universal sense but by the specific hardships and
injustices of their life under a colonial regime. Thus this dream of
double non-recognition, or partial recognition, is overdetermined. It
also hints at an anxiety that the pederastic-pedagogical option will not
always be available: the children no longer smile, not only because
they do not recognize him but also perhaps because they are no longer
open to his advances.

There are moments in 'Le Renoncement' when the physical
characteristics or the inhabitants of a particular place seem to restore
the narrator's youth, erasing his sense of time having elapsed, only for
this very restoration then to be revoked:

> Je rentre au coeur de ma jeunesse. Je remets mes pas dans mes pas. Voici
> les bords charmants de ce sentier que je suivais, ce premier jour où, faible
> encore, échappé de l'horreur de la mort, je sanglotai, ivre du simple
> étonnement *d'être*, du ravissement d'exister. Ah! qu'à mes yeux encore
> fatigués l'ombre des palmes était calmante! Douceur des ombres claires,
> murmures des jardins, parfums, je reconnais tout, arbres, choses... le seul
> méconnaissable, c'est moi![35]

---

[34] Gide, 'Le Renoncement au voyage', *Journal*, I, p. 414.
[35] Gide, *Journal*, I, pp. 399-400 (Biskra, 30 November 1903). The passage alludes to
the tubercular episode which also features in *Si le grain ne meurt*.

As he retreads this path of memory, the resemblance proves so perfect that it serves to undo the initial aspiration, the idea that this is youth revisited. In the movement of this passage, the unchanging environment recalls and momentarily restores Gide's youth, only for this to be snatched away again. The place provides a perfect marker, a paradigm of self-coincidence against which the gap between 'mes pas' and 'mes pas' can only become more apparent, the gap of senescence which entails a degree of alienation, rendering him 'méconnaissable'.

The willingness to travel and be surprised by new experience is closely related to Gide's sense of his age. At twenty-seven, while touring Belgium, he complains: 'Je crois que je me fais déjà un peu vieux pour voyager. La ressemblance des choses m'ennuie déjà plus que leurs différences ne me dépaysent, et les pays que j'ai traversés aujourd'hui manquent de ce confortable qui ferait désirer y demeurer.'[36] Here again we find Gide's *se faire vieux*, implying, I have argued, some pretence of control over the ageing process. And as in the previous paragraph, an observation of resemblance in the outer world is associated with a sense of being old – that is, of no longer being the same. Thus in his travel-writing, the scenery is very often invested with the power of a spatial marker against which his own sense of having aged may then be read. Yet this scenery does not actually have to remain the same. It suffices that it be apprehended as such:

> Si peu nombreux sont les éléments de l'accord, que le moindre changement reste le plus souvent inaperçu lui-même, pour celui dont l'esprit répugne à l'analyse et qui cueille sans tige sa joie; mais il s'étonne, repassant aux mêmes lieux, de ne plus regoûter mêmes délices, et, ne sachant qu'accuser de la diminution de leur charme, s'en prend à soi, se vieillit.[37]

Here the process of measuring and inferring is more clearly apparent than in the other examples, above; the conclusion of age is a desperate last resort, in the absence of any other hypothesis. The reflexive *se vieillir*, according to Littré, means 'se faire paraître, se dire plus vieux qu'on n'est', and is thus a matter of volition: Gide's *se vieillir* annexes a degree of control (and hence responsibility) to the individual over what is usually considered the paradigm of an uncontrollable process,

---

[36] Gide, *Journal*, I, p. 262 (January 1897).
[37] Gide, 'Le Renoncement au voyage', *Journal*, I, p. 414.

ageing.[38] The travelling subject attributes to senescence the obscure feelings of disappointment provoked by places which seem to have remained the same yet that have, in fact, changed with a subtlety that eludes direct apprehension. Yet the returning traveller's self-diagnosis of senescence (and corresponding projection of a prematurely aged self) is, Gide's passage suggests, often the wrong conclusion, stemming from an inability to detect subtle changes in the environment.

Historical and political change provides another of the diary's favoured models of the ageing process. In long sections of the *Journal* from the 1930s – which veer between autocritique and self-justification as Gide tries hard to reconcile his new-found political beliefs with both his class privilege and his own brand of non-institutional Christian spirituality – the prize is a politics of Youth. As for Beauvoir and Sartre in the 1960s and '70s, Communism and Youth are closely associated, with the demand for Revolution in the political creed mapping onto the stereotypical moment of revolt and discontent in the human lifespan, an association concretized, for example, in the involvement of Communist and Maoist students in Mai '68, as well as that of students in other revolutionary movements. Gide explicitly associates Communism with the decline of 'ce vieux monde'.[39] This attempt to tag political movements with the sign of Youth is not, of course, restricted to Communism: in a similar vein, Gide remarks of Fascist slogans daubed on Italian walls that they are 'propres à galvaniser la jeunesse', though does not himself place Fascism under the aegis of Youth.[40] There is nothing particularly original about this association of Gide's: the link between revolutionary change and youth is hardly new, whether in the political sphere or the aesthetic (cf. Futurism). What is interesting about Gide's engagement with Communism in the 1930s, however, is the extent to which the *Journal* suggests that his political conversion was bound up with anxiety about his own age and an attempt to recover the zeal of youth. I am suggesting that this engagement with Communism constitutes a political analogy of his pederastic-pedagogical

---

[38] Littré (1889) and *Le Robert* (1985) are in agreement on this point: both see *se vieillir* as denoting a voluntary act.

[39] Gide, 'Feuillets' (1933), *Journal*, II, p. 446.

[40] Gide, *Journal*, II, p. 562 (5 August 1937).

negotiation of the ageing process: central to both is the idea of vicarious experience and prosthetic youth.

The use of political and historical models for the ageing process in Gide's self-writing is not, however, confined to Communism. In 'Morale Chrétienne', an early text incorporated into the new Pléiade edition of the *Journal*, an extended political simile characterizes the ageing individual's religious development:

> Il est vrai que tous n'ont pas également à combattre pour se vaincre et mourir à eux-mêmes – dit l'Imitation (I, xxv, 4). Je crois à présent, sinon qu'il est inutile de "se vaincre", du moins qu'après des victoires remportées, la jeunesse doit se conclure, et, par des traités de paix intime et perpétuelle, préparer ce qu'on appelle l'âge mûr. Ainsi ne voyons-nous, pour les Etats, les ères classiques s'établir que sur l'achèvement des luttes intestines. Alors les forces éduquées, au lieu de s'antagoniser, peuvent s'occuper aux frontières et permettre de s'épanouir à l'harmonie de la cité.[41]

This passsage is clearly related to the topic of self-fashioning, or 'autopedagogy', which I discussed above. Yet it is considerably more complex than any of the examples considered there: it combines religious, political and historical elements to produce a model of moral development with age. Moreover, 'les forces éduquées' not only refers to the taming of unruly forces in the Classical city-state but also recalls the pseudo-scientific terms of a vitalist psychological analysis. Thus the range of elements incorporated into this particular comparison is remarkably wide. In addition, the rhetorical nature of the comparison is itself grand: an extended, or epic, simile, pivoting on 'Ainsi'. Such grandeur of content and form could easily conceal the dangerously uncertain character of the parallel: what exactly would the equivalent be, in the inner life of the individual, of a 'traité de paix' between the warring factions of a city-state? What guarantee is there that this peace will be 'perpétuelle'? What happens to those

---

[41] Gide, 'Morale Chrétienne', *Journal*, I, p. 259. Compare the similar: 'J'aime assez me représenter que nos parents si chers, qui nous paraissent si calmes à présent, ont eu comme nous leurs jours de révolte et de trouble; mais comme le temps calme! comme il ruine! comme il meurtrit! Ne laissons pas trop faire au temps; enlevons-lui de ses victoires, et prenons-les nous-mêmes avant, pour en avoir au moins un peu d'orgueil. N'attendons pas qu'il nous apaise; il apporte une paix trop en deuil. Apaisons-nous nous-mêmes' ('Feuillets' (1894), *Journal*, I, pp. 195-6). Here the familiar autopedagogical insistence upon the subject's volition meets the politco-historical analogy of self-pacification.

factions that are defeated – are they entirely eliminated or is there a risk of the repressed returning? Finally, why is this comparison so introverted, implying that peace is entirely an internal matter, independent of whatever lies beyond the frontiers of the polis or individual – an 'outside' which may still have a decisive impact upon them? The simile is intended to illustrate the individual's spiritual progress from 'la jeunesse' to 'l'âge mûr' and, like all such normative models of age-related personal development, inevitably raises many questions.[42] From an autobiographical perspective, many of these questions seem particularly pertinent to Gide: he who signed innumerable treaties (and treatises) in the search for peace – marriage and, eventually, *Corydon*, among others – before realizing that peace in one province could mean war in another; he whose introverted model of non-institutional Christian spirituality eventually collapsed into a sentimental Communism; he whose literary classicism seems to flourish not on the basis of 'l'achèvement des luttes intestines', but rather upon their exacerbation.

The above model of personal development with age, from 'Morale Chrétienne' (1896), which posits a peaceful transition from the strife of youth to the harmony of maturity, stands in marked contrast to the following remark from Gide's diary for 1919, which could almost have been written as a riposte to the earlier pamphlet:

> Pour ma part je puis vous dire que je n'ai jamais senti le vieillissement que dans cette quiétude précisément à quoi votre morale invite, mais que souvent vous atteignez d'autant moins que vous vous efforcez davantage et plus nostalgiquement d'y atteindre. Votre croyance en la survivance des âmes est nourrie du besoin de cette quiétude et de l'*inespoir* de la pouvoir goûter durant la vie.[43]

From the context it is clear that Gide's imagined interlocutor is a Christian reader, which makes the relationship to the earlier pamphlet all the more striking. The aspiration to quietude, to 'l'harmonie', which the earlier text characterized positively in terms of an age-indexed developmental process, is here dismissed as 'vieillissement' – not simply ageing in a neutral sense, but a defeat, far too willing a surrender to the inevitable. To cultivate quietude is not development

---

[42] Please see my discussion of Jung and Erikson in Chapter Four, below.

[43] Gide, *Journal*, I, p. 1101 (20 January 1919).

but a hastening toward the grave, the 'rest' and 'peace' – meaning death – of the Victorian hymnal. Immediately before this passage, Gide insists upon the importance for him not of quietude but rather 'cette cohabitation en moi des extrêmes', 'cet *état de dialogue*'.[44] Although the scope of this remark is clearly wider than just this, the context allows it to be read as having a particular bearing upon the question of subjectivity and ageing. Thus in spite of his espousal of the quietist model in 'Morale Chrétienne', Gide as he ages comes to favour instead a model of inner variety, dialogue and 'cohabitation'.

Indeed it would appear that far from being peacefully resolved, the diarist's 'luttes intestines' become progressively more violent with age. We move here from a model of dialogue between inner forces to one of fragmentation:

> Ce n'est pas les gros bras très forts que j'aime, c'est l'harmonie de tout le corps. De même certaine harmonie de l'esprit. A mesure que l'âge vient, je sais plus malaisément m'en passer [...] Je vieillis par morceaux qui deviennent sujets d'étonnement pour le reste.[45]

And similarly:

> [...] et ma volonté qui se lamente de vieillir. Encore si l'usure était constante et régulière, si elle attaquait à la fois, et également, âme et corps; mais non, elle procède par bonds; je vieillis par morceaux, qui deviennent un sujet de stupeur et de désolation pour le reste.[46]

There is here a sense that the attrition, or wear ('usure'), of the ageing process attacks unevenly: this is not a case of simple diminution. Rather, the body and mind are split into fragments which change at different speeds ('je vieillis par morceaux') and the overall picture verges on the grotesque or monstrous. Later on, Gide returns to this model of fragmented parts when he complains that 'ce qui de moi a le plus vieilli, c'est ma voix'.[47] Bound up with this fragmentation is a loss of self-control, both conceptual and physical: both of the above formulations remark on the sense of bafflement or confusion ('étonnement', 'stupeur') caused by this *morcellement*. In the case of

---

[44] Gide, *Journal*, I, p. 1100 (20 January 1919).
[45] Ibid., p. 425 (17 March 1904).
[46] Ibid., p. 479 (3 September 1905).
[47] Gide, *Journal*, II, p. 823 (12 July 1942).

his voice, the emphasis is very much on loss of control: this was once 'une voix dont j'étais parfaitement maître' and is no longer. I have already argued that the idea of volitional control is key to both Gide's youthful model of ageing as self-fashioning and to later, desperate, attempts to redescribe an inevitable process in volitional terms. Although these are by far the dominant constructions, the few remarks on fragmentation which I have just examined suggest a very different model. The emphasis is no longer on volition – indeed it is 'ma volonté qui se lamente de vieillir' – and the integrity of the subject is undermined by a fragmentation and warping induced not by failings for which he can be held responsible, but by an inevitable and external process of 'usure'.

Although not the dominant model of the ageing process in Gide's diary, *morcellement* remains a significant alternative to the volitional model so much in evidence elsewhere in this text. It is striking how similar this alternative version is to Beauvoir's conflictual model of the ageing process, as outlined in Chapter Five of *La Vieillesse*.[48] Both involve inexorable and widening inner division, a conflict between different parts of a fragmented subject and, as such, stand resolutely – and in Beauvoir's case, explicitly – opposed to the model of old age as quietude outlined in, for example, 'Morale Chrétienne' and Marcel Jouhandeau's *Réflexions sur la vieillesse et la mort*. In Gide's case, however, we have a generalized fragmentation into several parts whereas in Beauvoir's, a schizoid split, in two, between the inner conviction of enduring self-sameness and the objective but alien fact of old age. Beauvoir's position is closer, in this sense, to the 'état de dialogue' between two extremes, which precedes *morcellement* in this alternative and less prominent model of the ageing process in Gide's *Journal*.

I have examined, in this subsection, three other ways in which Gide's diary approaches the ageing process, in addition to the autopedagogical and pedagogical-pederastic modes. The first of these, travel-writing, is invariably bound up with a weighing of similarities

---

[48] Indeed Beauvoir uses Gide's *Journal* to illustrate her thesis in Chapter Five of *La Vieillesse* (see, in particular, p. 314 of her study). She suggests rightly that he speaks often of 'Ces oscillations, de notre conviction intime à un savoir objectif'. Yet as this chapter demonstrates, Gide's engagement with the ageing process in his *Journal* is multifaceted and very much more complex than Beauvoir's primarily illustrative use of the text implies.

and differences, an attempt to pinpoint age-related changes in the individual or environment: places are used as spatial markers of temporal processes. Second, history and politics offer a model of Youth in Communism and a grand vision of mature harmony in 'Morale Chrétienne'. Yet this quietist hope is explicitly rejected in the third model I examined, gleaned from later passages which construe ageing first in terms of an inner split ('dialogue' and 'cohabitation') and then as fragmentation or *morcellement* ('je vieillis par morceaux'). Indeed the early passage from 'Morale Chrétienne' proves to be something of an exception. For rather than espousing a quietist model of the ageing process, Gide's diary is haunted, as I shall argue in the next section, by a fear of desire ebbing away, both from the life of the individual and concomittantly from the texture of his writing.

Anorexie and ressassement in *Ainsi soit-il ou Les Jeux sont faits*

In all of the models which Gide's diary uses to frame the ageing process, desire plays a central role. This is particularly true of the dominant models, namely the autopedagogical and pederastic approaches examined in the preceding section: narcissistic desire and intellectual curiosity are closely related in the project of self-fashioning and the rejuvenating effects of pederasty are only made available on the basis of a minimal bond of interest from the older partner. But what if desire itself is lacking? The possibility of desire's simply dying, before the individual does, threatens all the various models, in their elaborate detail, that I have examined thus far.

The death of desire is something Gide contemplates in *Ainsi soit-il*, an unduly neglected postscript to the *Journal* which forms the main focus of my discussion in this section. In this work, he uses the term 'anorexie' to denote the absence of desire as such rather than, more narrowly and more usually, the desire to eat.[49] The term is

---

[49] Gide, *Ainsi soit-il*, p. 14. Gide's 'anorexie' recalls what Ernest Jones described as 'aphanisis', namely the ebbing away or terminal decline of desire. Aphanisis is, however, a condition seldom experienced in either psychoanalytic theory or practice; but then what could be more threatening to a theory of desire than the idea of its central quantity failing? See Ernest Jones, *Papers on Psycho-Analysis* (London: Baillière, Tindall & Cox, 1950).

introduced within the first few pages of the text and glossed as follows:

> mon inappétence physique et intellectuelle est devenue telle que parfois je
> ne sais plus bien ce qui me maintient encore en vie sinon l'habitude de
> vivre. Il me semble que je n'aurais, pour cesser d'être, qu'à
> m'abandonner.[50]

Gide has, he claims, been in the grip of 'anorexie' for several months. Yet 'anorexie' proves to be a particularly elusive subject in the pages that follow, which digress into anecdotes about recent republications, adaptations and complaints about contemporary novelists and the theatre. These are interrupted briefly by two short *reprises* of the initial theme – desirelessness – to which he eventually returns for a third time, offering a more prolonged discussion and cutting short the litany of complaint: 'Arrêtons: j'en aurais trop à dire. Je reviens à l'anorexie'.[51] Thus a contrapuntal relationship is established: the theoretical discussion of *anorexie* takes place against the backdrop of a textual mode characterized by anecdote and meandering, often repetitive, reflection. Thus *anorexie* is suspended within the text and, correspondingly, the writing of that very text is cast as a way for the author to evade the closure of desirelessness: 'Anorexie. Il a suffi pour en triompher, momentanément du moins, de ces quelques pages que je viens d'écrire à plume abattue'.[52] The balance is delicate here: *anorexie* is both a leading theme of these meditations and that which they are designed to circumvent, at least for a while. Writing serves to defer the closure of desirelessness yet can only do so by engaging with the reality of that state. It seems that the threat of desirelessness – of closure – can be countered only by embracing a more relaxed and conversational form of textual expression, by indulging the urge to repeat anecdotes and rehearse grievances. The generalized threat of *anorexie* seems to have spared the narrator's appetite for anecdote: 'Je reste extrêmement friand des "bons mots" et des anecdotes.'[53]

The narrator of *Ainsi soit-il* does indeed indulge this one desire: anecdote follows anecdote with little hint of any overarching

---

[50] Gide, *Ainsi soit-il*, pp. 14-15.
[51] Ibid., p. 23.
[52] Ibid., p. 26.
[53] Ibid., p. 29.

structural logic. The work as a whole bears some resemblance to the very 'recueil' of 'bons mots' which its author had, he says, planned at one time to produce.[54] And even this act of internal self-reference, a familiar gesture from Gide's earlier works (in particular, *Paludes* and *Les Faux-monnayeurs*), is here more relaxed, less insistent, than its more celebrated precursors. The progression from one anecdote to the next is generally by association and the way in which these connections are made, as the following examples suggest, intensifies the conversational tone that is an inherent feature of anecdotal discourse: 'Ils me font penser à […]' (p. 67), '[…] me fait penser à […]' (p. 73), 'Cela vous amuse? Alors, écoutez encore celle ci […]' (pp. 68-9), 'Ou encore […]' (p. 69) and 'J'en connais vingt autres' (p. 69). Anecdotal discourse is, in addition, inherently repetitive: anecdotes are always already repeated, being stories of events and utterances that circulate, passing from one individual to another. Moreover, a number of the anecdotes in *Ainsi soit-il* are even repeated from within Gide's own corpus of work, particularly from the *Journal*. Thus he remarks, for example, that 'puisque ceci n'est pas un *Journal*, je veux profiter de la licence de cet écrit pour reparler (j'y prends plaisir) de l'admirable enfant […]'.[55] Whereas the diary is structured around the writing self and tends to minimise repetition by virtue of its rigorous chronological framework, the relative 'licence' of anecdotal discourse allows it to indulge in pleasure-seeking *ressassement*.

The possibility of *ressassement* is viewed very differently in the *Journal* and *Ainsi soit-il*. Returning to his diary in 1949, after a short break, Gide writes with some regret: 'le sujet me paraissait épuisé. Rien de neuf à dire sur moi-même; je ne pouvais que ressasser'.[56] Whether the 'sujet' is, as here, the author himself or the topic of a possible future work, such as Gide contemplates in other passages, the fear is one of *ressassement*. In *Ainsi soit-il*, Gide describes his fantasy of writing a work which could not be placed within his *oeuvre*, before admitting: 'Rien à faire: je retombe dans des thèmes déjà ressassés'.[57] He notes a little later:

---

[54] Gide, *Ainsi soit-il*, p. 30.
[55] Ibid., p. 145.
[56] Gide, *Journal*, II, p. 1069 (4 January 1949).
[57] Gide, *Ainsi soit-il*, p. 35.

> J'ai plus ou moins bien dit ce que je pensais que j'avais à dire et je crains de
> me répéter [...] Me rebute surtout le caractère concentrique de ce que je
> pourrais encore entreprendre... Ah! qu'il est difficile de bien vieillir![58]

Whereas Beauvoir reserves a uniquely privileged position for the
ageing writer (by contrast with workers in almost every other field, in
her account), the vision here is bleak. Whereas for Beauvoir, the fact
that writers do not 'retire' but rather continue with their life's work is
very positive. Yet for Gide, the fact that ageing writers can do nothing
but write is something of a curse: they are doomed to repeat and
exhaust themselves in a desireless winding down, in the 'concentric'
gravitation of senescent *ressassement*. The text turns inexorably
around a fixed point. Yet if the *Journal* is haunted by (and breaks off
at the prospect of) *ressassement*, *Ainsi soit-il* embraces this particular
textual mode, even going as far as to revisit material from the diary.
Gide notes: 'dans ce que j'écris aujourd'hui, il m'arrive souvent de me
redire. C'est ce que l'on appelle irrévérencieusement: radoter'.[59] If
Gide is prepared to accept that his form of senescent textuality is
characterized by *ressassement*, he is clearly less keen on the term
radotage. Not so in the case of Violette Leduc: *radotage* will form the
basis of my discussion of her practice of senescent textuality in
Chapter Three. I want to consider now how the inherent possibility of
repetitiveness in anecdotal discourse affects the position of the
speaking subject.

Anecdotal discourse tends to eclipse the speaking subject: the
anecdote moves indifferently from one speaker to the next. Wheras
the diary projects a writing self, anecdotal discourse points to the
dissolution of that self:

> Ce n'est pas très intéressant, ce que je raconte là. Je le sais, mais je l'écris
> quand même; comme je vous le dirais très simplement si vous étiez assis là,
> près de moi, tous deux fumant une cigarette. Je voudrais tant que vous ne
> sentiez pas de distance entre nous! que vous puissiez penser: je n'avais pas
> besoin de lui pour penser cela... alors, naturellement, je suis amené à sortir
> quelques platitudes.[60]

---

[58] Gide, *Ainsi soit-il*, pp. 45-6.
[59] Ibid., p. 127.
[60] Ibid., p. 92.

In this reflection on the nature of anecdotal discourse, the desire for conversational proximity ('près de moi') becomes a fantasy of merging ('pas de distance'), which in turn gives way to one of self-effacement ('je n'avais pas besoin de lui'). The dissolution of the self, realized here in anecdotal discourse, is also reflected in an arresting omission of the word 'je' in the first two paragraphs of the work, 'Tâcherai', instead of 'Je tâcherai' and 'n'affecterai', instead of 'je n'affecterai'.[61] Similarly, because the word 'jeux' in the work's secondary title inevitably recalls its homonym, 'je', this may suggest that in place of the self stands a series of games (games, perhaps, of self-representation), which are now coming to an end, for the chips are down. This suppression of the 'je' and the title's dissolving of 'je' into 'jeux' both echo the effect of self-dissolution produced by anecdotal discourse.

It will be recalled, as I showed in the preceding section, how firmly Gide emphasised volitional control, or moral rigour, in his earlier modelling of the ageing process in terms of self-fashioning. In *Ainsi soit-il*, facing the dissolution of that self in advanced old age and, ultimately, in death, Gide looks back on that very project of self-fashioning: 'À combien de sollicitations je regrette aujourd'hui de n'avoir pas cédé! Pour mon plus grand enrichissement sans doute; mais peut-être aussi pour la dissolution de mon caractère'.[62] The rigour and tension of resistance, of desire, played a central role in Gide's attempt to shape his 'character': dissolution was the risk to be resisted. Yet in this last work, Gide's response to the final inevitability of dissolution, in extreme old age and death, is to ease this tension: he resolves to 'se laisser aller (un peu)' and to 'écrire au hasard', striving thereby to embrace the decline of desire.[63] Yet there is something paradoxical about *resolving* to let go, even a little: the resolve deliberately to embrace dissolution suggests that, in fact, the project of autopedagogical self-fashioning has not yet been entirely abandoned, even at this late stage.

Yet desire is not subject to volition and its decline cannot be halted or even slowed by an act of will. As a theorist of *anorexie*, in *Ainsi soit-il*, Gide suggests that the cause of his generalized lack of

---

[61] Gide, *Ainsi soit-il*, pp. 11-12.
[62] Ibid., p. 27.
[63] Ibid., pp. 12, 11.

desire lies in the waning of his sexual interest with age. Returning to the subject of *anorexie* for the third time, after numerous anecdotal digressions, Gide distinguishes between its various forms (principally alimentary and intellectual) before advancing an underlying sexual-hormonal explanation: 'mon anorexie vient aussi, vient surtout, d'un retrait de sève'.[64] This is an explanation he has already entertained in the *Journal*:

> Non, je n'ai plus grand désir de forniquer; du moins ce n'est plus un besoin comme au beau temps de ma jeunesse. Mais j'ai besoin de savoir que, si je voulais, je pourrais; comprenez-vous cela? Je veux dire qu'un pays ne me plaît que si de multiples occasions de fornication se présentent. Les plus beaux monuments du monde ne peuvent remplacer cela.[65]

Even as the waning of sexual desire is acknowledged, the vital importance of knowing that it remains in some form – if more as a matter of potential – is asserted. And the suggestion, too, in the anxious 'comprenez-vous cela?', a demand for reassurance or recognition, is that *anorexie* threatens a withdrawal from the world of mutual human understanding. Although this may appear to be merely another excerpt from Gide's handbook for the sex tourist, it is important to note in the context of the present discussion that it constitutes a blunt refusal of sublimation: the works of culture, be they 'les plus beaux monuments du monde', cannot compensate for the loss of sexual pleasure with age. This runs resolutely against the grain of traditional (and particularly religiously-inspired) narratives of senescence, in which the sexual ardour of youth mercifully gives way to the desexualized culture and wisdom of later years. It likewise echoes Freud's recognition of the element of irrecoverable loss in sublimation.[66]

In 'Morale Chrétienne', as I noted above, Gide does himself look forward to a sublimatory model of senescence. Yet when confronted in his old age by the spectre of *anorexie*, he rejects this earlier position. He once prayed that age would bring the extinction of

---

[64] Gide, *Ainsi soit-il*, p. 25.

[65] Gide, *Journal*, II, p. 648 (3 February 1939).

[66] See Monique Schneider's discussion of Freud's *Moses and Monotheism*, 'Répudier le féminin', *Généalogie du masculin* (Paris: Aubier, 2000), pp. 77-102 and, in particular, pp. 91-3.

sexual desire, yet writes in the *Journal*, as an old man: 'Abstraite, ma pensée même s'éteint; c'est, encore aujourd'hui, ce que j'ai de charnel en moi qui l'alimente, et je prie aujourd'hui: puissé-je rester charnel et désireux jusqu'à la mort!'.[67] This sentiment is echoed in *Ainsi soit-il*, where Gide refers to Montaigne's example: 'il savait, et je le sais aussi, que la sagesse n'est pas dans le renoncement, dans l'abstinence, et prend soin de ne pas laisser tarir trop vite cette source secrète, allant même jusqu'à s'encourager vers la volupté, si je l'entends bien…'.[68] The rejection of religiously-inspired models of ageing in terms of sexual quiescence is explicit here. Note that Gide draws upon Montaigne's authority here in support of his campaign to remain sexually active. Moreover, there is something paradoxical here in this determination to keep desire alive – just as there was in his resolving to 'se laisser aller' – for desire is not subject to volitional control. These paradoxes suggest clearly that Gide, while embracing, to some extent, *anorexie* and the inevitability of *ressassement*, in *Ainsi soit-il*, at the same time remains attached to his earlier model of ageing, from the *Journal*, in terms of willed self-fashioning.

Whereas, in the *Journal*, the waning of desire was cast as a major threat to the self-writing project and excluded wherever possible, in the post-script that is *Ainsi soit-il*, desirelessness is named (*anorexie*) and becomes one of the main themes of the text. The reliance on anecdotal discourse is accompanied by an acknowledgement of the inevitability of *ressassement*, by contrast to the position in the *Journal*. Anecdotal discourse also eclipses the speaking subject and thereby prefigures the dissolution of the self. Thus Gide's practice of senescent textuality in *Ainsi soit-il* embraces the repetitive, foreshadows the dissolution of the subject and strives paradoxically both to accept and resist the waning of desire.

*

While it appears at times that the level-headed representation of senescence is, according to Gide, the highest task of any *journal intime*, at others considerable effort is expended in equivocation and denial, as though the function of the diary were not to confront the

---

[67] Gide, *Journal*, II, p. 807 (10 April 1942).
[68] Gide, *Ainsi soit-il*, p. 25.

ageing process but rather to bolster its writer's increasingly implausible juvenile self-image. There is a sense of the diary being intimately involved in a subject's experience of the ageing process, part of the lived reality of that process. At times the diary suggests that self-writing is a crucial part of the subjective experience of the ageing process, yet at others, old age is itself just another text, one that can be rehearsed but never known 'by heart'.

I have endeavoured to show that the experience of old age in Gide's *Journal* is complex and multi-faceted, involving a range of different models, some of which appear a small number of times before vanishing, while others – in particular the concepts of self-fashioning and pederastic pedagogy – are major themes running through the entirety of the work. Throughout, however, there remains a sense of moral danger attached to the act of *naming* old age (hence the importance of other 'explanations' such as tiredness) and a tendency to insist on the importance of volitional control over and responsibility for what is ususally assumed to be an uncontrollable process (the use of *se faire vieux*, I have argued, and the clearer case of *se vieillir*). Thus the thought that this diary could provide a movingly unsentimental account of 'le lent travail de la vieillesse'[69] coexists alongside an artful practice of equivocation. Indeed the text plays with, acts out, models of the ageing process, trying them on for size before partially discarding them or putting them into question.

Even in the earliest diary entries, we find a cult of Youth: it is not enough simply to be young: what is required is an art of living young, an age-specific ethic. The transition to pederastic pedagogy allows this cult of Youth to be retained and lived vicariously through the younger partner. Examined in the context of the ageing process, Gidean pederasty seems to imply a far greater degree of dependency on the part of the older partner than other critical perspectives have suggested; it offers, after all, a defence against the narcissistic trauma of senescence. The younger partner has not just beauty but also truth on his side, which represents a significant departure from the Classical precursor.

Travel and historical change also provide the diary with ways of negotiating the ageing process: both involve marking distances, registering or failing to notice changes – and thereby hold up a mirror

---

[69] Gide, *Journal*, II, p. 93 (22 October 1928).

to the ageing subject. The idea that old age will bring harmony, as in some notional Classical city-state, comes to be rejected in favour of a coexistence of opposites, which in turn gives way to an inner *morcellement*.

Yet this process of experimentation which the diary undertakes requires desire. The prospect of desire's extinction before the end of a life – the spectre of *anorexie* – comes increasingly to haunt the pages of the *Journal*. By contrast with other writers, who embrace the decline of desire by emphasising the compensations to be found in cultural artefacts, Gide refuses to think in these terms in the *Journal*. In *Ainsi soit-il*, by contrast, he strives both to embrace (in writing) and to hold off (in life) the decline of desire in a senescent textuality of anecdote and *ressassement*.

Chapter Three

Violette Leduc and the problem with psychoanalysis

I turn now to Violette Leduc's autobiographical trilogy: *La Bâtarde*, *La Folie en tête* and *La Chasse à l'amour*. Ambivalence and senescent textuality, which emerged as key themes in my readings of Beauvoir and Gide, will continue to be at the forefront of discussion in this chapter. My exploration of these facets of Leduc's work will prepare the way for a broader discussion of the place of ageing in psychoanalytic theories of the subject in the next chapter.

Leduc's autobiographical trilogy is a work rich in references to age.[1] Violette's short self-descriptions are invariably age-indexed: 'une vieille qui veut être la championne de la désolation'[2], or more demeaningly, 'cette vieille carcasse'[3], 'une vieille actrice à la retraite'[4], a 'pauvre vieille'[5], 'cette vieille femme avec un gros nez'[6], a 'vieille guenon quadragénaire'[7]. She also speaks, for example, of 'mes mains d'enfant de cinq ans'[8]; she remarks elsewhere that 'j'aurai bientôt soixante ans. Je suis plutôt fière de le signaler'.[9] She says of

---

[1] I shall be concentrating in this chapter mainly on the three sequential volumes of Leduc's autobiography proper: *La Bâtarde* (Paris: Gallimard, 1964), *La Folie en tête* (Paris: Gallimard, 1970) and *La Chasse à l'amour*, published posthumously (Paris: Gallimard, 1973). There is, however, a pronounced autobiographical dimension to all of Leduc's works: by the time she began writing *La Bâtarde*, she had already evoked formative experiences of her childhood in four preceding texts (viz. *L'Asphyxie*, *L'Affamée*, *Trésors à prendre* and *Ravages*), works which, by contrast with *La Bâtarde*, made little or no impression on the wider reading public in France.

[2] Leduc, *La Chasse à l'amour*, p. 85.

[3] Ibid., p. 230.

[4] Ibid., p. 243.

[5] Leduc, *La Folie en tête*, p. 149.

[6] Leduc, *La Bâtarde*, p. 453.

[7] Ibid., p. 102.

[8] Leduc, *La Folie en tête*, p. 321.

[9] Ibid., p. 212.

Cocteau, whom she visits, 'Je suis ici pour vous voir vieillir'[10]; she gets embroiled in exploitative relationships with adolescent male readers in a bid for rejuvenation; she worries intensely about her mother's old age; she may or may not be going through the menopause in the second volume. I shall examine the picture of the ageing subject which emerges from these isolated characterizations and a number of the many more developed passages on old age in the autobiography. In the second part of the chapter I shall discuss the relationship between the ageing subject in Leduc's work and psychoanalysis as it is depicted as therapeutic technique in the autobiography.

Ambivalence

Ageing is sometimes recognized in Leduc's autobiography and sometimes denied. This ambivalence of representation affects both Violette's ageing and that of others.

Leduc sometimes finds a kind of grim solace in the passing of the years: 'Des femmes trichent, des femmes souffrent. Elles plaisaient: elles effacent leur âge. Je claironne le mien puisque je ne plaisais pas, puisque j'aurai toujours mes cheveux d'enfant'.[11] More extreme still, at the close of *La Bâtarde*: 'Vieillir, c'est perdre ce qu'on a eu. Je n'ai rien eu. J'ai raté l'essentiel'.[12] Whereas the sense of the loss involved in ageing is tied in Beauvoir's autobiographical account to a fear of her growing inability to inspire desire in others, a firm belief in her own ugliness is the overriding and constant feature of Leduc's body-image throughout her work and, by all accounts, throughout the life which the work writes. For Leduc internalizes the patriarchally-conditioned judgement of herself as an ugly woman – and therefore less of a woman – while putting up a show of defiance, which presupposes an acceptance of this very judgement, by proclaiming proudly that she is ugly, defiance in which (as in Sartre's description of all such attempts to assume or reject categories imposed by others, *mauvaise foi*), alienating self-reification and free resistance

---

[10] Leduc, *La Folie en tête*, p. 222.
[11] Leduc, *La Bâtarde*, pp. 19-20.
[12] Ibid., p. 462.

are ambivalently intertwined.[13] Old age – and in particular the patriarchal stereotype of the ugly, non-sexual, old woman – seems to offer a kind of release and a compensating last victory over those women who 'cheat' and suffer with the years. Whereas Beauvoir's autobiography largely tells the story of her success – her brilliant intellectual and social achievements, her steady rise to public prominence and her political activism – a sense of failure and self-abnegation are constants throughout Leduc's life and work. Whereas the scandal of ageing for Beauvoir is that all her achievements should, in a sense, come to nothing, Leduc suggests here that ageing could hardly detract from the 'nothing' that is all she ever had.

Indeed Leduc, far from recoiling at the thought of old age, seems at times to embrace it with anticipation:

> 15 juin 1961 [...] J'ai soif, j'ai faim et je me baigne dans le gosier de l'oiseau. J'écoute, je regarde, je ne meurs pas. Ma vieillesse, dis que tu seras mon oreiller. Les flocons de mes vieilles années accrocheés aux haies me plaisent tant. Dis-moi, ma vieillesse, que ma solitude sera mon petit enfant à cheveux blancs. Mon âge se fane, je n'ai plus peur des enfants qui rient. La nuit je patiente: ne pas dormir c'est vivre les heures qui sonnent, c'est être aimée d'un clocher. Je vieillis donc je vis: mes linceuls sont argentés dans l'écorce de l'arbre qui meurt. Rentrons, ma Violette, remuons sur les divans le tilleul que nous avons cueilli. Je cueillais sous le dôme du jeune tilleul, je me mariais à ce monde de fleurs, d'hélices, de feuilles dans lequel les abeilles tissaient mon voile.[14]

For all that ageing tends towards death, the experience of getting older described in this passage is one of persistence and survival: 'je ne meurs pas', 'Je vieillis donc je vis', 'je patiente'. This will perhaps recall Beckett's Malone, whose protracted failure to die has been suggestively characterized by Christopher Ricks as an anguished double negation: Malone is 'not *not*, cruelly'.[15] Yet there is less anguish and a different kind of ambivalence in Leduc's approach to old age: there is the prospect of repose ('dis que tu seras mon oreiller'), albeit mixed with the anxiety suggested by the way this is

---

[13] Cf. Isabelle de Courtivron: 'Haunted by what she continued to perceive as her ugliness, she assumed this burden and made it into the defiant symbol of her destiny as a bastard'. *Violette Leduc* (Boston: Twayne, 1985), p. 100.

[14] Leduc, *La Bâtarde*, p. 331.

[15] Ricks, *Beckett's Dying Words* (Oxford: Oxford University Press, 1995), p. 117.

phrased, as a demand for reassurance, and by the subsequent negation of rest, 'ne pas dormir'. There is also an approach to the natural world, a dispersal of her 'vieilles années' among the hedgerows, a shroud in the dying tree and the hope of union with nature, a union both referred to ('je me mariais') and suggested at the level of the signifier in the close sound and graphic patterning of 'gosier'/'oiseau', and 'tilleul'/'cueilli'/'feuilles'/'abeilles', a closural patterning which mimes the weaving of the shroud or veil. And it is difficult not to see in this 'tilleul' an allusion to Proust, a cipher for the act of remembrance, emphasizing and authorizing the separation between remembered narrative and this, the metanarrative of remembrance. Another reflexive reference, then, to the act of self-writing. The aegis of Proust is, moreover, entirely fitting for such a passage, which offers, above all, the texture of 'le temps sensible'. The advance into old age longed for here is a quiet 'not dying' which nevertheless borders death, just as the 'voile' of the old woman is close to the 'linceul'. It is a brute experience of time passing, 'vivre les heures qui sonnent', as in insomnia. It is the banal story which remains even when nothing else happens, a dispersal of the subject into the natural world, prefiguring but also allaying death. The curt *cogito* of the ageing subject, 'je vieillis donc je vis', suggests that getting older is the first thought, the fundamental experience: being alive is an inference from decline. Decrepitude is primary; the life which remains, by contrast, is slight, its presence discernible only by induction. And 'je vieillis donc je vis' performs this contraction at the level of the signifier, from 'vieillis' to 'vis' ('v[ieill]is'), emphasising the diminutiveness of the life which remains, as well as contributing to the closural patterning of rhyme and graphic resemblance in this passage. Thus we have a multifaceted description and indeed a performance of ageing as a real process. The passage is also a reflexive reference to the autobiographical act as such, in its simultaneous recognition of both the distinction between and the continuity of the older and younger, writing and written, selves.

I have already indicated that Leduc mobilizes the patriarchal category of the ugly old woman, often in an attempt to harm both herself and others. In the passage I turn to now, an exchange from *La Folie en tête*, the patriarchal socio-medical category of the menopausal woman is brought into play.[16] A recurring theme in Leduc's autobiography, especially in the second and third volumes, is its evocation of acute mental illness. The title of the second volume, *La Folie en tête*, suggests the prominence of this 'case history' aspect: madness is not only in the mind, but comes first, 'en tête', is embossed in the paper (as an 'en-tête') and remains stubbornly prominent (exhibits 'entêtement'). Violette's paranoid symptoms are pronounced: she believes that others, above all her benefactors, are conspiring against her and that an 'Organization' of unseen enemies is persecuting her, in particular by defacing treasured possessions in her absence. In addition, she often experiences feelings of disorientation and mild delirium, such as those she describes to her mother in the following passage:

> — La vie me quitte, le sol va s'ouvrir, je ne suis plus sûre de rien... J'avance le long des murs, ils croient que je suis ivre, je n'ai plus rien dans le corps. C'est grave? Tu crois que c'est grave?
> Ma mère a respiré, aussi fort qu'un professeur de culture physique:
> — Mais non ce n'est pas grave! je vois ce que c'est.
> — Qu'est-ce que c'est?
> — Sotte, tu devrais être contente.
> — Pourquoi?
> — C'est ton retour d'âge.
> Elle me souriait, j'avais un sexe anodin de petite fille, j'étais digne de sa confiance.[17]

There is no confirmation of, nor indeed any further reference elsewhere in the autobiography to, this quick 'diagnosis' of menopause ('ton retour d'âge'), in response to Violette's psychic or existential complaint and it must surely be viewed with some circumspection, given the presence of the other paranoid symptoms

---

[16] For a rigorous discussion of the nature and uses of this category, see Linda Gannon's *Women and Aging. Transcending the Myths* (London: Routledge, 1999). Under patriarchy, Gannon writes, 'menopause is not a change in life, a life transition, a mildly irritating event, but a definitive and all-consuming disease – a deficiency disease – one that is said to be the cause of any and all changes that are designated as age-related when occurring in men. Not only does this interpretation effectively put and keep women in their place, but it also puts men at their ease. They need not worry about age-related deterioration because they are not women; their experience of aging is determined by their life experience and their accumulated wisdom, not by their biology' (p. 9).

[17] Leduc, *La Folie en tête*, p. 166.

accompanying these feelings of disorientation and corporeal emptiness. Such a 'diagnosis' also reflects a consistent desire of Violette's mother in this autobiography and indeed of the mother in other texts by Leduc to gloss over her daughter's distress, fearing that to linger would be to aggravate. That Violette is experiencing an early menopause is, for her mother Berthe, an appealing explanation because it replaces the daughter within the natural order, reasserting the banal but comforting story of predictable changes indexed by chronological age, thereby erecting a barrage against Violette's turbulent inner world. Berthe's is a 'diagnosis' of menopause – an attempt to reduce a complex array of physiological and existential problems to a stable medical category – one which seeks to legitimize her daughter's distress. To *legitimize* Violette, 'la bâtarde', by binding her to the banal logic of chronological age, which is not just medical but also closely related to the social and administrative temporality of the birth certificate. Violette at once becomes more like her mother – together they are, as she says elsewhere, 'deux vieilles, chère mère' – but at the same time her mother's diagnosis seems to throw Violette back into the murky world of infantile sexual innocence, by restoring her 'sexe anodin de petite fille'. This innocence is not absolute, for sex is innocent, in Berthe's eyes, if it carries no risk of pregnancy. She suggests later in this exchange that Violette take advantage of her new situation to 'prendre quelqu'un'; when her daughter objects with the familiar refrain, 'je suis moche', the mother's response is simply, 'sois femme'.

Thus in the course of this one exchange, Violette is aged with a diagnosis of menopause, rejuvenated by being thrown back to the sexual innocence of a 'petite fille' and exhorted to 'be a woman' (which for Berthe means to 'catch' a man, 'comme le restaurateur prend les truites dans un vivier'). In this pivotal exchange, Violette alternates between youth and age, between sexual innocence and experience, between the subjective pole of extreme psychosomatic inner turbulence and the public safety of a socio-medical category, menopause, which has traditionally deigned to licence a degree of mental, as well as physical, unrest. Violette is pulled, too, between her mother's recognition of the magnitude of her distress and the familiar need to contain or even ignore it. So the mother's diagnosis of menopause represents recognition and affective denial, a new phase in life and the restoration of an earlier state, supposed sexual freedom (from the horror of pregnancy) and yet an acceptance of the norm of heterosexuality that is stronger than ever. This diagnosis-scene inaugurates a more equal, lateral, relation to her mother – 'deux vieilles, chère mère' – which is nonetheless offset by the reassertion of vertical relationality in this return to the scenario of parent and 'petite fille' and the subtext of a power relation in which a woman presents her symptoms to a male authority-figure, a doctor or, as Leduc suggests explicitly, 'un professeur de culture physique'.

The text neither conclusively confirms nor rejects outright the application of this category of age and gender – the menopausal woman – to Violette. The way that the diagnosis is 'staged', in what is both a dialogue between mother and daughter and an exchange between a woman patient with symptoms and a male authority-figure, highlights and to some extent undermines the patriarchal implications of this category. The introduction of uncertainty and ambivalence into this diagnostic situation undermines the very categories and power dynamics which it seeks to mobilize. Rather than a diagnosis to close the case, the reader is left with a series of new questions. Is Violette menopausal or just mad? Is she now a sexless old crone or a sexualized older woman free to 'prendre un homme' at liberty? Is Berthe trying to get closer to Violette, to help her, or is the categorization an attempt to keep her at a distance, a dismissively oversimple rationalization of complex psychic and somatic misery? Young or old, innocent or experienced? These questions are all left open and consequently Violette emerges with a certain degree of contestatory freedom, of elusiveness, in relation to these societal categories.

If Violette's age is quite often the subject of spoken exchanges with her mother in the autobiography, this is not true of her mother's age, which remains a matter of silent rumination. In the passage below (from the very beginning of *La Bâtarde*), her mother's age surfaces in thought:

> Tu deviens mon enfant, ma mère, quand vieille femme tu te souviens avec une précision d'horloger. Tu parles, je te reçois. [...] je deviens lyre et vibraphone pour ta crinière de poussière. Tu es vieille, tu te délaisses, j'ouvre la bonbonnière. Tu me dis: "Tu as sommeil? Tu fermes les yeux." Je n'ai pas sommeil. Je veux me défaire de ta vieillesse. J'enroule mes cheveux dans mes bigoudis, mes doigts chantent tes vingt-cinq ans, tes yeux bleus, tes cheveux noirs, ta frange modelée, ta guimpe, le tulle, ton grand

chapeau, ma souffrance à cinq ans. Mon élégante, mon infroissable, ma courageuse, ma vaincue, ma radoteuse, ma gomme à m'effacer, ma jalouse, mon injuste, ma commandante, ma timorée.[18]

Violette closes her eyes to her mother's age in order to reimmerse herself in the elegance of her clothing and bearing in times past. The mother's age, then, is disavowed, in Freud's sense of being simultaneously seen and yet not seen. There is an analogy of this act of disavowal in the way that the mother's question is both heard and, as it were, not heard, in the passage. Leduc spent several years working as a fashion journalist and the world of *haute couture* features prominently in her autobiography; yet here clothes are implicated in the very act of remembrance itself. It is only as Violette tries on her mother's clothes of yesteryear that she recovers the language to describe her, the list of clothes giving over into a list of epithets.

So clothing in a literal sense gives way to the (metaphorical) clothing of descriptive language. Her mother's clothing prepares the ground for Violette's autobiographical project. It functions as a kind of fetish, saturated with the past. Yet this clothing, like a fetish in Freud's terms, hides an absence: it hides the absence of attention, of the mother's interest; it hides an experience of neglect. And this passage is, in its own way, a re-production of neglect. For the first of these enumerative sequences begins with Violette attending to her own body-image, putting her hair in curlers; yet these attentions and the self to which they refer are quickly submerged in the catalogue of the mother's clothes which follows. And in both series – in the list of clothes and in the list of epithets – the scars of neglect ('ma souffrance à cinq ans' and 'ma gomme à m'effacer') lie almost buried in the linguistic profusion of the mother's youthful elegance. The passage suggests that Berthe's old age, her 'crinière de poussière', can be removed just as clothes can be removed: Violette undresses and redresses her mother, who thereby becomes her child, or mannequin, casting aside the years that have elapsed and restoring the play of brilliant surfaces that was her mother's elegance. Similarly, by taking this route back to her suffering as a child, she casts off the experiences of her intervening years as so many inessential garments. The

[18] Leduc, *La Bâtarde*, p. 20.

autobiography begins, then, with this act of double divesture in which
the disavowal of the mother's age returns the daughter to the inaugural
experience of her childhood suffering. The mother is undressed and
reclothed and so, thereby, is Violette. This process of double divesture
suggests that her childhood suffering is her essence, her original body,
which is merely clothed by the passing years and their experiences.

Yet time's passing and the traces it leaves on the mother
cannot always be so easily disavowed. In the following extract from
La Folie en tête, the physical and emotional softening occasioned by
her decrepitude contrasts markedly with the image of crystalline
maternal indifference in one of Leduc's earlier published works,
L'Asphyxie, where the mother is indeed implacable, distant and
largely self-regarding:

> Je ne peux pas décrire ma mère. Elle vieillissait. C'était un chef-d'oeuvre
> qui partait à la dérive. Le temps, si je posais réellement mon regard sur ses
> traits, le temps me dérobait ses jabots, ses grands chapeaux [...] La dureté de
> son visage, où était-elle? Qu'est-ce que tu penserais d'une blanquette de
> veau pour midi? me disait-elle. Réponds, où es-tu encore? Je me cache dans
> tes linons, dans tes boas, j'erre dans tes dentelles et tes alpagas, je me raidis
> dans tes guimpes, je retiens mes larmes dans tes voilettes, je t'offre tes
> épingles à chapeau; ouvre les pages de *L'Asphyxie* [...] Ecoute, maman,
> écoute bien, j'ai été peintre dans mon enfance, je te contemplais, tu te
> contemplais dans le miroir; crois-le, j'ai réussi nos deux portraits, je les ai
> peints avec ma passion, ma fraîcheur, tu ne peux pas les voir, je les porte
> mélangés en moi. Ne détruis pas mon oeuvre avec tes craquelures, ne
> t'effrite pas.[19]

Violette's mother is not what she was – not as elegant and not as
indifferent to her daughter's welfare and very being – yet this change
is not only unbearable but indescribable. The mother was once the
distant object of her daughter's adoration, a remote painting or a
model rapt in the silent contemplation of her own self-image.[20] The
mother's fall from the cold indifference of youthful grace is nowhere
clearer than in her question about lunch, yet this question not only
goes unanswered but is not even allowed full textual expression as a
spoken question; it is, rather, submerged in reminiscence of the

[19] Leduc, *La Folie en tête*, pp. 167-8.
[20] This mix of idealization and derision of the silent woman certainly recalls Lacan's
tribute to Bernini's St. Teresa in *Encore* (Paris: Seuil, 1975), pp. 70-1.

elegance of her mother's youth. This glorious past is more present than the indescribable reality – and banality – of decrepitude. Again, Violette immerses herself in her mother's clothes of yesteryear. As she says elsewhere of her mother, 'Elle a toujours près d'elle une enfant de sept ans qui la veut élégante devant un miroir. Je suis une maniaque de ses toilettes'.[21] She is made manic, driven slightly mad, by the absence, the neglect, which these garments clothe. The two questions which cross, as letters do, in the passage above – Violette's 'La dureté de son visage, où était-elle?' and her mother's 'Réponds, où es-tu encore?' – suggest that the two women are both lost in their own thoughts and lost to one another. The mother's ageing distances her from a daugther who remains entirely invested in the 'deux portraits' of an earlier era. As her mother has softened, so the distance between them which her self-absorption created in Violette's childhood is replaced by the distance of her indescribable fall into old age: they remain separated, if differently. Though they share space, they remain apart, the daughter hardly registering her mother's question and hardly asking her own; her mother's age – ineffably but implacably – comes between them. So this is a familiar, if less successful, attempt to disavow the mother's decrepitude.

In the four passages I have just analysed – Violette's anticipation of her old age, her being 'diagnosed' as menopausal, the inaugural disavowal of her mother's old age and a second, more difficult, disavowal from *La Folie en tête* – the ageing process attains a degree of reality: it means something to get older, to become old. Ageing signifies. Even where ageing is disavowed, as in the mother's case, this still involves a measure of recognition: that which is disavowed is both seen and not seen. Yet there is an opposing current in this autobiography with respect to ageing, which I shall turn to now, one which tries to deny altogether it meaning as a process. In the following passages, for instance, ages are confused or run together:

> Dix-huit ans. Quelle farce, un acte de naissance. J'avais cent quatre-vingts ans lorsqu'une élève massacrait une sonate dans le Jardin d'enfants, j'avais quatorze ans lorsque je recevais une lettre de ma mère, j'avais mes dix-sept ans lorque l'élève-complice glissait une lettre d'Hermine dans la manche de mon tablier.[22]

---

[21] Leduc, *La Folie en tête*, p. 164.
[22] Leduc, *La Bâtarde*, p. 113.

> J'étais une adolescente de trente-huit ans, je découvrais le bonheur d'adorer, celui d'admirer. Je suis une adolescente de cinquante-sept ans, je découvre le bonheur d'adorer, celui d'admirer.[23]

> J'ai huit ans, j'ai dix ans quand un inconnu se propose.[24]

Such confusions of chronological age imply a rejection of ageing as unreal or meaningless. The first quotation, in particular 'Quelle farce, un acte de naissance', suggests that this is, in part, a defiant refusal to accept the official time of civil administration, bound up as it is for Violette with the social stigma of illegitimacy. The nuances of age which this quotation uses to characterize affective states give way elsewhere to extreme inversions:

> Souvent je me perdais, je m'oubliais. J'avais six ans, j'étais vieille. Une centenaire, une désabusée sans épreuves et sans expérience.[25]

And as a fifty-something patient in the clinic:

> Une enfant malheureuse découpait son peignoir en petits morceaux avec de petits ciseaux. Tout recommençait. Je ne variais pas. Le sanglot suivant imitait le sanglot précédent.[26]

The child of six is a jaded old woman and the old woman is an unhappy child, her life characterized by repetition, by an absence of variation. Not only is she always miserable but the misery is always of the same sort, the misery of her ever-present childhood. Age and experience are incidental; what really signify are the formative deprivations of childhood. Oxymorons, or age descriptions which are oxymoronic in context, for example the 'vieille enfant' or 'enfant malheureuse' of fifty, effectively make present once again the unhappy child in the adult's suffering, suggesting that adult experience is mediated by the enduring and unchangeable patterns established in childhood. It is not just that Leduc talks a lot about the formative influence of her childhood on the course of her later life;

---

[23] Leduc, *La Folie en tête*, p. 113.
[24] Leduc, *La Chasse à l'amour*, p. 137.
[25] Leduc, *La Bâtarde*, p. 33.
[26] Leduc, *La Chasse à l'amour*, p. 121.

her writing, with its age oxymorons and identifications of different phases in the lifespan, produces the abiding reality of her childhood experience as a perpetual present. These features of Leduc's writing combine to convey a strong sense of the enduring presence of the suffering child in Violette's adult experience: they are localized techniques of fixation or obsession. Their effect is reflected and magnified in the 'macro'-level fixation on her childhood which is a feature of Leduc's work as a whole: different texts renarrate the same, or very similar, episodes from that childhood, each text in Leduc's *oeuvre* to some extent reworks this same fertile ground of meaning. Critics have indeed characterized her work as 'obsessional' (Alex Hughes), 'circular, cumulative, repetitive' (Isabelle de Courtivron) and 'circular' (Susan Marson).[27] I would contend that these ways in which Leduc's work constantly makes present again ('re-presents') the reality of childhood suffering in adult experience – obsessively, on both a local and a global level within her *oeuvre* – make her work a textual analogy of Freud's regressive model of human mental development. It is not just that Leduc is writing in a post-Freudian cultural context and has accordingly absorbed some of his insights in vulgarized form. The connection is stronger than that: the repeatedly performed return to childhood in the autobiography, the resulting, regressive, demonstration that the child's experience is an enduring present occluding and penetrating adult life, make for an analogy which is considerably more substantial and insistent than the mere notion that both Leduc and Freud think of childhood as formative.

I shall return, in the following chapter, to Freud's view of human development. First, however, I would like to give some indication of the ways in which Leduc's work offers not only an analogy but also a critique of psychoanalysis with respect to the ageing process.

Psychoanalysis as such features in Leduc's autobiography: it not only features, but actually *fails* in its therapeutic function. In *La Chasse à l'amour*, Violette describes her one and only visit to Lacan and the several years of treatment she underwent with René Diatkine.

---

[27] See Alex Hughes, *Heterographies: Sexual Difference in French Autobiography* (Oxford: Berg, 1999), pp. 13-23; Isabelle de Courtivron, *Violette Leduc* (Boston: Twayne, 1985), p. 18; Susan Marson, 'The Beginning of the End: Time and Identity in the Autobiography of Violette Leduc', *Sites* 2:1 (1998), 69-87, p. 79.

According to Leduc's biographer, Carlo Jansiti, the visit to Lacan was suggested and arranged by Beauvoir.[28] Leduc describes her 'escapade' with Lacan in the following terms: 'je parlais, je lisais des aveux de vieille toquée dans les yeux de Lacan'.[29] So Lacan (she thinks) dismissed her as a mad old woman. Leduc then saw René Diatkine, with the encouragement of Beauvoir and other friends. Diatkine was later (in 1964) to become the analyst of Louis Althusser and eventually also of his wife, Hélène Rytman.[30] Although Jansiti maintains that Leduc's treatment with Diatkine was more of 'une psychothérapie de soutien' than psychoanalysis as such, by his own admission he has no evidence to support this assertion.[31] The precise nature of Leduc's treatment remains unclear, though it appears to have combined elements of both psychoanalytic and psychiatric technique (including, on the psychiatric side, medication, a sleeping-cure and, in a private clinic, electroshock 'treatment').[32] Whatever the precise nature of her treatement with Diatkine, there can be no doubt that it involved significant psychoanalytic elements. Diatkine was both a qualified psychiatrist and a practising psychoanalyst, having trained under Lacan in the early 1950s.

So how, if at all, might this representation of psychoanalytic treatment within an autobiography affect the way readers approach that work? There have been a number of attempts by critics to subject

---

[28] Carlo Jansiti, *Violette Leduc* (Paris: Grasset, 1999), p. 299.

[29] Leduc, *La Chasse à l'amour*, p. 94.

[30] See Althusser, *L'Avenir dure longtemps* (Paris: Stock/IMEC, 1994). He became engaged in a public dispute with Diatkine in 1976-7, accusing the latter of treating him with too much respect: 'je lui reprochai en bref de ne pas savoir ni pouvoir maîtriser son propre *contre-transfert à mon égard*'. Althusser presented Diatkine with a semi-parodic theoretical text in which he maintained that, from the outset, countertransference rather than transference is dominant in psychoanalytic treatment.

[31] Diatkine, citing the reason of patient confidentiality, apparently refused to discuss Leduc's case with Jansiti. Note, however, that Beauvoir suggests he discussed Leduc's treatment with her while it was taking place. See Beauvoir, *Tout compte fait* (Paris: Gallimard, 1972): 'J'obtins qu'elle [Leduc] consultât un psychanalyste: il me laissa entendre qu'il considérait le cas comme désespéré' (p. 70).

[32] Carlo Jansiti claims that 'Violette n'a jamais suivi de cure psychanalytique. Dans les années cinquante les analystes ne traitaient pas ce genre de troubles' (Jansiti, p. 300). He gives no indication of his evidence for this generalization about psychoanalysis in the 1950s, which seems entirely questionable in view of the fact that, by all accounts, Leduc's symptoms were principally paranoid and psychoanalytic treatment for 'ce genre de troubles' had been common in France since the 1930s.

'Violette' to a kind of psychoanalysis in their reading of the autobiography: Pièr Girard[33] and Isabelle de Courtivron[34] have both adopted this rather reductive strategy, attempting to treat 'Violette' (or the leading female character in *L'Affamée*, in Girard's case), analyzing her as though she were a real person rather than a textual entity, or at most a *persona*. And both critics present what is rather a pale imitation of psychoanalytic method by ignoring its fundamentally dialogic (or dialectical) character: neither really allows the autobiography a chance to talk back. Alex Hughes, by contrast, avoids the trap of attempting to treat 'Violette' as though her autobiography were a case history. Hughes makes considerable use of psychoanalytic concepts (those of Klein, Anzieu and Kristeva in particular) in her discussion of Leduc's work and argues, for example, that *Ravages* constitutes 'a powerful critique of a (Freudian) model of feminine evolution'.[35] I shall be advancing a similar case with respect to the autobiography, namely that it constitutes a critique of the regressive and age-indifferent model of human development which is a feature not only of Freud's world-view but indeed of psychoanalysis in all its forms. However, in the autobiography, unlike *Ravages*, psychoanalysis as such is represented and explicitly contested in the text and thus the dialogue with Freud – the 'answering back' – is necessarily more direct, less parenthetical, than in Hughes's chosen work.

For psychoanalysis is implicated in the texture of the autobiographical trilogy, both in the context of Violette's therapeutic treatment in *La Chasse à l'amour* and throughout, in maxims and turns of phrase: 'je me dominais, j'emmagasinais les crises, les dépressions pour plus tard'[36]; 'Complexes. J'ai appris le mot après. Je me voulais à la proue de mes complexes'[37]; 'Nous courons après ce que nous avons perdu, enfant'[38]; 'Transfert ici, transfert là-bas,

---

[33] Pièr Girard, *Oedipe masqué. Une lecture psychanalytique de L'Affamée de Violette Leduc* (Paris: des femmes, 1986).
[34] Courtivron, *Violette Leduc.*
[35] Alex Hughes, *Violette Leduc: Mothers, Lovers, and Language* (London: Modern Humanities Research Association, 1994), p. 10.
[36] Leduc, *La Bâtarde*, p. 60.
[37] Ibid., p. 167.
[38] Leduc, *La Folie en tête*, p. 183.

transfert dans tous les coins. Pas de transfert, mon vieux'[39];
'J'inventais des mains crispées d'hystérique'.[40] In sum, I think these
comments suggest a certain contempt for the technical terms and
mechanisms of psychoanalysis, an assertion of liberty with respect to
its categories – which can be mimed or refused – but coupled with a
shared commitment to the primacy of the child's experience.[41] This is
a combination of quips at the expense of psychoanalytic terminology
and a deeper congruence which will be familiar from Sartre's work, in
particular *Les Mots*.[42] René de Ceccatty has also drawn attention to the
fact that, in Leduc's life, the composition of this autobiographical
trilogy begins only after the failure of her analysis with René
Diatkine.[43] According to Ceccatty:

> Je ne crois pas, malgré plusieurs tentatives faites dans ce domaine, que
> l'oeuvre et la vie de Violette Leduc se prêtent aisément aux différentes
> grilles analytiques possibles. Du reste, la matière ne pourrait en être fournie
> que par elle et non par ses livres qui sont déjà une interprétation trop
> maîtrisée, trop orientée d'événements passés au crible de la transfiguration
> littéraire. Violette Leduc était donc à mes yeux beaucoup plus qu'un cas
> psychologique. C'était, plutôt, une forme de résistance à la théorie.[44]

Ceccatty is half right here, even though he does not elaborate on the
precise nature of this resistance to psychoanalysis. Only half right,
however, because as I have suggested, Leduc's work is not just a way
of resisting psychoanalysis but also a basic formal analogy of it.
While being explicitly and implicitly sceptical about Freud, the
autobiography and Leduc's other work nonetheless simultaneously

---

[39] Leduc, *La Chasse à l'amour*, p. 104.
[40] Leduc, *La Chasse à l'amour*, p. 339.
[41] Violette's self-aware performance of hysterical symptoms recalls that of Charcot's
patients. Cf. Appignanesi & Forrester, *Freud's Women* (London: Penguin, 2000,
second edition): 'Maybe the doctors, their science and the hysterics were all
accomplices in a complex game of give and take, whose microsocial habitat was the
Salpêtrière for the period of Charcot's ascendancy, from the early 1870s to his death
in 1893' (p. 65).
[42] This is moreover Christina Howells's argument with respect to Sartre's relation to
Freud in her *Sartre: The Necessity of Freedom* (Cambridge: Cambridge University
Press, 1988).
[43] René de Ceccatty, *Violette Leduc, Eloge de la Bâtarde* (Paris: Stock, 1994), p. 30.
[44] Ibid., p. 43

echo his theme in their continual reworking, their 're-presenting', of childhood suffering in adult experience. Leduc's resistance to psychoanalysis in the autobiography crystallizes around its lack of understanding of the ageing process. Thus: 'Je ne croyais pas en Freud pour me guérir. J'étais trop vieille pour être soignée par lui. Mes névroses, sclérosées. Mes complexes, du tartre, du calcaire'.[45] It will be my contention in the next chapter that this judgment is, broadly speaking, correct: Freud's work and psychoanalysis in general lack both an interest in and understanding of the role played by ageing in subjectivity. Before leaving Leduc's work, however, I would like to examine its own particular form of what, in the preceding chapters, I have called senescent textuality, namely *radotage*.

Leduc and *radotage*

In this section I want to suggest that if Leduc turns away from psychoanalysis, her text finds its own way of expressing the significance of ageing in the life of the subject. The absence of ageing from psychoanalytic accounts of the subject, which Leduc so astutely identifies, is unsurprisingly reflected in modes of literary criticism informed by psychoanalysis; which is to say almost all contemporary criticism. The influence of psychoanalysis is particularly clear in the work of Julia Kristeva and perhaps no more so than in *Soleil noir*, a text which purports to be both a work of psychoanalytic theory, on depression, and a critical analysis of works of art premised on the idea of a relationship between imagination and depression.[46] When these 'depressive' works are literary texts, they display the following characteristics: 'musicalisation des signifiants, polyphonie des lexèmes, désarticulation des unités lexicales, syntaxiques, narratives'.[47] This 'musicalité frugale'[48] in art is thought by Kristeva

---

[45] Leduc, *La Chasse à l'amour*, p. 211.
[46] Kristeva, *Soleil noir. Dépression et mélancolie* (Paris: Gallimard, 1987). Kristeva analyses works of art which exist 'en intimité constitutive avec la dépression en même temps qu'en déplacement nécessaire de la dépression vers un sens possible' (p.112).
[47] Ibid., p. 112.
[48] Ibid., p. 45.

to be a direct reflection of the same characterisic in the ordinary speech of the depressed:

> Rappelez-vous la parole du déprimé: répétitive et monotone. Dans l'impossibilité d'enchaîner, la phrase s'interrompt, s'épuise, s'arrête. Les syntagmes mêmes ne parviennent pas à se formuler. Un rythme répétitif, une mélodie monotone, viennent dominer les séquences logiques brisées et les transformer en litanies récurrentes, obsédantes.[49]

According to Kristeva, this degenerating textual music is essentially regressive in character, testifying to the subject's 'deuil inaccompli de l'objet maternel'.[50] It is not just the musicality of the signifier in depression that points to the early history of the subject; similarly, in *La Révolution du langage poétique*, certain privileged kinds of poetic utterance, distinguished by their broken musicality, are conceived of regressively as reflecting the pre-oedipal state.[51] I shall argue in this section that Leduc's autobiography also demonstrates, intermittently, the 'musicalisation des signifiants', the elaboration of an impoverished musicality, but that rather than referring back, regressively, this is a forward-looking, or projective, performance of the degeneration of ageing in text, with a closural function.

I have already touched upon this notion of sensecent textuality in relation to the first of the passages discussed in this chapter. I emphasised the close sound and graphic patterning of 'tilleul', 'cueilli', 'feuilles' and 'abeilles', to which might be added three further pairs – 'vieillesse' / 'oreiller', 'linceuls' / 'tilleul' and 'gosier' / 'oiseau'. I suggested that these (re)produce at the level of the signifier the weaving of the veil and the gradual union with with the natural world which are described in the passage as characteristics of ageing. The patterning produced by the mirror-effect in 'le tilleul que nous avons cueilli' is a frequent enough feature of Leduc's prose style, especially where the passage of time is concerned: 'Je fatiguais les horloges, les horloges me fatiguaient'.[52] Compare the mirroring in this textual reenactment of obsession: 'Je courais de ma chambre à la

---

[49] Kristeva, *Soleil noir*, p. 45.
[50] Ibid., p. 72.
[51] See Julia Kristeva, *La Révolution du langage poétique* (Paris: Seuil, 1974).
[52] Leduc, *La Bâtarde*, p. 113.

cuisine, de la cuisine à la chambre'.[53] The association of close rhyme with decrepitude will be familiar from another remark I have already quoted: 'Nous sommes deux vieilles, chère mère', where it performs the new-found closeness of mother and daughter in old age.[54] Similarly, in the cadence of 'Je suis vieille, donne-moi cette joie', 'moi' echoes 'joie' in what is a sentence of senescent closure which immediately precedes a sectional break in the text.[55] This 'musicalisation' or 'musicalité frugale' which shares many of the characteristics of Kristeva's various forms of regressive textuality, I think in Leduc tends in a very different direction. Such 'musicalisation' and 'litanies récurrentes, obsédantes', to redeploy Kristeva's terms, together characterize a form of textuality in Leduc's work which I propose to call *radotage*, in order to draw attention to its intrinsic relation to old age and its self-consciously repetitive, borderline obsessive, dimension.

Although what I understand by *radotage* is principally a textual mode of the autobiography, it is also exemplified in the behaviour of characters. In the following passage from *La Folie en tête*, a 'pauvre vieille', presumably Violette, though she is not named, is apparently going slightly mad in the métro. The description is all in the third person:

> Approchons, approchons-nous d'elle. Que peut-elle balbutier, pauvre vieille, elle n'a pas ses esprits? [...] Madame fait son numéro, elle imite les saintes avec ses yeux fermés qui regardent, Madame est habitée, elle récite, sa tête est prête à tomber dans le panier [...] Qu'elle a vieilli! pourtant elle était vieille. [...] Elle récite son chapelet, elle suit son idée.[56]

On this occasion, her obsession, her 'chapelet' or 'idée fixe', happens to be a hatred of men with glasses; yet if there is nothing terribly significant about the content of the obsession as such, note the specifically age-indexed terms in which it is described. This is an old woman who encounters *aliénation* in two senses – firstly, in an appearance, or show, a 'numéro', of mild senility and secondly, in that Violette is here 'alienated' in her own autobiography by this

---

[53] Leduc, *La Chasse à l'amour*, p. 308.
[54] Ibid., p. 350.
[55] Ibid., p. 308.
[56] Leduc, *La Folie en tête*, p. 149.

dismissive description in the third person. Old age is a double otherness, mental and textual, and in this passage, the 'balbutiements' of her delirious *radotage* are likened to the divine rapture of martyrs facing death. This mystical strand is taken up in the mystified, hermetic, utterance: 'Qu'elle a vieilli! pourtant elle était vieille', which evokes wonder and an entranced fascination, turning around the idea of old age. This is reflexive or involuted *radotage* – repetitive, fixated, elderly murmering – the very subject of which is old age. This is a fairly common move in the autobiography, as indeed it is in another of Leduc's works, *L'Affamée*.[57]

In *L'Affamée*, Leduc's semi-autobiographical *récit* of obsession and infatuation, we find two related examples of *radotage* which weave old age and the name. The text contains no mention of the name of its narrator, nor indeed of that of 'Madame', the object of her unrequited love. Critics, however, have tended to assume that the text is a fairly transparent evocation of Leduc's passion for her mentor, Beauvoir. The heroine at one point recalls 'Madame' having mentioned her name:

> Je pleure chez moi parce qu'elle a prononcé mon nom la veille des fêtes de Pentecôte. Vieillir plus vite. Sortir avec une voilette. Ne regarder que la terre.[58]

In this recollection, which precedes a break in the text, 'veille' becomes 'vieillir' which in turn becomes 'voilette', the veil of the stooped old woman which also recalls the name Violette. And at the end of the *récit*, on the very last page, the narrator recounts a vision of 'Madame' seated outside a café opposite her window, which takes up, once again, this so suggestive 'voilette':

> Je me rasseyais. Je me levais. Enigme et rapprochement. A travers le vitre, je voyais mieux son visage. La voilette mouchetée qui était devant, je

---

[57] For example in *La Chasse à l'amour*, in the narrative of her holiday with a younger lesbian couple, when Violette feels her age: 'Je me demande pourquoi elles ont besoin de cette vieille. Ce n'est pas catholique. Voici Cahors. Je vieillis. C'est lourd, deux valises. Ne dis pas toujours je vieillis. Tu ne le crois pas. Je me vois vieillir dans les yeux des autres. Je ne me déguiserais pas en jeune fille si je croyais à la mort' (p. 352).

[58] Leduc, *L'Affamée* (Paris: Gallimard, 1948), p. 128.

l'avais imagninée. Cette voilette évoquait les centaines, les milliers d'heures studieuses de son existence, cette voilette tempérait sa beauté.[59]

What, or indeed who, is the imagined veil in this imagined final sighting of 'Madame'? A 'voilette', or perhaps a Violette whose obsessive *radotage* is all about the passage of time, 'les centaines, les milliers d'heures studieuses', and the tempering, or fading, which this entails. A 'voilette' which emerges in the close sound and graphic patterning, the 'musicalité frugale' and the written resemblances of 'la veille' and 'vieillir'. The closural function of *radotage* is clear from the position of these two, interwoven, examples. In her analysis of *L'Asphyxie*, Alex Hughes argues that Leduc's obsessive texts betray signs of encryptment[60]; here, then, is another and a rather different example of encryptment from the type which Hughes identifies, in which the name 'Violette' becomes embroiled in the *radotage* of obsession. The subject, 'Violette', is linked to old age and the secrecy of the veil. This particular example of *radotage* is a neat reminder of the fact that Leduc's work, unlike psychoanalysis, offers the raw materials for an account of the role of ageing in subjectivity.[61]

    Radotage is, then, the local textual mode of obsession, and obsession is the characteristic which critics seem to concur is the red thread linking all of Leduc's work: *radotage* expresses the senescent dimension to a body of work in which the same basic material of an unhappy childhood and impossible interpersonal relationships is revisited over and again. That Leduc's more overtly autobiographical texts, in particular, are works of *radotage* is suggested by her own description of how she came to begin writing about her life (with *L'Asphyxie*), which in part seems to have been by driving the none too tolerant Maurice Sachs to exasperation: 'je lui parle de ma mère sans me lasser de radoter'.[62] The term *radotage* seems particularly apt in Leduc's case because not only does it refer semantically to old age but

[59] Leduc, *L'Affamée*, p. 197.
[60] Hughes, *Heterographies*, ch. 1, pp. 13-23.
[61] *Radotage* is to be found elsewhere in *L'Affamée*, in similarly closural positions: 'J'appartiens, malgré moi, à la race inutile des glaciers.' (p.62, 'race' / 'glaciers'); 'Le bleu décoloré des glycines était vieillot, le toit de chaume de la guinguette reblondissait, sur la colline, le château effrité vieillissait' (p.189): 'vieillot' / 'vieillissait' and 'effrité' / 'vieillissait'.
[62] Leduc, *La Bâtarde*, p. 396.

also, etymologically, to childhood: *radoter* comes from the old Dutch meaning 'tomber en enfance'. Moreover, Leduc's work, unlike psychoanalysis at present, seems to me to be able to combine both this regressive and this projective dimension, to offer a more developed sense of the role of ageing in subjectivity.[63]

The Leduc who emerges from my discussion in this chapter is, I hope, an accomplished thinker, not a semi-literate and inferior precursor of *écriture féminine*, confined to 'immediacy', as Courtivron and others have regrettably and implausibly suggested.[64] Her autobiography frames a key insight into psychoanalysis by correctly identifying its resistance to ageing and also performs a simultaneously progressive and regressive totalizing movement with respect to childhood and old age. Leduc's work manages, in its deployment of *radotage*, to suggest a view of subjectivity in which ageing signifies, one in which ageing can be spoken. And moving beyond Leduc, with this notion of *radotage*, I am suggesting that certain quirks usually thought derisively to be characteristic of elderly discourse be taken seriously as expressive of a mode of subjectivity in which repetition moves forward: the repetition of episodes from the past affirms their enduring persistence while simultaneously reorganizing and structuring them. *Radotage* works towards a kind of impoverished integrity, or totality, by co-ordinating disparate memories through repetition, shuffling them together in accordance with the logic of the signifier, through sound and graphic patterning.

Radotage is not, of course, a neutral term: it bears the full force of a negative cultural stereotype. Numerous are the examples of derisory old men and women who ramble on in literary texts of every period and in other forms of cultural representation. *Radotage* is, then, a mode of discourse which creates a measure of social isolation: the old man or woman who rambles on, going over the same ground of

---

[63] As a literary mode, *radotage* might find a precursor in Madame de Sévigné's sub-genre of the *radoterie*, or 'histoire décousue'.

[64] 'As a writer Leduc is less interested in self-analysis than she is in self-presentation and the unmediated transposition of experience into imagery. She does not interpret; she relives' (Courtivron, p. 54). 'Leduc never understood with sufficient clarity the forces of patriarchal culture that she was opposing. For this reason, she channeled most of her creative and psychic energy into the collision with these obscure forces rather than in the production of alternative symbolic worlds where female imagery and values could be sung' (ibid., p.62).

remembered fragments for the thousandth time, is isolated from others by a mixture of their own self-absorption and the derision, boredom or even indulgence of the listeners. As a discursive mode, *radotage* tends to bring about the disengagement of the older person from their immediate surroundings, from places and people.[65] Their immediate reality is elsewhere, borne witness to only in words which repeat, testifying to their slow exile.

*

Leduc's autobiography alternates between two opposing poles with respect to the representation of the ageing process: ageing is sometimes recognized and sometimes denied. When recognized, Violette tends to look forward with expectation and only a small measure of anxiety to her own decrepitude while disavowing that of her mother. When her own ageing is denied, confusions and oxymorons *perform* the abiding present of childhood suffering in adult experience. Thus ageing in Leduc's work is characterized by ambivalence, a dual ambivalence: the approach of old age is alternately welcomed and feared, acknowledged and denied access to representation. I suggested that the way in which ageing is blocked from representation, by re-presenting the suffering child in the adult's experience, made Leduc's work an analogy of psychoanalysis, with its essentially regressive model of human mental development. This is true both in the local textures of her writing and globally, in the reworking of the same (or very similar) ground of childhood suffering from work to work within the *oeuvre*.

Yet Leduc's autobiography is not just an analogy of, but also offers resistance to, psychoanalysis. I proposed that the focus of this resistance is the lack, in psychoanalysis, of an account of the role of ageing in subjectivity. A resistance too, of course, in that the autobiography depicts the failure of psychoanalytic treatment in Leduc's case: Violette is, she thinks, dismissed as a 'vieille toquée' by Lacan and is, she judges, 'trop vieille pour être guérie par Freud'. I

---

[65] Disengagement of various kinds, among them social and discursive, is, according to some psychologists, characteristic of old age. See William E. Henry, 'Engagement and Disengagement', in Lawton & Salthouse (eds.), *Essential Papers on the Psychology of Aging* (New York: New York University Press, 1998).

will go on to argue, in the next chapter, that the thrust of these criticisms of psychoanalysis is correct: Freud's model of the development of the human mind is essentially regressive and that prerequisite for psychoanalytic treatment, the transference, exploits precisely this regressive tendency. Of course the aim of treatment will be to reestablish some measure of forward-looking movement for the analysand, although Freud has comparatively little to say about this. And although Lacan expands Freud's account of the role of temporality in the life of the subject, his view of the aim of analysis is, if anything, even more pessimistic, less 'teleological', than Freud's.

The representational ambivalence of ageing in Leduc's autobiographical writing corrects the mainly regressive emphasis in psychoanalytic theory. In what I have chosen to call its *radotage*, her autobiography both revisits the fertile ground of meaning that is childhood suffering – as though the intervening years could be cast off as so many inessential garments – and yet also meditates on her approaching senescence. This dual directionality of Leduc's *radotage* is reflected in the contrast between the etymology of *radoter* ('tomber en enfance') and its semantic association with old age. The 'musicalisation des signifiants', which is a feature of *radotage*, both recalls and augments (with a forward-looking, senescent dimension) Julia Kristeva's characterization of the regressive significance of the speech of depression or the language of revolutionary poets. The re-orchestration of memories effected in the *radotage* of Leduc's autobiography, in accordance with the logic of the signifier in sound and graphic patterning, shuffles the subject towards an impoverished and isolated totality. And in *L'Affamée*, the name 'Violette' is drawn into a web of *radotage*, in which associations with the veil and old age as such are cryptically but insistently established: the implication of ageing in the life of the subject, Violette, is both suggested and encrypted in the ambivalence of these closural patternings.

If Leduc's writing remains ambivalent about the onset of old age, at times looking forward to it with anticipation, this is not so in the case of Simone de Beauvoir, to whose memoirs and biographical texts I turn in Chapter Five. In Beauvoir's autobiographical work, in keeping with her findings in *La Vieillesse*, the awareness that one is *becoming old* inevitably constitutes a moment of crisis for the subject, one in which life's promise of infinite, projective, expansion stands cruelly contradicted by psychic and somatic frailty. Yet it is also a moment at which the ageing self turns to other people, eschewing the isolation of Leduc's style of senescent subjectivity. Before turning to Beauvoir, however, I take my cue from Leduc's observations about the failure of psychoanalysis to understand ageing and look in the next chapter at some recent theoretical and clinical work on the ageing process.

Chapter Four

Towards a psychoanalytic approach to senescent subjectivity

This chapter will present a critical overview of some of the most important theoretical and clinical work by psychoanalysts on ageing and subjectivity, in France, the UK and the US, in the years after Leduc's experience of its failure. My discussion will aim to establish connections and mark differences between work done in France and research by analysts from very different institutional and theoretical backgrounds in the UK and US. However, these more encouraging recent developments must be seen in the context of a long history of resistance to ageing from within psychoanalysis and it is this that I shall examine briefly first.

Freud

Leduc encountered psychoanalysis when she was in her late forties and early fifties and the complaint that she felt 'too old' to be cured by Freud refers to this period of her life.[1] In his essay, 'On Psychotherapy', Freud asserts, as though in anticipation, that 'Near or above the fifties the elasticity of the mental process, on which the treatment depends, is as a rule lacking'.[2] Both Leduc and Freud speak in terms of hardening. For Freud, the 'elasticity' of the mental apparatus has been lost and, for Leduc, mineralization has occurred: neuroses and complexes have become too ingrained. This trope, itself age-old, of hardening as characterisitic of the ageing of bodies and temperaments will be familiar from the closing scene in *Le Temps retrouvé*, where Proust's vision also reflects contemporary medical thinking (Cazalis's theory in particular) which objectified the

---

[1] Jansiti, *Violette Leduc*, pp. 299-300.
[2] Freud, 'On Psychotherapy' (1905), SE 7, 255-68, p. 264.

stereotype by suggesting that hardening of the arteries was the cause of ageing and, eventually, death.

Simon Biggs argues that Freud's comments in 'On Psychotherapy' must be read in context: the paper was delivered by Freud in 1904 to a meeting of the Viennese medical establishment. As Biggs suggests, the audience was potentially hostile and Freud was playing safe, cautiously excluding from the therapeutic purview of the 'talking cure' any potentially difficult or seemingly inappropriate cases.[3] Older patients are not alone in being shut out: psychosis, confusion, deeply-rooted depression and cases in which the quick removal of dangerous symptoms is required are also declared to be beyond the reach of psychoanalysis.

In the same address, Freud also voiced objections to older people undergoing psychoanalysis which were of a more pragmatic kind: he felt they would have little time to enjoy any resulting benefits and was concerned that, in older patients, 'the mass of material to be dealt with would prolong the duration of the treatment indefinitely'.[4] In the first of these objections, Freud seems to be taking a particularly utilitarian view of psychoanalysis as a cure and is perhaps pandering here too to the expectations of a sceptical audience. As for the mass of material, his second objection, Freud never suggested that psychoanalysis should be a systematic working-through of *all* of the analysand's experiences, so it is not clear that being older and having had quantitatively more experiences should necessarily matter. As for the risk of an interminable analysis, it is clear from other texts that this is inherent in the process itself, whatever the age of the analysand may be.[5]

While of course these comments of Freud's in 'On Psychotherapy' must be taken seriously and argued about, there is a danger of becoming fixated on what may, as Biggs argues, have been to a great extent context-specific cautionary rhetoric. It may be true that Freud's notion of the hardening of the mental apparatus is an unscientific cliché and it is certainly the case that Freud's own old age

---

[3] Simon Biggs, 'The end of the beginning: a brief history of the psychoanalysis of adult ageing', *Journal of Social Work Practice*, vol. 12, no. 2 (Nov. 1998), *Special Issue: Counselling and Psychotherapy with Older People*, pp. 135-6.

[4] Freud, 'On Psychotherapy', p. 264.

[5] Freud, 'Analysis Terminable and Interminable' (1937), SE 23, pp. 209-54.

was characterized by an intellectual creativity all the more remarkable for its coexisting alongside the pain of his failing body. Yet even if we leave aside Freud's comments on old age in 'On Psychotherapy' and elsewhere, it seems to me that there are other, more significant and more deeply-rooted, causes of the resistance to ageing which psychoanalysis has displayed.[6]

It could be argued that psychoanalysis is founded on a refusal to recognize that the ageing process has meaningful effects on the inner life of the subject. Consider Freud's account of human development as it is encapsulated in the following passage, from 'Thoughts for the Times on War and Death':

> The development of the mind shows a peculiarity which is present in no other developmental process. When a village grows into a town or a child into a man, the village and the child become lost in the town and the man. Memory alone can trace the old features in the new picture; and in fact the old materials or forms have been got rid of and replaced by new ones. It is otherwise with the development of the mind. Here one can describe the state of affairs, which has nothing to compare with it, only by saying that in this case every earlier stage of development persists alongside the later stage which has arisen from it; here succession also involves co-existence, although it is to the same materials that the whole series of transformations has applied. The earlier mental state may not have manifested itself for years, but none the less it is so far present that it may at any time again become the mode of expression of the forces in the mind, and indeed the only one, as though all later developments had been annulled or undone. This extraordinary plasticity of mental development is not unrestricted as regards direction; it may be described as a special capacity for involution – for regression – since it may well happen that a later and higher stage of development, once abandoned, cannot be reached again. But the primitive stages can always be re-established; the primitive mind is, in the fullest meaning of the word, imperishable.[7]

What this purported account of human development does not account for is precisely development. What sets human mental development apart, Freud argues here, is that 'succession also involves co-

---

[6] Much has been written in recent years against these comments of Freud's, often by analysts who are interested in justifying the expansion of their business to meet increased demand from a growing elderly population. See, for example, Robert Nemiroff & Calvin Colarusso (eds.), *The Race Against Time: Psychotherapy and Psychoanalysis in the Second Half of Life* (New York: Plenum, 1985).

[7] 'Thoughts for the Times on War and Death' (1915), SE 14, pp. 285-6.

existence': this is not an account of change but rather one of coexistence, of cohabitation in the unconscious. In a sense, nothing is ever lost or definitively abandoned, moved beyond: as Freud writes elsewhere, 'We can never give anything up; we only exchange one thing for another'.[8] The 'extraordinary plasticity' of human mental development is, Freud specifies, primarily a regressive or retrospective 'plasticity'; it is not, in the first instance, a flexibility which favours adaptation to new circumstances, but rather expresses the ever-present risk of relapse. Regression, or the resurgence of a primitive past into the present, is a surprising characteristic not only of Freud's account of the development (and particularly the sexual development) of the individual, but also of his view of the history of civilizations, of the mechanism of dreams and of psychopathology. Freud, who insists then that human development is unlike any other developmental process, also posits a corresponding form of psychic causality that is unlike any other: retroaction, *Nachträglichkeit* or 'reverse' causality. Discussing Freud's concept of retroaction and the developmental process to which it corresponds, Malcolm Bowie makes a distinction between Freud as theorist and as therapist:

> An entire dimension of Freud's work redramatizes the myth of the Furies: the past is visited upon the individual in a series of violent incursions, and his future, if he has one, can be envisaged only as a prolongation of these and a continuing helpless desire to lift their curse. The retroactive mode, operating alone, produces a backward-looking hope, a wish to create for oneself a past that can be lived with. As a therapist, Freud was keenly aware that his patients brought with them their intentions, goals and ambitions as well as their painful memories, but as a theorist he had been reluctant to grant any causal authority to merely possible worlds. Anticipated events had no notable influence upon the present, no pre-effects or fore-shocks emanated from them and they did not trigger anything.[9]

Yet this distinction between Freud as theorist and as therapist with respect to temporality is arguably difficult to sustain. For there could be nothing more distinctive about psychoanalysis *as therapy* than its use of the transference. And transference is characterized by Freud, theorist of therapy, precisely in terms of regression. The tendency to

---

[8] Freud, 'Creative Writers and Day-Dreaming' (1908), *Art and Literature* (London: Penguin, 1990), pp. 129-41, p. 133.
[9] Malcolm Bowie, *Lacan* (London: Fontana, 1991), p. 182.

regress is held to be an inevitable feature of the analytic encounter and the very condition of the possibility of its therapeutic effect. Freud declares that 'the transference is itself only a piece of repetition'[10] and adds that:

> The patient's state of being ill cannot cease with the beginning of his analysis and [...] we must treat his illness not as an event of the past, but as a present-day force. This state of illness is brought, piece by piece, within the field and range of operation of the treatment and while the patient experiences it as something real and contemporary, we have to do our therapeutic work on it, which consists in a large measure of tracing it back to the past.[11]

Yet if the transference is regressive, the *use* of the transference in psychoanalysis is not purely regressive: the aim is to show that what the analysand experiences 'as a present-day force', is in fact an undead remnant of the past that has simply reasserted itself. In using the transference, itself regressive, the aim is precisely to create the possibility of development by establishing some degree of separation between the past and the present. As past resurges into present in the neurosis and again in the transference, the analyst shuttles back and forth, on the trail of their connections and, paradoxically, in an attempt to (re-)establish their separateness. When the past irrupts into the present, when the past is present, time and age are simply irrelevant: they have no meaning, or their meaning is without effect. Yet the analytic work is about establishing layers and separations, some of them temporal; it is to some extent about restoring time and the possibility of real development. If the human capacity for regressive resurgence is a necessary prior condition for Freud's theory and therapy, one of the aims of the analytic work is surely to reassert the possibility of development, however limited this may be. The Freudian concepts of working-through and the 'even suspension' of the analyst's attention both point to the importance of extended and *non-regressive* temporal processes in the analytic sesssion, yet sadly none of this even approaches an account in which ageing as such is allowed to signify.

---

[10] Freud, 'Remembering, Repeating and Working-Through' (1914), SE 12, p. 151.
[11] Ibid., pp. 151-2.

Yet there is what might be called a hidden history, even a hidden pre-history, of ageing in psychoanalysis. Charcot had begun his career in 1853 with a thesis on two diseases of old age, rheumatoid arthritis and gout.[12] Concurrently with his studies of the neuroses and hysteria at the Salpêtrière between 1862 and 1892, Charcot was also working and lecturing, on different wards in the same institution, on the peculiar characteristics and pathology of old age. 1868 saw the publication of his *Leçons sur les maladies des vieillards et les maladies chroniques*.[13] In the first of these lectures, he remarked to the audience that the Salpêtrière offered particularly favourable conditions for studying old age and its illnesses, because the advance of both can be carefully monitored over a long period of time; moreover, the sample size was large, readily available and, reading between the lines, generally compliant. These remarks exactly parallel those made in his infamous lectures with hysterics. It seems implausible to suggest that Freud would not have been aware of, even if he did not actually attend, these parallel but lesser-known performances during his time at the Salpêtrière in 1885-6.

By the following decade, it is clear that Freud was himself interested in ageing as such as well as other phases of the human lifespan. The exchange of letters between Freud and Fliess in the 1890s testifies to a vertiginously speculative interest in the possible patterning of the human lifespan. Fliess had proposed in his notion of periodicity that the menstrual cycle was paralleled – or rather, not exactly paralleled – in men by a twenty-three day biochemical cycle, on which both mood and sexual potency depended. These cycles were correlated to larger-scale patterns which shaped the entire lifespan of the individual. Periodicity, in Freud's letters to Fliess, is reminiscent of a secular, scientific, Kabbalism, one that seems to share the vast explanatory ambitions of its religious counterpart. Yet if Freud parted company with Fliess on various levels – personally, as well as theoretically in the 'Three Essays' – a vestige of this passion for the idea of patterning throughout the lifespan survives in his later work.

---

[12] See Georges Guillain, *J.-M. Charcot. His Life, His Work*, translated by P. Bailey (London: Pitman, 1959), p. 85.
[13] Charcot, *Leçons sur les maladies des vieillards et les maladies chroniques* (Paris: Delahaye, 1868).

In 'Beyond the Pleasure Principle', some of these earlier preoccupations reemerge. The essay is punctuated by references, often in footnotes, to contemporary scientific research on the demise of organisms. Senescence, as Charcot's work on the subject demonstrated, had in the nineteenth century been considered a mysterious process which it was the task of scientific theorizing and experimentation to explain. The mysteries of senescence and death are precisely those which preoccupied Weismann, Fliess and the other members of a shadowy cast of biologists lurking at the margins of Freud's essay. Yet in spite of a rather abstract reference to the 'circuitous paths to death' followed by the organism under the influence of the 'conservative instincts', there is no sense in the essay as such of the extended and gradual processes of senescent degeneration which precede the moment of death. Death, which Freud speculates is the 'aim' of life, is nonetheless *beyond*, beyond the experience of the organism even as it constitutes the very end and possibility of that experience. In Freud's minimal living organism, a 'protective shield' is formed by the reversion of the outer layer toward the inorganic, allowing the organism to resist stimuli.[14] Thus dead, or half-dead, matter borders and is bound to living matter, at least in the minimal organism, yet there is no indication of the way in which dead matter in the ageing adult human gradually colonizes the entire organism.

In fact, senescence, as a complex psychosomatic process, has been written out of this essay of Freud's: death, as the end, or 'beyond', of life is certainly present, but the 'circuitous paths' of senescence which lead to it remain mysterious. It is rather tempting to think of the emphasis in this essay on the 'beyond' of death as, in part, a defensive projection of the immanent processes of senescence: for projection, as Freud defines it here, is a way of bringing the cortical shield into play by making out that the threat that is really inside is in fact outside. Thus death, the final outer beyond, stands in for senescence, the slow inner peril. In a letter to Jung in 1910, Freud remarked: 'I am resigned to being old and no longer even think continually of growing old.'[15] It would indeed seem that thoughts of

---

[14] Freud, 'Beyond the Pleasure Principle' (1920), Penguin Freud Library, vol. 11, *On Metapsychology* (London: Penguin, 1991), pp. 269-338, p. 298.
[15] *Freud/Jung Letters* (London: Penguin, 1991), p. 177.

death, and especially of war and death, came more readily to Freud
than thoughts about growing old.

Lacan

That time is central to psychoanalysis as a therapy is also
suggested by the very mechanism of the analytic session: the
regularity of sessions, the insistence on the prescribed hour and the
corresponding resistance from within the psychoanalytic profession to
Lacan's 'short sessions'. Lacan characterized the role of the analyst in
terms of providing the 'ponctuation dialectique' in the analysand's
speech.[16] Punctuation makes 'articulation' possible by introducing
divisions which separate and unite, thereby constructing both breaks
and sequences in space and time. If futurity remains under-theorized
in Freud's work, as Bowie rightly suggests (even though, as I have
argued, his work implies it so thoroughly), temporality in general and
futurity in particular will rank high among Lacan's clinical and
theoretical preoccupations. Indeed, in the form of the short session,
this will serve as the punctuation, his own 'ponctuation heureuse',
marking his separation from the analytic mainstream.

The short session aside, Lacan's concern with temporality
comes to the fore in his essay from the 1940s on logical time[17] and
again in 'Fonction et champ de la parole et du langage en
psychanalyse'.[18] He characterizes the present of the subject in terms of
the tension, or state of suspension, between a past anticipation of
future certainty[19] and a future past, indeed a 'future perfect'.[20] I do not
want to enter here into a detailed discussion of these essays but would
like instead to make the simple point that Lacan never entertains the

[16] Lacan, 'Fonction et champ de la parole et du langage', *Ecrits* (Paris: Seuil, 1966), p.
310.
[17] Lacan, 'Le temps logique et l'assertion de certitude anticipée', *Ecrits*, pp. 197-213.
[18] Lacan, *Ecrits*, pp. 237-322.
[19] Referring to his 1945 essay on logical time, Lacan writes: 'On y démontre que c'est
la certitude anticipée par le subjet dans le *temps pour comprendre* qui, par la hâte
précipitant le *moment de conclure*, détermine chez l'autre la décision qui fait du
propre mouvement du sujet erreur ou vérité' ('Fonction et champ de la parole et du
langage', *Ecrits*, p. 287).
[20] See, in particular, Lacan, *Ecrits*, pp. 300, 521.

possibility of a relation between his new and original characterization of psychic temporality and the psychosomatic phenomenon of ageing. For this new account of temporality and futurity is constructed and exemplified in language and the topological diagrams which serve mainly to recall that language: it is not a temporality of bodies, however subtle.[21] The fact that, once again, the body is passed over for language will come as no surprise from Lacan. Yet if the relatively slight violence of curtailing an analytic session is held to be capable of precipitating 'le temps de conclure', then why should there not be an analogous role for the impending curtailment of the human lifespan and its somatic foreshocks, illness and infirmity? Thus while his engagement with temporality and futurity undoubtedly develops an under-theorized aspect of Freud's work, it is really no advance on Freud's position with respect to ageing.

Jung and Erikson

In the space left open by Freud's avoidance of ageing as a potentially meaningful process within the frame of psychoanalysis, some enthusiastically prescriptive prophets of the human lifespan have set up stall. Most significant among these is Jung, whose metaphor of the morning and afternoon of life has had enduring appeal. Erik Erikson's 'eight ages of man' is, I would argue, simply a more detailed and considerably more prescriptive working-out of Jung's metaphor.

In his essay 'The Stages of Life', Jung argues that between the ages of thirty-five and forty, 'a significant change in the human psyche is in preparation'.[22] He suggests that this change is often manifested in mental illness, particularly depression, a view which prefigures Elliott Jaques's now commonplace notion of the midlife crisis. Jung suggests in this essay that the 'morning' and the 'afternoon' of life have different, indeed opposing, goals associated with them: in the case of the former, it is 'to win for oneself a place in

---

[21] See Lacan, *Ecrits*, p. 301.

[22] Jung, 'The Stages of Life', in *Modern Man in Search of a Soul* (London: Routeldge, 2001 reprint), pp. 97-116, p. 107.

society'.[23] The second half of life is, according to Jung, the time for culture[24] and spiritual development or 'the illumination of the self'.[25] Jung's descriptive manner often lapses into implausible and unhelpful polarizations and I would argue that this is the case here.[26] However, it should be acknowledged that Jung's portrayal of the *process* of change is considerably more nuanced:

> Often it is something like a slow change in a person's character; in another case certain traits may come to light which had disappeared in childhood; or again, inclinations and interests begin to weaken and others arise to take their places. It also frequently happens that the convictions and principles which have hitherto been accepted – especially the moral principles – commence to harden and to grow increasingly rigid.[27]

This is a description which allows for variations in the manner of change yet which, for this very reason, is difficult to reconcile with the narrowly-defined and opposing goals which Jung posits for the first and second halves of the lifespan. What emerges clearly from this essay, however, is Jung's insistence that the price of not accepting some form of radical change in outlook with age will be psychic distress: 'we cannot live the afternoon of life according to the programme of life's morning'.[28] It is conceivable that Jung's alternately wide and narrow formulations of this process of change might assist an analyst faced with a certain kind of analysand, or indeed a reader looking to help him- or herself. Yet this essay stops a long way short of offering a coherent theoretical model of the ageing process. If Jung displays a degree of self-awareness about the metaphorical character of much of this essay[29], it is greatly to be regretted that many of the Jungians in the self-help business, who claim to draw on its insights, do not. A particularly turgid example of Jungian self-help literature about ageing is Brennan & Brewi's

---

[23] Jung, 'The Stages of Life', p. 106.

[24] Ibid., p. 112.

[25] Ibid., p. 111.

[26] See on this point my 'Theorizing Writerly Creativity: Jung with Lacan?', in *Post-Jungian Criticism: Theory and Practice*, ed. by Baumlin & Jensen (Albany: State University of New York Press, 2004).

[27] Jung, 'The Stages of Life', p. 107.

[28] Ibid., p. 111.

[29] See, for example, ibid., p. 109.

Passion for Life: Lifelong Psychological and Spiritual Growth: 'This we do know: aging is for soul making. Aging is for the growth and becoming of the magnificent human spirit. It is a spiritual enterprise, a godly thing'.[30]

Although very different from Jung in many other respects, the ego psychologist Erik Erikson's work on the life-cycle is best understood as a development of Jung's metaphor of the morning and afternoon of life into a series of 'eight ages of man'. Each stage has its set of 'tasks' and 'criteria'. In *Childhood and Society*, Erikson describes these as follows:

> a list of ego qualities which emerge from critical periods of development – criteria (identity is one) by which the individual demonstrates that his ego, at a given stage, is strong enough to integrate the timetable of the organism with the structure of social institutions.[31]

The resulting psychosocial and psychosexual timetable is remarkably prescriptive, socially conservative and, not altogether unsurprisingly, narrowly heterosexual (see 'generativity' in the table below). What is more surprising is how remarkably uninformative Erikson is about the content of each stage. In *The Life Cycle Completed: A Review*, he provides a table of the eight stages and for each stage there is an ego goal and a corresponding danger:

1. Infancy	basic trust vs. basic mistrust
2. Early childhood	autonomy vs. shame/doubt
3. Play age	initiative vs. guilt
4. School age	industry vs. inferiority
5. Adolescence	identity vs. identity confusion
6. Young adulthood	intimacy vs. isolation
7. Adulthood	generativity vs. stagnation
8. Old age	integrity vs. despair[32]

On 'integrity', the ego goal for old age, Erikson tells us that 'What is demanded here could be simply called "integrality", a tendency to

---

[30] Brennan & Brewi, *Passion for Life: Lifelong Psychological and Spiritual Growth* (New York: Continuum, 1999), p. 21.

[31] Erik Erikson, *Childhood and Society* (New York: Norton, 1950; repr. Penguin, 1965), p. 238. This and all subsequent references are to the 1965 edition.

[32] Erik Erikson, *The Life Cycle Completed: A Review* (New York: Norton, 1982), adapted from Erikson's table.

keep things together'.[33] Quite, though it could be argued that Erikson here is simply dressing up some very conventional wisdom about the life-cycle in rather loose-fitting psychoanalytic clothes. The role of the analyst in Erikson's generational scheme is simply to help the analysand back into the right slot for his or her age, which corresponds, not entirely coincidentally, to their appropriate niche within heteronormative consumerist society.

Segal, Jaques and King

This section will review some recent contributions to discussion of the role of ageing in psychoanalysis. In the case of Hanna Segal and Elliott Jaques, by contrast with Erikson, their papers on ageing represent a small part of their overall work. However, I would argue that both are considerably more suggestive of new theoretical and therapeutic possibilities than Erikson's scheme. Pearl King has become something of a specialist in this field and I shall come to her work last.

In her short paper, 'Fear of Death. Notes on the Analysis of an Old Man', leading Kleinian analyst Hanna Segal discusses the case of a male patient who began treatment with her at the age of seventy-three.[34] He had experienced, she reports, an acute psychotic breakdown at the age of seventy-two, with depression, hypochondria, paranoid delusions, and attacks of rage, none of which responded to the usual psychiatric treatments. The analysis with Segal lasted eighteen months and she divides this period into three phases. In the first phase, she comes to the conclusion that it is the unconscious fear of death which led to his psychotic breakdown and adds that, in her view, 'the same problem underlies many breakdowns in old age'.[35] She suggests that, in this first phase, the analysand was in a state of complete conscious denial of his approaching death. This gave way in the seond phase to his idealization of her as 'the only protection against death', as 'the source of food, love, and warmth', yet equally

---

[33] Erikson, *The Life Cycle Completed*, pp. 64-5.
[34] Hanna Segal, 'Fear of Death: Notes on the Analysis of an Old Man', *International Journal of Psycho-Analysis* 39 (1958), 178-81.
[35] Ibid., p. 178.

she became 'the killer, since I could bring him death by withdrawing them'.[36] These persecutory fears in turn gave way to a third phase in which his attitude to the idea of his own death had profoundly altered:

> The end of the treatment had then been already fixed, and symbolized for him his approaching death, of which he now spoke very freely. It appeared to him as a repetition of meaning, but now not so much as a retaliation and persecution, but as a reason for sorrow and mourning about the loss of something that he deeply appreciated and could now enjoy, which was life.[37]

So here the analysis works by rendering a powerfully repressed, unconscious fear of death a matter for conscious mourning and, in so doing, frees the subject to live better. Segal's hypothesis that the fear of death can often be all the more powerfully repressed with old age seems, as a matter of common sense, entirely plausible. From a psychoanalytic perspective, however, it invites further comment. For Freud famously insisted both that time plays no role in the unconscious and that the unconscious knows no such thing as death.[38] These principles are central and basic. Yet implicit in this case history of Segal's is the notion that, with age, the vigour with which certain fears are repressed and the corresponding violence with which they nevertheless produce their unconscious effects are both prone to increase. In other words, the qualities of timelessness and immortality which Freud attributed to the unconscious may not prevent ageing as such signifying in psychoanalytic terms. This is a significant theoretical step, albeit not one taken explicity in the paper. Yet Segal's admittedly brief paper leaves the reader wondering whether, beyond the circumstances of this one particular case, ageing is only ever a matter of the increasing fear of death or the repression of that fear. What of the psychoanalytic significance of diminished physical and mental functioning, for example? These aspects are, as I show below, prominent in much of the French work on this question.

Elliott Jaques first coined the term 'mid-life crisis' in a paper entitled 'Death and the mid-life crisis'. Like Jung, he suggests that

---

[36] Segal, 'Fear of Death: Notes on the Analysis of an Old Man', p. 180.
[37] Ibid., p. 180.
[38] Freud, 'The Unconscious', Penguin Freud Library, vol. 11, *On Metapsychology* (London: Penguin, 1991), 159-222, pp. 190-1.

around the age of thirty-five there occurs a more or less fraught period of transition which lasts 'for some years'.[39] What characterizes this critical moment is, Jaques argues, the realization of both 'the inevitableness of eventual death, and the existence of hate and destructive impulses inside each person [...] that is to say, both death and the death instinct'.[40] Jaques's account is phrased in Kleinian terms: successfully traversing the mid-life crisis is held to be a matter of working through the depressive position once again. Just as the infant, according to Klein, is called upon to succeed against 'the chaos inside him' (which is the depressive position), so the individual who in mid-life becomes conscious of the prospect of his or her impending death must also traverse this position.[41] In early adulthood, Jaques argues, depressive anxiety is invariably kept at bay by a series of manic defences, the existence and operation of which are concealed by successful activity of an economic, social, physical and sexual nature.[42] The mid-life crisis confronts the individual with the depressive anxiety which had hitherto been suppressed.

Whether or not the individual can work through the depressive position again in mid-life is said to depend, as it does for the infant, upon 'the prevailing balance between love and hate'.[43] Jaques says little about what it is which tips this balance in favour of love, though what he does say suggests that this is a matter both of the individual's inner world and his or her relationships with others. In the case history of his analysand Mr N., which Jaques presents in the paper, these prevailing conditions seem to amount to 'the positive factors in his personality make-up' which 'enabled him to utilize his analysis, for which he developed a deep sense of value and appreciation'.[44] This cannot but seem self-important on Jaques's part, although I would suggest that analysis can be seen as simply one

---

[39] Jaques, 'Death and the mid-life crisis', *International Journal of Psycho-Analysis* 46 (1965): 502-14, reprinted in Bott Spillius (ed.), *Melanie Klein Today: Developments in Theory and Practice*, vol. 2 (London: Brunner-Routledge, 2004), 226-48, p. 226. This and all subsequent references are to the 2004 reprint.

[40] Ibid., p. 232.

[41] See Melanie Klein, 'Mourning and its relation to manic depressive states', *The Writings of Melanie Klein*, vol. 1 (London: Hogarth Press, 1940), 344-69. See also Jaques, op. cit., p. 242.

[42] Jacques, 'Death and the mid-life crisis', p. 237.

[43] Ibid., p. 242.

[44] Ibid., p. 241.

example of a number of situations in which what he calls 'love' predominates. In spite of some rather involved Kleinian packaging, one aspect of Jaques's mid-life crisis is brutally straightforward: it is the advance realization of death and finitude, 'this sense of there being no more changing'.[45] What complicates the picture and makes Jaques's a richer concept is that the need for acceptance of death and finitude is accompanied by a need to recognize one's own destructive, death-dealing, impulses or instincts. In this sense Jaques's notion of the mid-life crisis can be seen as a developmental opportunity, where the prospect of death offers an occasion for reconciliation, 'reparation', and insight. The expression 'mid-life crisis' has, of course, long since passed into common usage and in so doing seems to have lost this nuance of potential growth, denoting merely a nervous breakdown in middle age.

Pearl King, a British analyst who qualified in 1950 and who for a time was a colleague of Jaques's at the Tavistock, has since become something of a specialist on psychoanalysis and ageing.[46] King is particularly attentive to the psychosomatic aspect and takes her cue here from Freud's remarks in 'Types of Onset of Neurosis' on the possibility that biological development may sometime produce an alteration in psychic equilibrium and lead to neurotic breakdowns at key moments in the lifecycle, notably puberty and menopause.[47] King notes that Freud also discusses, in this essay, the possibility of 'falling ill from an inhibition in development'.[48] I have already described how Jaques suggests that it is the working-through of the infantile depressive position which must be undertaken again in the first encounter with ageing which is the mid-life crisis. By contrast, King argues that:

> for analysis to be successful for middle-aged and elderly patients, the traumas and psychopathology of puberty and adolescence must be re-

---

[45] Jacques, 'Death and the mid-life crisis', p. 246.

[46] See Pearl King, 'In My End is My Beginning', *Psychoanalysis and Culture: A Kleinian Perspective*, ed. by David Bell (London: Duckworth, 1999), pp. 170-88, p. 170.

[47] Pearl King, 'The Life Cycle as Indicated by the Nature of the Transference in the Psychoanalysis of the Middle-Aged and Elderly', *International Journal of Psycho-Analysis* 61 (1980), 153-60, p. 155.

[48] Freud, 'Types of Onset of Neurosis' (1912), SE 12, pp. 227-38.

experienced and worked through in the transference, whatever early infantile material is also dealt with.[49]

She suggests, moreover, that this is because the middle-aged individual is having to experience *in reverse* many of the changes associated with adolescence: both biological changes and 'role changes'. In a number of obvious ways this is rather an imprecise parallel yet I would suggest that the basic point about the reliving of adolescent experiences in transference with ageing patients can stand without it. In the analysis of middle-aged and elderly patients, King argues, the analyst (regardless of his or her age in years) comes to be experienced in the transference as 'significant adults' from the patient's adolescence.[50] Rather than the implausibly neat mechanical progression from stage to stage that Erikson's timetable seems to demand, King presents a vision of a backward-looking psyche determined to relive its most recent developmental traumas, with an indomitable stubbornness and a context-defying fidelity to an earlier state of things. This feels closer to Freud.

King manages to be refreshingly positive about the advantages of working with older patients, without ever lapsing into the sort of blithe gerontological optimism I criticized in my Introduction. These advantages include a sense of urgency which may, she suggests, give rise to a more productive therapeutic encounter and also the immediacy of real loss which may make it harder to deny paranoid and depressive anxieties, thus allowing mourning to begin more readily.[51] There are specific dangers too, according to King: there is a risk of the analysand behaving as though he or she had the same amount of time ahead of them as in adolescence and leaving the analyst to carry the burden of the 'truth' of the matter. There is also, she argues, a risk that the analysis will be difficult to terminate if it becomes associated with staying alive.[52] Overall, King's approach is pragmatic and plausible, even if there is arguably too little by way of case material to support her point about the reliving of specifically adolescent experiences. The question arises of how her work relates to Jaques's paper on the mid-life crisis. I would suggest that while, in

---

[49] King, 'The Life Cycle as Indicated by the Nature of the Transference', p. 156.
[50] Ibid., p. 155.
[51] King, 'In My End is My Beginning', pp. 184-5.
[52] Ibid., pp. 185-7.

theoretical terms, they seem to be poles apart, the clinical difference might be rather smaller, for if adolescence itself involves the working-through of infantile conflicts then its reliving in middle- or old age will inevitably involve some infantile material too. The difference is more than one of emphasis, however, for King's approach comes closer to offering a psychoanalytic account of ageing which does rather more than reheat the leftovers of infantile conflicts.

Psychoanalysis in France: Herfray, Messy, Danon-Boileau and Guillaumin

Charlotte Herfray, in her *La Vieillesse en analyse*, argues that Jaques's mid-life crisis is followed, in old age, by a series of other crises which are similar in type in the sense that all involve the subject envisaging his or her own death and all of which occasion loss.[53] The psychoanalytic concept of castration plays an important role in Herfray's account: the sense of loss which the ageing subject experiences in no longer being able to do, or to remember, things reawakens the fear of something being forcibly taken away, which is what the notion of castration in broadest terms signifies in psychoanalysis. She also suggests that this anxiety can be communicated to younger onlookers, making the spectacle of ageing unbearable and giving rise to a range of defensive behaviours. Herfray hypothesises that ageing can be conceived as a gradual undoing of the developmental process of early childhood, an ungainly descent of the sublimatory ladder: 'l'enfance *fait retour*'.[54] The reemergence in advanced old age of displays of gluttony, of scatalogical pranks and masturbatory gestures, Herfray suggests testifies to a relaxation of ego (or superego) control analogous to the failure of vigilance which Freud saw as the source of dreams.[55] The banality of all this makes it all the more difficult to accept, for the individual and their entourage alike: 'Arriver à vieillir et sur-vivre aux difficultés que le Moi affronte à cette occasion ne sont, au fond, que des choses éminemment banales qui exigent, comme toute vie dans sa banalité un grand courage et une

---

[53] Charlotte Herfray, *La Vieillesse en analyse* (Paris: Desclée de Brouwer, 1988).
[54] Ibid., p. 30.
[55] Ibid., p. 84.

grande humiltié'.[56] Drawing on Lacan's concept of primitive infantile
hate, 'hainamoration', Herfray suggests that this is very often the last
defence against the complete undoing of the subject.[57]

For Herfray, the crises of old age are just particularly intense
moments in human living, which is at all times a struggle between the
forces of life and death:

> Ce qu'on appelle l'existence devient toujours ainsi une résultante (toujours
> problématique) du dépassement dialectique de la contradiction entre les
> forces qui la constituent: forces qui tirent vers la vie et forces qui tirent vers
> la mort. Articulées l'une à l'autre, l'une dans l'autre en quelque sorte, le
> contraire de l'une comme de l'autre serait ainsi la non-existence qui est à la
> fois non-vie et non-mort.[58]

It is the complexities of this struggle which it would be interesting to
hear more about from Herfray because this bare notion of struggle
seems an unduly reductive version of psychoanalysis. Laplanche's
remarks with respect to the place of the death instinct within the
Kleinian tradition are relevant here:

> In the Kleinian tradition, the whole psychology of the passions is simplified,
> as the opposition between the two great instincts re-appears on every level.
> Henceforth, concrete phenomena are explained through mixtures or simple
> dialectics, in a sort of Manichean logomachy: in this respect, one cannot
> avoid emphasising the boredom which exudes from Kleinian texts, and to
> compare them with such nuanced and insightful works by great
> *Menschenkenner* such as Stendhal or Proust would be extremely
> uncharitable.[59]

One response to this kind of criticism, which might also be used in
defence of Herfray, would be that the aim of psychoanalysis is not to
be interesting but rather to be effective. I would suggest, however, that
if this struggle between the forces of life and death is not to be
'Manichean logomachy' and a reductive account of human life and, in
particular, of human ageing, then there is still a great deal more to be

---

[56] Herfray, *La Vieillesse en analyse*, p. 91.
[57] Ibid., p. 96.
[58] Ibid., p. 23.
[59] Jean Laplanche 'The So-Called "Death Drive": A Sexual Drive', in Rob Weatherill
(ed.), *The Death Drive: New Life for a Dead Subject?* (London: Rebus, 1999), pp. 40-
59, p. 53.

said about the complex detail of this interplay, of the imbrication of life in death.

It will be clear by now that Herfray's account draws extensively on the language and the ready-formed conceptual apparatus of psychoanalysis, yet I would argue that it does not constitute a significant advance in the way that psychoanalysis theorizes the ageing process. Indeed by suggesting that the crises of old age imitate or run in parallel to those of early childhood, it seems to typify the refusal of psychoanalysis to conceptualize ageing in its own terms.

Jack Messy's *La Personne âgée n'existe pas: une approche psychanalytique de le vieillesse* also, like Herfray, links ageing with castration and its related anxiety: the inability to perform tasks reactivates these fears of early childhood.[60] And like Herfray, he too is interested in the role played by the death instinct. Yet in Messy's account, castration anxiety gives way at a certain moment to another kind of anxiety. Messy suggests that, after this moment, ageing can be understood psychoanalytically in terms of a gradual increase in what he calls death anxiety ('l'angoisse de mort'), which is not, however, anxiety about death as such but rather anxiety in the face of the death instinct.[61] Death anxiety is, he says, unconscious.[62] It is anxiety about the self-destructive potential represented by the death instinct: 'Pour le moi elle [l'angoisse de mort] avertit du danger, c'est-à-dire: elle signale la déliaison, ou coupure, ou séparation entre l'objet et le moi'.[63] This theorization of ageing in terms of an increase in unconsious anxiety about an ongoing tendency towards unravelling or disconnection ('déliaison'), both within the self and with the outside world, rather than death as such, can in fact be seen a second-order reworking of Segal's notion that it is unconscious anxiety about death itself which increases in old age, although Messy does not himself refer to Segal's work.

The moment in the life of the subject when castration anxiety gives way to death anxiety, Messy names that of 'le miroir brisé'. This

---

[60] Jack Messy, *La Personne âgée n'existe pas: une approche psychanalytique de la vieillesse* (Paris: Payot & Rivages, 1992, repr. 1994 and 2002). All subsequent references are to the 2002 edition.
[61] Ibid., pp. 60-3.
[62] Ibid., p. 65.
[63] Ibid., p. 63.

is when the individual is confronted, in a mirror or in some other reflecting medium (including other people), with the image of the elderly other which they have become. The image reflected back is, Messy suggests, an antithesis of the ego-ideal,'le moi hideur', and this moment also reactivates the fear of 'le corps morcelé' and the disintegration which this betokens.[64] Before this moment, Messy suggests that castration anxiety is the dominant anxiety in the life of the subject; after this point, however, it is death anxiety, in his special sense, which begins to take over. Although Messy's moment of 'le miroir brisé' clearly and overtly alludes to Lacan's 'stade du miroir', even going as far as to evoke by name the disintegrated state of 'le corps morcelé', which played such a key role in the infant's encounter, Messy's moment of the broken mirror is not simply a rerun, nor even a straightforward reversal, of this critical moment in (or idea about) the very early life of the subject. For it gives way to an entirely new kind of anxiety, one specifically related to the age of the subject and their experience of unravelling or 'déliaison'. What is not clear from Messy's account is the role which the body and its failings plays in death anxiety: presumably the body, or its image, is involved intimately in the moment of the broken mirror, which is quintessentially an experience of the disjunction between the age which the body looks, or acts, and the age the subject thinks of himself or herself as being. But to what extent do the body and its infirmities play a role after this critical moment? Is this mainly psychic or mainly somatic 'déliaison', or both?

Henri Danon-Boileau's *De la vieillesse à la mort* begins by examining the social taboo on elderly sexuality. There is a good amount and a wide range of clinical material, including two perceptive pages on age difference in gay relationships, remarkable by their very presence and for the lack of obvious reproof: the older partner is invariably in the grip of a double identification, Danon-Boileau argues, with both the generous, giving, permissive mother he would have liked to have had and with the younger man who is showered with good things, just as he would have wanted to be.[65] His explanation of the taboo on elderly sexuality in elderly (straight)

---

[64] Messy, *La Personne âgée n'existe pas*, p. 50.
[65] Henri Danon-Boileau, *De la vieillesse à la mort. Point de vue d'un usager* (Paris: Hachette, 2002), pp. 41-3, p. 42.

couples of the same age is similarly ingenious: it is the unconscious revenge of the son on the father. If the father once forbade the son from having sex with the mother, or so the story goes, now the son forbids the father's sexual relationship with the mother, with a similar 'castrating' effect.[66] An elaborate discussion of the anxiety which often surrounds the forgetting of names in old age is also worthy of note: Danon-Boileau suggests that to forget the names of others, of places, corresponds to the desire to forget one's own name, for to avoid being named is to avoid being claimed by death.[67] Yet at the same time this desire to forget one's own name creates anxiety because, were it to be realized, this would be madness. If Danon-Boileau's study is at times densely speculative, it is also rich in case material and is characterized by an engaging lightness of touch. There is, however, little attempt to build on the work of other analysts, either in France or elsewhere, making this a somewhat idiosyncratic and isolated book.

Jean Guillaumin, in his paper 'Le temps et l'âge: réflexions psychanalytiques sur le vieillir', argues that Freud's original conception of time, particularly as manifested in *Nachträglichkeit*, which he takes to imply that the meaning of events which took place in the past can be established after they have taken place, should allow us to free our thinking about ageing from the tyranny of simplistic 'biological' and 'chronological' time. Thus according to Guillaumin, the psychoanalyst's engagement with ageing is of an entirely different kind from that of the geriatrician and demands that:

> on questionne dans leur intériorité les effets du choc, ou des chocs successifs de l'âge, envisagés comme des traumas désorganisateurs, et, inséparablement, comme des chances tardives, parfois jusqu'au bout maintenues, de réarticuler et de resignifier la vie entière.[68]

Thus psychic and somatic changes can be used as opportunities to reinterpret life to date, as I suggested might be the case with Jaques's mid-life crisis and the working-through of adolescence theorized by

---

[66] Danon-Boileau, *De la vieillesse à la mort*, pp. 75-83.

[67] Ibid., pp. 145-56.

[68] Jean Guillaumin, 'Le temps et l'âge. Réflexions psychanalytiques sur le vieillir', in *Le Temps et la vie: les dynamismes du vieillissement*, ed. by Guillaumin & Reboul (Lyon: Chronique Sociale, 1982), p. 134.

King. One avenue Guillaumin is alone among these psychoanalysts in pursuing is his reflection on the significance of the tendency towards 'radotage' or 'rabachage' in old age, a phenomenon we have already encountered in the context of Leduc's work. He suggests that this fixation on the past could be seen as:

> une manière de cuirasse caractérielle tardive, qui absorbe et traite automatiquement, à la périphérie du psychisme, par des réponses émotionnelles et sensori-motrices totalement dépendantes des stimuli déclencheurs, des afférences devenues impossibles à élaborer sur un mode souple et créateur.[69]

He adds that 'radotage' also has an interpersonal dimension, for those who exhibit it very quickly come to be treated as old bores, which reduces considerably the creative potential in any given encounter and begins a downward spiral. The danger of 'radotage', Guillaumin suggests, imposes upon the analyst the delicate duty of locating the analysand's level of tolerance to challenge and questioning: there is an obligation to get through and dismantle this shield of 'radotage', yet too vigorous an attempt to do so will be experienced as a threat and have the opposite of the desired effect.

*

Psychoanalysis has been reluctant to consider ageing as a meaningful process for reasons which are more than merely circumstantial. Both as theory and practice, psychoanalysis is intensely backward-looking. Indeed as Adam Phillips has put it: 'what was radically puzzling originally about Freud's work was the implication that, in one sense, after childhood there was nowhere to go'.[70] Yet there is no reason why this essential concern with the infantile should necessarily exclude an engagement, both theoretical and clinical, with the ageing subject. I would suggest that, in spite of the variety of work examined in the foregoing chapter, there is still much to be done here. It would be wrong, however, to expect more of psychoanalysis than it can give: the demand to give account for the irreversible singularity of the human lifespan is better addressed

[69] Guillaumin, 'Le temps et l'âge', p. 136.
[70] Adam Phillips, *The Beast in the Nursery* (London: Faber, 1998), p. 103.

elsewhere, if not forgotten altogether, yet those who suffer from that demand and who suffer from the process which leads them to frame it, can perhaps be helped.

Chapter Five

Beauvoir as biographer and autobiographer of the ageing subject

By contrast with Leduc, in whose writing ageing is associated with introversion and a withdrawal from others, senescence in Beauvoir's late work brings the subject into an encounter with the other. This is not, however, always a felicitous encounter. It will be recalled from Chapter One that Beauvoir's account of ageing in *La Vieillesse* is essentially one in which the subject is alienated, split in schizoid fashion between its sense of inner self-sameness and the reality of becoming old: ageing is *othering*. I shall argue that the precursor of this abstract formulation is to be found in Beauvoir's experience of the ageing process in *La Force des choses*. Critics have seldom taken this book seriously enough, finding it easier to dismiss Beauvoir's bleak analysis here as evidence merely of a depressive tendency. After having discussed this work at some length, I shall then go on to examine two of Beauvoir's biographical texts, both concerned with the ageing and death of another person. I conclude my discussion in this chapter by examining a documentary film about old age in which Beauvoir not only featured but in the making of which she also collaborated.

Autobiography: *La Force des choses*

I shall be concentrating in this section on the third volume of Beauvoir's four-volume autobiography, *La Force des choses*. The main body of this work is essentially a catalogue of events, arranged in linear chronological order. To the extent that this episodic narrative has, in addition, thematic unity, it is Beauvoir's ageing that provides this. Although it might be thought that the prominence of senescence in this later volume of Beauvoir's memoirs is foreshadowed in the titles of the first two (*Mémoires d'une jeune fille rangée* and *La Force*

de l'âge), these are otherwise relatively free of material related to
ageing and will accordingly play only a small part in my discussion
here. Similarly, the fourth and final volume, *Tout compte fait*, lacks
sufficient relevant material: although Beauvoir readily describes
herself as old in this work, she has little to say about this state as such
and the process that led her to it.

A striking but neglected feature of Beauvoir's memoirs in
general and *La Force des choses* in particular are their several
paratexts.[1] These are easily overlooked, for they are short by
comparison with the main body of the text on which they pass
comment. Their distribution, however, is far from uniform through the
four volumes that constitute Beauvoir's memoirs. The *Mémoires
d'une jeune fille rangée* contain no such passages; *La Force de l'âge*
begins with a 'Prologue' of some two pages, as does the last volume
of the series, *Tout compte fait*. Yet in *La Force des choses*, we find an
introductory passage of some four pages (which is italicized but bears
no title), an 'Intermède' (at the end of the first part, of some six pages)
and the notorious 'Epilogue', running to around twenty pages, which
concludes the entire volume. So there are three times as many
paratexts in *La Force des choses* than in both the preceding and
following volumes and each of these paratexts is considerably longer
than the one before. Although varying in emphasis, all are concerned
with justifying the autobiographical project. And all are concerned
with the ageing process. I shall, in this section, look first at the role

---

[1] In Philippe Lejeune's case, the neglect of these paratextual passages is part and
parcel of his perplexing reluctance to accept the legitimacy of Beauvoir's choice of
linear chronology. See Lejeune, *Le Pacte autobiographique* (Paris: Seuil, 1975).
Lejeune considers linear chronological narrative to be the lowest form of self-writing,
assuming that it prevents totalization and is not, therefore, autobiography proper. Yet
it is he who arbitrarily stipulates that totalization is a necessary condition of true
autobiographical writing. In a chapter of *Le Pacte autobiographique* which is
supposed to be about Sartre's autobiography, he nonetheless finds time for a side-
swipe at Beauvoir: 'elle devrait plutôt pratiquer franchement le journal intime, au lieu
d'essayer de le déguiser en autobiographie' (p. 236). In addition to the gendered
implications in Lejeune's paternalistic attempt to consign Beauvoir to the extra-
literary (and traditionally 'feminine') field of diary-writing, on account of her choice
of linear chronology, is his neglect of those paratextual passages in which she justifies
this choice. Lejeune suggests merely that they evince Beauvoir's 'tant de difficultés'
with autobiography as a genre (p. 234). However, as I demonstrate above, these
paratextual passages attempt to justify Beauvoir's choice of linear chronological
narrative as most conducive to the representation of the ageing process.

ageing plays in this process of paratextual self-justification before turning to its role in the main body of the account.

The short 'Prologue' to *La Force de l'âge* provides a useful point of comparison: here Beauvoir attempts both to justify continuing to write the memoirs and to excuse herself in advance for any slight factual errors and for those omissions necessitated by the need to be discreet.[2] Her justification for going on is framed in fairly vague terms: a desire to show what she did with the hard-won freedom she had acquired by the end of the *Mémoires* and to explain why she wrote the books she did thereafter. Later, she addresses a similar, though on this occasion temporally specific, question, in the prologue to *La Force des choses*: why continue *now* rather than in a few years' time? Here her answer is much more pointed:

> L'indifférence, sereine ou désolée, de la décrépitude ne me permettrait plus de saisir ce que je souhaite capter: ce moment où, à l'orée d'un passé encore brûlant, le déclin commence.[3]

So Beauvoir suggests that the principal aim of her memoirs (and, presumably, of this volume in particular) is to represent the process of her decline into old age. The account must go on, and she must continue to tell the story now, because Beauvoir wishes to 'grasp' (*capter*) her own decline as it happens, before the anticipated 'indifférence' of old age. In other words, this is to be an account of ageing in process, in 'real time'. Because there is so very little in the preceding volumes, their titles aside, with much of a bearing on ageing, this radically new justification may come as something of a surprise. It may also come as a surprise that the representation of so banal a process as ageing should become the principal aim, the preoccupying drama, of the memoirs: not the events but the human fabric against which they are set is to be brought to the fore. Beauvoir's stated aim here will recall the suggestion of Gide's, in his *Journal*, that I examined in Chapter Two: the greatest achievement of any diarist, he intimated, would be to provide a persuasive representation of the experience of human ageing. Beauvoir reiterates her position in the 'Intermède' at the end of Part One of *La Force des*

---

[2] Beauvoir, *La Force de l'âge* (Paris: Gallimard, 1960), pp. 11-13.
[3] Beauvoir, *La Force des choses* (Paris: Gallimard, 1963), I, p. 7.

choses, where she links this new overriding representational aim to her choice of linear chronology:

> Ce qui compte avant tout dans ma vie, c'est que le temps coule; je vieillis, le monde change, mon rapport avec lui varie; montrer les transformations, les mûrissements, les irréversibles dégradations des autres et de moi-même, rien ne m'importe davantage. Cela m'oblige à suivre docilement le fil des années.[4]

This may seem a particularly bleak focus for a memoir and it is tempting to wish to dismiss patronisingly her assertion that what matters most in her life is the fact she is getting older either as overstatement or as evidence of a tendency towards depression.[5] Yet her proposition deserves to be taken more seriously. For as Beauvoir herself remarked of old age: 'si elle m'effraie, c'est donc qu'elle est effrayante'.[6] Moreover, it raises an important question about the genre. How far is it possible for an autobiography, which must, however told, be a story of events in which an individual was implicated, to bring into focus the ground against which those events are set, namely the ageing of the person concerned? Ageing is universal and, at first sight, banal. How far is it possible to dramatize this banal background, to make something of it?

These questions concerning the possibility of representing the writer's own ageing in her memoirs might be thought of figuratively as a question of the visibility of the background. This is an issue also raised in the 'Intermède' in *La Force des choses*, but on this occasion in the context of the visibility, or lack of it, in the main body of the text not of her ageing but of Beauvoir's work as a writer. She appears troubled by the fact that the main body of the narrative appears to convey little sense of the labour which led to its coming into being:

> Un défaut des journaux intimes et des autobiographies c'est que, d'ordinaire, 'ce qui va sans dire' n'est pas dit et qu'on manque l'essentiel. J'y tombe, moi aussi. [...] Le travail ne se laisse guère décrire: on le fait,

---

[4] Beauvoir, *La Force des choses*, pp. 375-6

[5] Depression is Toril Moi's verdict. This reductive diagnosis of depression as the explanatory matrix for all Beauvoir's late work is the weakest point in an otherwise persuasive study (Moi, pp. 243-52).

[6] Beauvoir, *Tout compte fait* (Paris: Gallimard, 1972), p. 165.

> c'est tout. Du coup, il tient dans ce livre peu de place, alors que dans ma vie il en occupe tant: elle s'organise tout entière autour. J'y insiste [...].[7]

So if the 'Prologue' to *La Force de l'âge* had sought to excuse small errors of fact and detail, here by contrast, in the middle of *La Force des choses*, we have anxiety about a far more serious narrative blind-spot. Beauvoir goes on after the passage above to describe the different stages in writing a book, emphasising the hard work involved, by way of compensating for the fact that the main body of her account appears to her to convey little sense of it. The possibility that the main body of her autobiography could have omitted something so central to Beauvoir's life as her work – work of which it is, in one sense, material evidence but of which it seems to her to bear few internal traces – is accordingly a cause of profound unease. Nor indeed is this irritation surprising in view of the fact that, as I mentioned above, one of the repeated paratextual justifications for these memoirs is the hope that they will demystify writing by casting light on the relation between the text and the life and person of the writer.[8] Yet however similar in structure these concerns of re-presenting her work and her ageing, Beauvoir clearly feels that whereas the main body of her account is deficient in the former case, it has succeeded in the latter. For this is precisely what linear chronology is good at, she indicates in the passage from the 'Intermède' which I quoted above, whatever its other problems and however much her critics derided this approach as laborious and unilluminating.

She expanded on this point in a lecture given in Japan in 1966, entitled 'Mon expérience d'écrivain', in which she responded to the criticism that her reliance on linear chronological narrative made for a disappointing read:

> J'ai eu cette même déception quelquefois, en lisant des autobiographies et des biographies; on suit le héros, on pense qu'il va vers une plénitude, vers un point culminant dans son existence; et puis soudain c'est fini, il y a comme une espèce de coupure, ce moment n'a jamais eu lieu.[9]

---

[7] Beauvoir, *La Force des choses*, I, p. 371.

[8] See Beauvoir, *La Force de l'âge*, p. 12.

[9] Beauvoir, 'Mon expérience d'écrivain' [lecture delivered in Japan on 11 October 1966], in Francis & Gonthier (eds.), *Les Ecrits de Simone de Beauvoir* (Paris: Gallimard, 1979), pp. 439-57, p. 453.

She suggests that the sense of disappointment created in the reader by narratives which follow a linear chronology maps onto the sense of profound disappointment which characterizes her experience of the ageing process: 'j'ai été flouée', she declares in her infamous last words from *La Force des choses*.[10] She suggests (it might be thought rather too conveniently) that linear chronology is successful insofar as it disappoints, for the experience of getting older that she most wants to represent is one of existential disappointment. What exactly is the nature of this disappointment? It is a feeling that life's promise of infinite self-expansion has been sorely contradicted: expectation has given way immediately to regret. The sense of a missing present that ensues is illustrated in the Japan lecture with an algebraic term ('une coupure', a hiatus) which Beauvoir first used in the Epilogue to *La Force des choses*:

> J'ai vécu tendue vers l'avenir et maintenant, je me récapitule, au passé: on dirait que le présent a été escamoté. J'ai pensé pendant des années que mon oeuvre était devant moi, et voilà qu'elle est derrière: à aucun moment elle n'a eu lieu. Ça ressemble à ce qu'on appelle en mathématiques une coupure, ce nombre qui n'a de place dans aucune des deux séries qu'il sépare. [...] Me remémorant mon histoire, je me trouve toujours en deçà ou au-delà d'une chose qui ne s'est jamais accomplie.[11]

The notion of 'oeuvre' here is used in this passage almost synonymously with 'mon histoire': forever either anticipating or recollecting, Beauvoir feels that she remains perpetually estranged from her story. The story of her own ageing cannot be *her* story: she is always either young and looking ahead or old and looking back. Thus Beauvoir seems to feel in the Epilogue that the ageing process cannot

---

[10] Beauvoir's readers have often tried to explain away the pessimism of these closing remarks. Yet they deserve to be taken seriously, as Beauvoir herself indicates in an interview with Francis Jeanson in 1966. Here she not only reiterates the closing formula but insists that it neatly encapsulates her entire world-view: '"J'ai été flouée", cela correspond bien entendu à tout un ensemble d'idées que j'avais, de pensées que je m'étais déjà formulées différemment, et qui d'ailleurs – ça me surprend qu'on ait été si surpris! – correspond à *toute* ma vision de l'existence: j'ai toujours pensé, comme Sartre, que l'existence est une vaine recherche de l'Être, que nous voulons l'absolu et n'accédons jamais qu'à du relatif'. See Francis Jeanson, *Simone de Beauvoir ou L'Entreprise de vivre* (Paris: Seuil, 1966), p. 270.

[11] Beauvoir, *La Force des choses*, II, p. 504.

be experienced by the subject, while it is happening, as a gradual process; only its two extremes, young and old, can be grasped. These various comments from the paratexts and the Japan lecture imply that the closest autobiography can come to representing the ageing process is to replicate in the reader that sense of having been cheated or short-changed, deprived of the experience of a continuous process by being presented retrospectively with a series of discrete events. Thus Ursula Tidd argues that chronological presentation, as Beauvoir uses it, 'in its ability to render "la déception ontologique" [is] particularly apt for representing the decline of the ageing self'.[12] Tidd is echoing Beauvoir's own view here, as expressed in the paratexts and the Japan lecture. Whether Beauvoir is right, whether in fact she realizes this representational potential in the main body of the narrative, is a question I shall consider in a moment.

Before moving on from the paratexts to the main body of *La Force des choses*, I want to suggest one further reason for the extreme pathos of the Epilogue which has to do with linear chronology but which does not figure in Beauvoir's own discussion of this approach. Linear chronology, as an autobiographical method, has closure built into it: by the end of *La Force des choses*, Beauvoir has caught up with herself. She cannot continue writing the autobiography because she has no more to tell. Her anguished sense, in the Epilogue, of having reached an age where she has no future, or no future that can change who she essentially is, is closely related to the self-closing aspect inherent in linear chronology: on reaching the Epilogue it is indeed true that her autobiographical account has no future. She could not go on writing autobiography, even if she wished to because the chronological account has reached the present and thus closure. That Beauvoir could have felt the closure of her autobiography signalled the closure of her life, could have momentarily confused *bios* and *graphos*, is unsurprising in view of the fact that she had, by 1963, spent the last seven years writing her life.[13]

I turn now from the paratexts to the main body of *La Force des choses*. Whereas the paratexts in this volume are overwhelmingly

---

[12] Ursula Tidd, *Simone de Beauvoir: Gender and Testimony*, (Cambridge: Cambridge University Press, 1999), p. 168.

[13] Beauvoir notes that she began work on the story of her childhood in 1956. See *La Force des choses*, II, p. 128.

concerned with the question of ageing, this topos emerges only intermittently in the main body of the account, during brief pauses in the catalogue of events. And just as the closing Epilogue stages a climactic crisis of ageing, so these references to old age in the main body often occur in a closural position, immediately preceding breaks in the narrative.[14] Yet close inspection of such material from the main body reveals a striking connection not discernible in the paratexts. This is the association between Beauvoir's feelings about getting older and her reaction of disgust to the French government's brutal response to the Algerian struggle for independence. Torture, in particular, forms the locus of this connection:

> "Pourquoi? pourquoi? pourquoi?": ce cri indéfiniment répété d'un petit Algérien de quinze ans qui avait vu torturer toute sa famille me déchirait les tympans et la gorge. Qu'elles étaient bénignes les révoltes où me jetaient jadis la condition humaine et l'idée abstraite de la mort! Contre la fatalité, on peut convulsivement se débattre, mais elle décourage la colère. Et du moins le scandale demeurait hors de moi. Aujourd'hui j'étais devenue scandale à mes propres yeux. Pourquoi? Pourquoi? Pourquoi devais-je me réveiller chaque matin dans la douleur et la rage, atteinte jusqu'aux moelles par un mal auquel je ne consentais pas et que je n'avais aucun moyen de conjurer? De toute façon, la vieillesse est une épreuve, la moins méritée, pensait Kant, la plus imprévue, disait Trotsky: mais qu'elle fît basculer dans l'ignominie une existence qui jusqu'alors me contentait, je ne le supportais pas.[15]

Torture and ageing are so thoroughly intertwined here that Beauvoir's reference to 'un mal auquel je ne consentais pas' seems to encompass both the use of torture in the Algerian conflict and the onset of old age: torture and old age are both an 'épreuve', both a scandal. Both involve the infliction of bodily pain and imply an internal contradiction in the very concept of the human. Whereas death once ('jadis') seemed to be an 'idée abstraite', a metaphysical concept and a distant, external, threat, it now inhabits her very being. Similarly, the young Algerian's cry not only tears into her eardrums, inflicting injury, but also her throat: it is as though she were screaming too. Thus torture is bound up in the main body of *La Force des choses*

---

[14] See Beauvoir, *La Force des choses*, I, p. 190, p. 234, and *La Force des choses*, II, pp. 236-7, p. 310.
[15] Beauvoir, *La Force des choses*, II, pp. 410-11.

with Beauvoir's experience of the ageing process. It might reasonably be objected that this elision of torture and old age is ethically suspect in that it tends to belittle the particular horror of the former practice.[16] There is no reason to think that Beauvoir had the slightest wish to do such a thing: her preface to *Djamila Boupacha*, many of her articles, interviews and speeches from the late 1950s and early '60s and indeed much of *La Force des choses* make it clear that she was utterly appalled by torture and wanted her compatriots to share her horror, that the practice might stop. But what are we then to make of the passage above and others like it, which suggest an analogy or elision between being tortured and growing older? I shall address this question by way of a closer inspection of other facets of Beauvoir's representation of torture in *La Force des choses*.

Beauvoir stresses in her account that government officials initially denied that torture was taking place at all. Her compatriots were, she implies, all too willing to believe these denials. The press, far from exposing the truth, 'était devenue une entreprise de falsification'.[17] The climate, she suggests, is one of lies and half-truths, grudging admissions and generalized indifference: 'Les Français flottaient dans une indifférence où les mots savoir et ignorer s'équivalaient et telle qu'aucune révélation ne leur apprenait jamais rien'.[18] Torture, it seems, has perverted language, truth and logic: to know and not to know amount to the same. Such is the extent of this linguistic corruption that Beauvoir is reluctant to dignify these utterances as 'lies':

> Des rafales de mots s'abattaient sur la France; le clair vocable de "mensonges" ne leur convenait même pas: c'était des *lecta*, sans relation positive ou négative avec la réalité, des bruits produits dans l'air par un souffle humain.[19]

Thus the ethical crisis of torture is coupled with a linguistic crisis, a breakdown of meaning. The French language seems to have lost its

---

[16] The connection between torture and ageing, if not their elision, is made in the work of Jean Améry, who wrote both of his experiences of the former, in Auschwitz, and his response to the ageing process in *Über das Altern* (Stuttgart: Klett Cotta, 1968).

[17] Beauvoir, *La Force des choses*, II, p. 121.

[18] Ibid., p. 259.

[19] Ibid., p. 238.

oft-vaunted 'clarté' and the purchase which this gave on the world.[20] The use of the verb *s'abattre* suggests that these lies, or senseless *lecta*, actually do violence to Beauvoir, echoing the torturer's violence. Similarly, Beauvoir remarks elsewhere in the same volume that 'j'eus à subir chaque jour, indéfiniment répétée, l'agression des mensonges crachés par toutes les bouches'.[21] Torture, a practice intended to elicit truth, is thus shown in Beauvoir's account to occasion a proliferation of falsehood, both in the form of lies about particular occurrences and a more general corruption of language and logic. That this miasma of deception should have permeated Beauvoir's account of ageing thus comes as no surprise. Her infamous closing comment on the ageing process in the Epilogue is 'J'ai été flouée': she feels she has been deceived, cheated, lied to. In an interview with Francis Jeanson, Beauvoir later commented on this period that, on account of French actions in Algeria, 'ce qui me dégoûtait, c'est qu'on nous faisait [...] une vieillesse horrible [...] ces années-là, il y a eu ensemble l'âge et ce dégoût'.[22] Yet close inspection of the main body of *La Force des choses* suggests that these two experiences do not merely sit 'ensemble', but are rather more closely connected. What is surprising is the way in which the two experiences seem in her account not just to be similar but to be intertwined. However ethically discomforting we may find the connection, growing old and being tortured are, for Beauvoir in the main body of *La Force des choses*, not only structurally similar but frequently intertwined experiences. Both involve a violation of the subject's psychic and somatic integrity, by another person (in the case of torture), or by otherness (in the case of ageing). For Beauvoir in the main body of *La Force des choses*, to age is to be attacked by otherness, to have otherness forced upon oneself. Dramatic and uncomfortable though this construction may be, in its 'use' of torture, it clearly foreshadows Beauvoir's philosophical account of the ageing process in *La Vieillesse*, as I described it in Chapter One, above.

---

[20] The way in which the French language is thought of here as degraded may be likened to the idea of the very language that is German having been tainted by the Holocaust.

[21] Beauvoir, *La Force des choses*, II, p. 120.

[22] Beauvoir, cited in Jeanson, *Simone de Beauvoir*, p. 274.

Beauvoir's interest in the ageing process grows steadily stronger as *La Force des choses* builds to its angry climax: 'je désire de plus en plus écrire sur la vieillesse'.[23] Yet this growth of her interest in ageing occurs just as she approaches the natural end of her linear chronological narrative. For, as I noted above, this particular autobiographical method, as Beauvoir employs it, has closure written into it. Having exhausted her material but not her subject, she is almost compelled to turn her attention to ageing in other people. I have already examined the theoretical dimension of this new turn, namely *La Vieillesse*, a global study which approaches old age from a variety of different perspectives. In the next section, I shall turn to Beauvoir's treatment of ageing and old age in two biographical works.

The Other: from autobiography to biography

The two biographical accounts I shall examine in this section are *Une Mort très douce* (1964) and *La Cérémonie des adieux* (1981). I showed in the last section that *La Force des choses*, by way of an analogy with torture, creates an account of ageing in terms of violation by otherness. Similarly in *La Vieillesse* (1970), as I showed in Chapter One, ageing is characterized both as a process in which the subject is progressively made other and as one the effects of which are revealed to the subject primarily through other people. It seems, according to this formulation, that the effects of ageing are destined to be more visible to others than to the subject: 'on n'est vieux que pour les autres', as Beauvoir remarks.[24] It could be objected that *Une Mort*

---

[23] Beauvoir, cited in Jeanson, *Simone de Beauvoir*, p. 212.

[24] At the philosophical core of *La Vieillesse* (Ch. 5), Beauvoir argues that the subject is gradually 'othered' with age: old age, even when it happens to me, is something that only happens to others, she maintains. To use the vocabulary and conceptual structure of *L'Etre et le néant*, as Beauvoir herself does frequently in that chapter, my age is a property of my 'être-pour-autrui', my 'being-for-others'. According to Beauvoir, ageing implies the encroachment and simultaneously the denial of inner alterity, the growth of an otherness which the subject is bound to reject even as s/he is gradually colonized by it: 'La vieillesse est particulièrement difficile à assumer parce que nous l'avions toujours considérée comme une espèce étrangère: suis-je donc devenue une autre alors que je demeure moi-même?' (p. 321). This *othering* of the subject with old age involves, as Beauvoir puts it, 'une contradiction indépassable' – a schizoid splitting in which the subject's inner conviction of enduring self-sameness is

très douce is more a text about dying than it is about old age.
However, though much of the work is indeed centred on Françoise's
deathbed, an emphasis reinforced by the reference to death in the title,
Beauvoir is no less attentive to the way in which her mother changed
her life in old age. Moreover, as I shall demonstrate, Françoise's
deathbed struggle is continuous with Beauvoir's account of ageing in
La Force des choses and *La Vieillesse*: there, ageing is a kind of slow,
protracted, dying.[25] Conversely, in *Une Mort très douce*, dying is a
kind of accelerated ageing. There is less room for dispute about the

---

continually confronted by, but always resists, the 'outer' evidence that it is no longer
what it was. Old age is 'une sorte de scandale intellectuel' because 'nous devons
assumer une réalité qui est indubitablement nous-même encore qu'elle nous atteigne
du dehors et qu'elle nous demeure insaisissable' (pp. 308-9). The elusivity, or
resistance to representation, exhibited in Beauvoir's autobiography by the old age of
the self-writing subject, can be explained in terms of this new ontological theory, for
'la vieillesse apparaît plus clairement aux autres qu'au sujet lui-même' (p. 302). Or in
other words, 'On n'est vieux que pour les autres'. The resistance to introspection, to
solitary autobiographical probing, of the ageing self both repeats and repositions
Sartre's argument in *La Transcendance de l'Ego*, a text to which Beauvoir was
particularly well-disposed and from which she quotes very frequently in the memoirs.
Sartre had argued that the individual in search of a self in introspection finds only this
very act of looking. The self, or ego, is 'transcendent', which means that it is as
accessible to other people as it is to the subject. By *L'Etre et le néant*, Sartre's
emphasis had shifted slightly and the self is held to be *more* accessible to others than
to the subject: indeed the self as static, reified, entity is here a fabrication of the
Other's gaze, a characterization imposed upon the subject which is both a partial
recognition and a misrecognition, or alienating reduction. Yet Beauvoir's
rearticulation of Sartre's argument is not (as it may seem to be from her gestures of
deference) simply a reproduction born of fidelity or habit. For by resituating the
Sartrean paradigm in the context of old age, Beauvoir inevitably modifies it. For
Sartre (in *L'Etre et le néant*), my being-for-others is only one aspect of my being: the
alienated 'self for others', robbed of its possibilites, may be contested by the subject,
who in rejecting it also recognizes it as a partial truth, that is, partially assimilates the
Other's view into its own self-image. Yet Beauvoir seems to be suggesting in *La
Vieillesse* that old age is precisely characterized by the overwhelming predominance
of my being-for-others and consequently by a much-widened gap between others'
views of me (for example, as "that old man") and my inner sense of ageless self-
sameness: there can be no assimilation, however partial, because the divide is too
extreme. Early Sartrean ontology, then, needs to be modified and supplemented if it is
to account for senescent subjectivity. The much-widened gap between *être-pour-
autrui* and *être-pour-soi*, which Beauvoir seems to suggest is a feature of senescent
subjectivity, is what leads her to speak of a 'contradiction indépassable' and to allude,
in addition, to psychoanalytic metaphors of schizoid splitting.
[25] See, for example, Beauvoir, *La Force des choses*, II, p. 39.

relevance of *La Cérémonie des adieux*, it clearly being an account of the last ten years of Sartre's life.

Both of Beauvoir's biographical subjects in these accounts, Françoise and Sartre, end up in hospital beds which become deathbeds. The deathbed scene has traditionally been associated with the establishment of a final truth about the individual concerned. This is an intersubjective truth in the sense that it concerns others' views of the individual, both in the immediacy of the present moment and for posterity. Both accounts are concerned with establishing, or re-establishing, this intersubjective truth: in the first, the portrait of Françoise from the memoirs is supplemented with the story of the accomplishments of her later years and revised to offer a more sympathetic appraisal. In *Cérémonie*, Beauvoir is keen to assert the truth of her version of the story of Sartre's final years at a time when others (notably Lévi) had been propagating very different accounts.[26] Beauvoir defends Sartre here, returning with renewed vigour in this text to one of her main projects as a memorialist: 'dissiper les malentendus'.[27] So intersubjective truth and the correction of error are key concerns in both of these *récits de vie*.

This connection between the deathbed and biographical truth is not new. Although Geneviève Idt is clearly right in some ways to say of *Cérémonie* that it is 'a scandalous breach of the rules of ritual', this is not true in every respect.[28] For although the portrayal of Sartre's incontinence and other bodily weaknesses was indeed received as a scandalous infringement of the unwritten rules of representational decency, what could be more in keeping with the rules of ritual than a deathbed scene? For such scenes have a long history in literature. Beauvoir's representation of the two deathbed scenes recalls the rites depicted in the *artes moriendi* of the fifteenth

---

[26] Urusla Tidd rightly argues that whereas *La Cérémonie des adieux* is concerned with the *completion* of a chronological account of Sartre's life-long achievements, *Une Mort très douce* undertakes the *revision* of the portrait of the mother presented in the memoirs. (Tidd, *Gender and Testimony*, p. 167) Yet other of the two texts' objectives are held in common: for example, as I have argued, both texts are similarly concerned to replace error with truth.

[27] Beauvoir, *La Force de l'âge* (Paris: Gallimard, 1960), p. 12.

[28] Idt, 'Simone de Beauvoir's ADIEUX: a funeral rite and a literary challenge', in Aronson & van den Hoven (eds.), *Sartre Alive* (Detroit: Wayne State University Press, 1991), 363-84, p. 373.

and sixteenth centuries, as Philippe Ariès describes them.[29] In
traditional Medieval Christian iconography of the deathbed scene,
while the last rites are being performed, the dying person is presented
with the book of their life, their *liber vitae*, effectively a 'moral
biography', in which the balance between good and evil deeds is set
down. In the fifteenth and sixteenth centuries, this iconography
acquired a new dimension which turned the deathbed into the scene of
an epic final struggle, with angels and demons in attendance:

> Cette épreuve consiste en une dernière tentation. Le mourant verra sa vie
> tout entière, telle qu'elle est contenue dans le livre, et il sera tenté soit par le
> désepoir de ses fautes, soit par la "vaine gloire" de ses bonnes actions, soit
> par l'amour passionné des choses et des êtres. Son attitude, dans l'éclair de
> ce moment fugitif, effacera d'un coup les péchés de toute sa vie, s'il
> repousse la tentation, ou, au contraire, annulera toutes ses bonnes actions,
> s'il y cède.[30]

The connection between biography and the deathbed in the *liber vitae*,
the dramatic sifting of good from evil and falsehood, the hope of a
final truth-telling and the temptation of relapse are all elements shared
by Beauvoir's accounts and these *artes moriendi*. In *Une Mort très
douce*, there is a parallel between the hordes of angels and demons
and the dutiful daughters pitted against both the might of medical
technocracy and the relentless pressure of Françoise's church-going
friends. Similarly, througout *Cérémonie*, a battle between good and
evil is waged between those in Sartre's entourage who smuggle him
alcohol and cigarettes and others, Beauvoir among them, who seek to
protect him by urging restraint. Both Françoise and Sartre, caught in
the midst of these various struggles, seem in their extreme old age and
above all on their deathbeds to be relatively powerless. Ageing, which
for Beauvoir in *La Vieillesse* involves the encroachment of otherness,
has finally delivered them into the hands of others. They require the
ministrations of other people, being unable to care for their own
physical welfare and ensure their bodily integrity. Correspondingly,
they both seem to invite the assistance of their biographer, being
alienated from themselves by the otherness of extreme old age:

[29] Philippe Ariès, *Essais sur l'histoire de la mort en Occident du Moyen Age à nos jours* (Paris: Seuil, 1975), pp. 34-37.
[30] Ariès, *Essais sur l'histoire de la mort en Occident*, p.36.

Beauvoir's role as a biographer in these accounts may thus be likened to that of the nursing staff. Whereas they are concerned primarily with the bodily wellbeing of the individuals concerned, Beauvoir's care is to portray a representation of her subjects in the final years of their life, years in which they are no longer able to project themselves in the world. As I shall now show, however, the precise nature of this biographical 'care' differs in each case.

Beauvoir's approach, as a biographer, to extreme old age in *Une Mort très douce* is clearly though unwittingly influenced by *La Force des choses*. The representation of physical pain in the deathbed scenes of *Une Mort très douce* recalls and develops the largely unconscious association between senescence and torture that I identified in the main body of *La Force des choses*. The description of Françoise as 'un pauvre corps supplicié'[31] must be read, in the context, as more than simply a hyperbolic attempt to indicate the extremity of her mother's physical pain. For Beauvoir also wants to make her mother talk: 'Je la faisais parler, j'écoutais, je commentais'.[32] She constantly evaluates her mother's fragmented utterances, sifting her speech in a desperate attempt to pick out glimmers of truthful self-awareness from the wreckage of bodily disintegration and class-bound prejudice. Speaking of her mother, Beauvoir refers to '[le] contraste entre la vérité de son corps souffrant et les billevesées dont sa tête était farcie.'[33] Yet not even the truth of this suffering flesh fully belongs to Françoise, whose body escapes her: 'l'extérieur même de son corps lui échappait'. She exists 'à une distance infinie de sa chair pourrissante, les oreilles remplies du bruit de nos mensonges'; she is 'complètement ignorante de l'histoire qu'elle vivait'. Bodies are the field of truth; speech (as with the senseless *lecta* of *La Force des choses*) is the domain of falsehood or non-meaning. In the case of Françoise, these lies are of two sorts: her daughters decided not to tell her that she had cancer, surrounding her with a comforting 'babillage menteur'[34], such that there is a real sense in which the truth of her body lay beyond her. Lies of a second kind that ensnare Françoise are the 'billevesées', which is how Beauvoir describes the class

---

[31] Beauvoir, *Une Mort très douce*, p. 75.
[32] Ibid., p. 97.
[33] Ibid., p. 26.
[34] Ibid., p. 135.

prejudices, as expressed with respect to the motivations of the nursing staff, of this typical *bourgeoise*. What remains of the mother's failing voice is held in the grip, alternately, of the ideology of her class and the well-meaning lies and evasions of her daughters and the hospital staff: thus even when Françoise manages physically to speak, she cannot speak the truth. So not only is her body and its truth not her own, but nor exactly is her voice: disembodied and voiceless, she really is 'étrangère à soi'[35] and may accordingly be considered a precursor for the characterization of old age in Chapter Five of *La Vieillesse*.[36]

If Françoise herself has been reduced by old age and illness to a voiceless and effectively disembodied state, Beauvoir's *récit* functions as a sort of second skin, a way of *holding together* the mother as a totality, as a person – a means of articulating this body and mind that share a common history.[37] Beauvoir articulates the silent truth of Françoise's failing body, describing in detail its perforations and mutations: she substitutes the truth of her analysis for the falsehoods and false hopes audible in her mother's voice. Thus the following scene might be thought of as a *mise-en-abyme* of the text in its entirety:

> Je parlai à Sartre de la bouche de ma mère, telle que je l'avais vue le matin et de tout ce que j'y déchiffrais: une gloutonnerie refusée, une humilité presque servile, de l'espoir, de la détresse, une solitude – celle de sa mort, celle de sa vie – qui ne voulait pas s'avouer. Et ma propre bouche, m'a-t-il dit, ne m'obéissait plus: j'avais posé celle de maman sur mon visage et j'en imitais malgré moi les mimiques. Toute sa personne, toute son existence s'y matérialisaient.[38]

---

[35] Beauvoir, *Une Mort très douce*, p. 61.

[36] Similarly, Idt argues that *Cérémonie* presents Sartre's case as the last of 'Some Examples of Old Age', that is, the last of the examples in the final chapter of *La Vieillesse*. Sartre's case provides, Idt argues, 'experimental verification of the hypotheses of the essay on *Old Age* [...] the confusion between old age and illness, indifference, resignation, old people's lack of curiosity, their taking refuge in habit, their harrowing feeling of physical, financial and emotional insecurity' (Idt, p. 375).

[37] Thus Beauvoir's text might be likened to Winnicott's 'holding environment'. See his 'Primitive Emotional Development', *Through Paediatrics to Psychoanalysis* (London: Tavistock, 1958), 145-56.

[38] Beauvoir, *Une Mort très douce*, pp. 43-4.

Here the text offers not an interpretation of what Françoise has been saying, but is anchored rather in the *physical* characteristics of her mouth. The mother's voice itself remains unheard here, her speech bypassed as her daughter deciphers her history directly from the traces on her body.[39] Thus Beauvoir attempts to restore the truth of the mother's life by reading straight off the body. *Une Mort très douce* strives to recompose, or hold together, a true – integrated – picture of Beauvoir's mother and is thus, in formal terms, more of a synthesis than the largely chronological account of the memoirs and of *La Cérémonie des adieux*. Françoise is presented with a latter-day *liber vitae*, a summary of the life as inflected by the deathbed trial of the final months. The pain in Françoise's aged body seems accessible, open to investigation and annexation by Beauvoir's account, and to offer a guarantee of representational accuracy. The specific bodily events of Françoise's senescent decline firmly anchor the account in truth. The relationship between biographer and subject may be likened to that between nurse and patient: Françoise surrenders to Simone's care her ailing and abandoned flesh; Simone provides Françoise with the strength of her interpreting voice. In this example of biographical nursing, there is no question but that Françoise is entirely exposed to the biographer's gaze. There are no hidden corners of obscurity in her extreme old age; she is alienated from herself but embraced by her interpreting biographer.

　　If Beauvoir's account in *Une Mort très douce* strives for integration and coherence, by directly interpreting the mother's broken body in the context of her personal history, *La Cérémonie des adieux*, by contrast, produces its 'effect of truth' by way of narrative discontinuities. These discontinuities, which might at first sight be thought to demonstrate the implausibility of the account, are in fact held up as evidence of its reliability. For they mime the very ups and downs of Sartre's physical and mental condition over the ten-year period. Thus Beauvoir writes, in a parenthesis:

---

[39] Woodward claims of this episode that 'It is as if, for a moment, the daughter becomes the mother and the mother, the daughter' (Woodward, 1988, p. 103). This evocation of ecstatic union is somewhat over-idealized in the wider context of a work which consistently leaves the mother voiceless: even here, Beauvoir is interpreting her mother's *mouth* rather than her voice, is fusing her own voice to her mother's broken body.

> Ce qu'il y a eu d'extraordinaire chez Sartre et de déconcertant pour son
> entourage, c'est que, du fond des abîmes où on le croyait à jamais enlisé, il
> resurgissait, allègre, intact [...] Ces résurrections, au sortir des limbes,
> expliquent que par la suite je puisse dire, d'une page à l'autre: "Il allait très
> mal. Il allait très bien".[40]

Unlike Françoise, Sartre, it seems, can pull himself together, emerging
'intact'; the text then neither needs nor attempts to hold him together.
Quite the reverse: by juxtaposing copious details of the many public
activities undertaken by Sartre in his last decade alongside the brute
(indeed brutal) facts of his gradual bodily collapse, an oscillating
rhythm is produced which effectively pulls 'Sartre' apart. Although
the account is even more overtly chronological in structure than the
memoirs, divided into subsections headed by the year in question, a
latent structural pattern of increasingly violent contrast is no less
significant. Above all, what Beauvoir's text will not allow Sartre is
serenity in old age followed by 'une mort très douce'. It consistently
undermines every apparent indication of his equilibrium and repose:

> J'admirais cette sérénité reconquise. (En vérité, quelle sérénité? Etait-ce
> l'orgueilleux consentement du sage? l'indifférence d'un vieil homme? la
> volonté de ne pas peser sur autrui? Comment décider? Je sais d'expérience
> que de tels états d'âme ne sont pas formulables. Orgueil, sagesse et souci de
> son entourage interdisaient à Sartre de se plaindre, même en son for
> intérieur. Mais entre chair et cuir, que ressentait-il? Personne n'aurait pu
> répondre, pas même lui.)[41]

Beauvoir's ambivalence here is striking: while she is glad that he has
recovered his 'sérénité', she is also anxious about the meaning of this
state and unwilling to accept it at face value. In the remarkable
parenthesis, a salvo of questions rains down on 'Sartre' and the reader,
as though trying to shake the former out of a mood of resignation
which comes too close to death to be tolerable to onlookers; these
questions concern the truth of his inner being but subside into
resignation and the belief that such 'états d'âme' as Sartre's are in fact
beyond expression, that in his decrepit state he is effectively as much
a stranger to himself, 'entre chair et cuir', as he is to his entourage.
This parenthesis represents both the attempt and the failure to know

---

[40] Beauvoir, *La Cérémonie des adieux* (Paris: Gallimard, 1981), pp. 55-6.
[41] Beauvoir, *La Cérémonie des adieux*, p. 107.

and expose Sartre fully: unlike Françoise, Sartre in extreme old age retains a degree of opacity to the biographer's gaze. Whereas in *Une Mort très douce*, Beauvoir's text tried to recompose and hold together its central character, Sartre here is allowed to be anything but together: better alien and inconsistent than integrated and intelligible.

And whereas Françoise is left effectively voiceless in her extreme old age, both by the lies of ideology and those well-intentioned falsehoods of her bedside visitors, Sartre is anything but. Indeed *Cérémonie* charts what is effectively a fall into orality, into the domain of the spoken word (when his failing eyesight leaves him unable either to read or write) and the culpable pleasures of eating, drinking and smoking. The oral becomes increasingly prominent: Sartre's interviews with Lévi and Beauvoir are recorded and then transcribed, those with the latter being published after the text of *Cérémonie*, in the same book. Introducing these, Beauvoir notes that they add nothing unexpected to Sartre's thought (a criticism is surely implied here of those with Lévi); rather, they simply 'permettent [...] d'entendre sa voix vivante'.[42] Thus Sartre's death is followed immediately by the resurrection of his disembodied speaking voice.

In *Cérémonie* it is in the area around Sartre's mouth that the signs of an attack first appear; Sartrean orality thus becomes charged with anxiety for his vigilant entourage.[43] In the following scene, as Sartre lies in hospital, the oral is again the site where Sartre's infirmity and imminent demise are made manifest:

> Il m'a tendu la bouche. J'ai embrassé sa bouche, sa joue. Il s'est rendormi. Ces mots, ces gestes, insolites chez lui, s'inscrivaient évidemment dans la perspective de sa mort.[44]

Gestures and speech signifying tenderness thus also, in Sartre's atypical acceptance of them, signify his resignation and the imminence of his death. The oral is a site of the disingtegration of personality no less than the other orifices that have tended to predominate in readers' responses to this text.[45] Sartrean orality is thus

---

[42] Beauvoir, *La Cérémonie des adieux*, p. 179.
[43] See, for example, ibid., p. 126.
[44] Ibid., p. 172.
[45] Beauvoir's mention of Sartre's incontinence was a crucial factor in hostile critical responses to this work at the time of publication and has continued to play a major

ambiguous in *Cérémonie*, for when he is no longer able to write but only to give interviews, it becomes the sole locus of expression for his thinking. It is also the locus, as in the qutotation above, of uncharacteristic tenderness in dealings with other people. Yet this very demonstrativeness, as a kind of 'letting go', is associated with dissolution and the imminence of death. The rich ambiguity of elderly orality in Beauvoir's work is a theme to which I shall return in my discussion of *PROMENADE AU PAYS DE LA VIEILLESSE* in the next section.

Old age, according to Beauvoir in *La Vieillesse*, is, for the subject, a time of extreme alienation. The subject's enduring inner sense of self-sameness clashes violently with the outer reality of their age. We do not see ourselves as old, she suggests: 'on n'est vieux que pour les autres'. Beauvoir's two biographical narratives of extreme old age and death reveal two rather different ways of seeing old age in another person. Whereas Françoise's voice is suppressed and indeed supplanted by her daughter's, who reads directly off her exposed and broken body, 'Sartre' retains a degree of impenetrable mystery. That the two biographies differ so radically in approach is not altogether surprising, for Françoise and Sartre could hardly be more different; both, moreover, are invested with great emotional significance for Beauvoir. In the next section, I turn to Beauvoir's collaborative filmic representation of herself and other aged and ageing individuals. Having examined in isolation Beauvoir's autobiographical engagement with the ageing process and then her biographical exploration of the matter, I now turn to a project about old age in which both self-representation and the representation of others are thoroughly intertwined.

PROMENADE AU PAYS DE LA VIEILLESSE

PROMENADE AU PAYS DE LA VIEILLESSE, a documentary film, was shot in 1974 under the direction of Marianne Ahrne, a

---

role in critical interpretations since. See Elaine Marks, 'Transgressing the (In)cont(in)ent Boundaries: The Body in Decline', in *Simone de Beauvoir: Witness to a Century* (*Yale French Studies*, no. 72), ed. by. Wenzel (New Haven and London: Yale University Press, 1986), 180-200.

Swedish film-maker and writer who was then near the beginning of what has since proved to be a long and distinguished career. This seventy-minute documentary, made for television, is based on *La Vieillesse* and features many of this work's key locations, in particular hospices, retirement homes and elderly couples in a domestic setting. Beauvoir not only appears in the film, but was also involved in various different stages of its production, including script-writing. The film was never shown on French television, despite winning the critics' prize at the 1975 Hyères film festival. It was, however, broadcast in Sweden (Swedish television having provided the funding) and did get screened in two Parisian cinemas, for some two weeks, in 1978. No mention is made of the film in Deirdre Bair's biography of Beauvoir and a mere paragraph alludes to it in that of Francis and Gonthier, albeit under an erroneous title. Although Beauvoir's work on old age has generally been neglected, the plight of this film is extreme. There has, to my knowledge, been no sustained discussion of this late collaborative project by any critic in the field of Beauvoir studies. The film itself is not generally available and appears not to be held in any of the French archives; my copy was kindly provided by the director herself. For a more detailed account of the production process and Beauvoir's role in it, the reader is referred to my interview with Marianne Ahrne, in Appendix 1, below.

Rather than attempting to comment exhaustively on the film in its entirety, the following discussion will focus on three clips of around six minutes each. I propose to demonstrate, in each case, how the film both echoes – representationally and formally – Beauvoir's experience of old age as I have outlined it in the other texts by her already discussed in this book and also to explore the ways in which it extends the state of current critical thinking about this phase of her work.

In the first clip (37:50 – 43:13), Beauvoir is filmed in her impeccably tidy flat. She descends from the upper level and puts on a record. The camera pans around the well-lit lower room, showing her many souvenirs from travel abroad and political activism at home. Looking into the camera, she says that once one has crossed a certain line in life, one looks back on one's former activities with the thought 'jamais plus', echoing her remarks in the Epilogue to *La Force des choses.*[46] The film cuts immediately to a very different interior: a dilapidated, dark and messy single-room flat, with an old woman, fully clothed, in bed. She talks about how she can no longer manage the stairs to her flat after being hit by a motorbike while crossing the road. During the remainder of the clip, we alternate between Beauvoir's flat and that of the bed-bound old woman, a contrast with striking effect.

This contrast must surely be seen as a form of autocritique, one which seeks to highlight class differences in the experience of old age by juxtaposing Beauvoir's living-space and her narrative with those of the old, bed-bound, woman. Thus proof of Beauvoir's active and privileged life, souvenirs from her travels and her political campaigning, are arranged (in a manner recalling the grave-relics of warrior-rulers) on shelves around her, whereas the old woman's flat has no such adornment. Whereas Beauvoir admits that "J'ai toujours envie de voyager", the old woman can hardly get up the stairs. The clip ends with Beauvoir taking a taxi to meet a friend; the old woman, by contrast, has been run over by a motorbike and left almost entirely alone. Throughout, Beauvoir's elegance and eloquence contrast sharply with the near-aphasic, repetitive and somewhat frantic utterances of the old woman, reflecting her physical and mental state and, no doubt, the educational disadvantages of her class background.

In addition to what I am suggesting is Beauvoir's clearly self-critical take on her view of senescence in the film, I also want to highlight a formal continuity between the confrontation staged in this clip and Beauvoir's view of senescent subjectivity in *La Vieillesse*, as I have analysed it. The abrupt cutting between Beauvoir and the bed-bound woman echoes the distance and incommensurability of the divide between the elderly individual's self-image and the view of others, the breadth of that 'contradiction indépassable', which Beauvoir suggests is characteristic of old age.

A similar sense of non-communicative juxtaposition is created in the second clip, which I shall now discuss. Beauvoir, in this scene (1:01:00 – 1:07:00), is interviewing, or at least is supposed to be interviewing, a nurse who works in a large, state-run, hospice at Chancueil. The nurse speaks of her disillusionment with her work and complains about the insults she is forced to endure from the patients.

---

[46] Beauvoir, *La Force des choses*, p. 506.

Beauvoir becomes increasingly terse, intcrrupting more and more often. The body-language of the nurse becomes increasingly defensive.

Much of the humour in this scene derives, I would suggest, from the way in which Beauvoir proves unable to respect the conventions of the interview, first by failing to allow the nurse to answer her questions and eventually by failing even to ask questions. Yet it is not only the interview situation that is subverted in this scene, for Beauvoir is herself a (relatively) old woman and the nurse's professional role is the care of elderly. This is, then, a parodic inversion of her everyday work: an elderly woman who answers back, not, as in the case with her patients, with a barrage of insults, but rather with pointed, rational, argument, one whose hyper-articulacy smothers the nascent responses of her younger interviewee, who, like the bed-bound woman in the first clip, is reduced to mute self-expression through gesture and body-language. And this body-language suggests that she feels the encounter is both too reminiscent of her professional life – having to deal with yet another demanding old person – and also too disconcertingly different: the power-relation has been inverted, she and the institution she represents are being called into question. Penelope Deutscher has argued that Beauvoir's late work serves perniciously to strengthen cultural stereotypes of old people, reinforcing 'violently, cultural views about ageing'.[47] Yet this scene suggests otherwise: Beauvoir here is gently challenging the stereotype of the defenceless, submissive and silenced old woman, prey to institutional violence. Ahrne and Beauvoir together present us here with a parodic inversion of institutional forms of interaction which tend generally to deprive the elderly of the capacity to express themselves freely.[48]

Yet Beauvoir's articulacy, her infamous strength of voice, is also juxtaposed in this film alongside less strident, far less encouraging, examples of elderly orality. In the third and final clip

---

[47] Penelope Deutscher, 'Three touches to the skin and one look. Sartre and Beauvoir on desire and embodiment', in Ahmed & Stacey (eds.), *Thinking Through the Skin* (London: Routledge, 2001), 143-59, p. 156.

[48] Those familiar with the documentary of Sartre, by Astruc and Contat, from 1972, will recall that Beauvoir is similarly hyper-articulate there, answering many of Sartre's questions for him; it is the context, in *PROMENADE*, and the direction, which makes this a subversion with signifance rather than a comedy turn.

(16:50 – 24:00), we are shown Marcel Jouhandeau at home, surrounded by richly-coloured paintings of himself as a younger man. He argues that old age represents deliverance from the passions: "Ma vie est une sorte d'apothéose". The film cuts to Beauvoir, who denounces this view of old age as serenity. We then return to Jouhandeau, who proceeds to sing a verse from the Magnificat while accompanying himself on an old harmonium. His fingers are contorted and arthritic. We continue to hear his repetitive "Magnificat, anima mea" while the camera slowly enters a hospice from its garden walkway; the building and its environs are an exceedingly drab grey. Nurses deliver water to patients on the wards, manoeuvre them into and out of beds; one old woman sings and others proceed to explain how they ended up in this particular institution.

Now Jouhandeau's claim that old age brings serenity is the very antithesis of Beauvoir's argument in *La Vieillesse*. When she mentions Jouhandeau in that text, it is to dismiss him just as perfunctorily as she does in this clip with the comment: "C'est tout à fait faux". Yet by allowing Jouhandeau to speak directly, the film inevitably accords rather greater weight to his experience of old age than Beauvoir did in *La Vieillesse*. Indeed, Beauvoir's abrupt dismissal in the film is somewhat undermined by its very brevity: it comes across as a little too cursory. Yet the interest of this particular scene lies most of all in its use of sound, in its presentation of the voices of old age. In both her Introduction to *La Vieillesse* and in the course of the film, Beauvoir characterizes her ambition with respect to the elderly in society as follows: 'donner une voix à ceux qu'on n'entendent jamais'. Yet the voices which this film allows to be heard are faltering and disintegrating. Whether singing, as Jouhandeau and some of the inhabitants of the hospice do, or relating how they came to be admitted, what the 'grain' of these voices betray is a striking hollowness, the near-death-rattle of broken bodies. In the first clip, the bed-bound woman's speech often breaks down into semi-expressive gesture; here, the mining of the subject is audible in the fading and fragmented delirium of the voices of the hospice residents. And this impression can only be heightened by the contrast with Beauvoir's vocal fortitude elsewhere in the film.

The overall impression is sobering: the political voice of the elderly as a social group, which Beauvoir strives to make heard in this film, as in *La Vieillesse*, a strong voice that demands improvements in material conditions, is juxtaposed to the thin and failing voices of particular individuals. No change, however radical, in the material circumstances of elderly people, nor in the way in which they are viewed, diminishes in the slightest the scandal of an individual's decline; social change, however profound, cannot sweeten the fundamentally bleak story of the human lifespan. Just as orality, in *Cérémonie*, was expressive of the paradoxes of Sartre's decline into extreme old age, so the contrasting voices audible in *PROMENADE* reflect the ambiguity of this process in general: Beauvoir's strident and reasoned demands for social change and her virtuoso performance, as an old woman, against the young nurse at Chancueil are placed alongside the failing and delirious voices of the hospice residents and Jouhandeau's thin singing.

*

I have examined, in this chapter, four of Beauvoir's late works – autobiographical, biographical and filmic – which are richest from the point of view of her engagement with the ageing process. The paratexts in *La Force des choses* argue that this is a text overwhelmingly concerned with the ageing process of its subject and that linear chronology is an approach to autobiography that is particularly favourable to conveying the sense of existential disappointment central to Beauvoir's experience of that process. I suggested, however, that in the main body of the text, Beauvoir's experience of growing older becomes thoroughly entangled with the phenomenon of torture. Unsettling and problematic though this elision is from an ethical standpoint, the resulting model of ageing as violation of the subject by otherness is one clearly carried over into Chapter Five of *La Vieillesse*. Beauvoir's interest in the ageing process becomes gradually more intense as *La Force des choses* builds to its bitter climax; this growth in interest corresponds, however, to the steady exhaustion of autobiographical raw material as her linear chronology draws ever nearer to the present in which she is writing.

As a biographer of ageing and death, in *Une Mort très douce* and *La Cérémonie des adieux*, Beauvoir displays two competing tendencies: in her mother's case, the text seeks to hold together an integrated picture of Françoise, replacing the lies in which she is steeped with the truth of an interpretation anchored in the suffering of her broken body. In the case of Sartre, by contrast, the urge to establish coherence is resisted and the text emphasises the erratic and unpredictable course of his decline. She does not presume to speak for Sartre here and emphasises his resistance to biographical scrutiny. In both works, the oral emerges as a privileged focus for the representation of the conflicts and ambiguities of extreme old age.

PROMENADE AU PAYS DE LA VIEILLESSE is a rather special case, not only because it is a collaborative work but because it combines self-representation with the representation of others. In other words, other people were involved in the process of its production and other people form part of its subject-matter. By involving others at the level of production and that of content, it represents a full enactment of Beauvoir's construction of ageing in terms of the encroachment of otherness into the life of the subject. When theorized in *La Vieillesse*, the *othering* that takes place with age implies a radical split in the subject. The schizoid alternation between a sense of inner youthfulness and outer decrepitude is reflected formally in the abrupt, often brutal, cutting which is so prominent a feature of the film. *PROMENADE* develops considerably our understanding of Beauvoir's late work on old age, by introducing a rigorously self-critical stance, by gently subverting social stereotype and, lastly, by developing the thematization of the oral from her biographical works. *PROMENADE* allows a distinction to be drawn between Beauvoir's approach to old age and the cheery optimism of gerontologists and advertisers: while Beauvoir is keen that the political voice of the elderly be heard and that their demands for better treatment be met, she does not pretend that this would change the fundamentally tragic character of the human life-story.

Chapter Six

Hervé Guibert's intergenerational photo-text

Beauvoir's work as a biographer of elderly subjects both influenced and was influenced by her own experience of the ageing process. The present chapter, by contrast, examines a biographical photo-text published by Hervé Guibert at the beginning of his career, at the age of only twenty-five. It takes as its subjects his elderly great-aunts. *Suzanne et Louise* (1980) had, until very recently, been a largely forgotten text by Guibert, a series of photographs of the two eponymous women accompanied by short narrative fragments.[1] It describes itself, on the front cover, as a 'Roman-Photo'.[2] The interest of this text in the context of the present study was, in the first instance, of an ethical nature. It seemed that Guibert's work might answer Beauvoir's impassioned plea for the young to empathise with and recognize themselves in the elderly:

> Devant l'image que les vieilles gens nous proposent de notre avenir, nous demeurons incrédules; une voix en nous murmure absurdement que *ça* ne nous arrivera pas: ce ne sera plus nous quand *ça* arrivera [...] Cessons de tricher; le sens de notre vie est en question dans l'avenir qui nous attend; nous ne savons pas qui nous sommes, si nous ignorons qui nous serons: ce vieil homme, cette vieille femme, reconnaissons-nous en eux.[3]

However, for reasons given below, I soon came to the conclusion that the ethical status of *Suzanne et Louise* was fraught with ambiguity. Meanwhile, my interest in the work in aesthetic terms had grown: it was clear that this is a text which can only be read alongside *L'Image*

---

[1] Guibert, *Suzanne et Louise* (Paris: Editions Libres/Hallier, 1980). As explained below, this work has recently been republished: *Suzanne et Louise* (Paris: Gallimard, 2005).

[2] The hybrid genre of the 'roman-photo' is defined by *Le Robert* (1985) as follows: 'récit romanesque ou policier présenté sous forme d'une série de photos accompagnées de textes succincts souvent intégrés aux images comme dans la bande dessinée'.

[3] Beauvoir, *La Vieillesse* (Paris: Gallimard, 1970), p. 11.

fantôme, Guibert's better known meditations on photography, and that these in turn can only be read in the light of *Suzanne et Louise*.[4] Furthermore, I was intrigued by the neglect which *Suzanne et Louise* had suffered, by its absence from almost all of the otherwise complete bibliographies of Guibert's work included in later texts.[5] Could this 'missing' text paradoxically be central to his oeuvre, 'inaugural', or germinal, like the Winter Garden photograph in Barthes's *La Chambre claire*, or the 'image fantôme' of Guibert's own mother in the text of that name?[6] Inevitably, I was interested in the vexed relationship between Guibert's engagement with photography, in *Suzanne et Louise* and *L'Image fantôme*, and that of his one-time friend and intertextual sparring-partner Barthes. After a brief overview of the text's background and contents, this chapter will expand upon the areas just outlined, namely the ethical status of *Suzanne et Louise*, its aesthetics of photography and its relationship to Barthes's work on the medium.

Overview of the text's history and contents

The pre-history of the work and its fate after publication are both worthy of remark. It had a number of previous incarnations, or *avant-textes*: Guibert wrote a play about his great aunts which he read at the Avignon festival in the Summer of 1977. His wry account of this experience, which he sent, speculatively, to *Le Monde*, was published there in August that same year.[7] This was the first piece of his to be published at the paper where he was to work as photography correspondent from 1977 until 1985. Guibert's first book, *La Mort*

---

[4] Guibert, *L'Image fantôme* (Paris: Minuit, 1981).

[5] Jean-Pierre Boulé, in his invaluable and scholarly study of Guibert's *oeuvre*, rightly recognizes the importance of *Suzanne et Louise* in Guibert's development, but does not discuss the many connections between it and his far better known work, *L'Image fantôme* (Boulé, *Hervé Guibert: Voices of the Self*, Liverpool, Liverpool University Press, 1999, p. 2). Boulé rightly notes that, in *Suzanne et Louise*, 'bodies provide the narrative' (p. 52), though does not comment on the fact that these are, first and foremost, *old* bodies. Similarly, in *L'Image fantôme*, he does not acknowledge the centrality of the ageing process in Guibert's account of photography.

[6] Barthes, *La Chambre claire: Note sur la photographie* (Paris: Gallimard/Seuil, 1980).

[7] See François Buot, *Hervé Guibert. Le jeune homme et la mort* (Paris: Grasset, 1999).

propagande (1977), contained a short story entitled 'Histoire d'une sainte', a hagiographic account of Louise's life which mixes the fantastic and the pedestrian.[8] As for the photographs, many of the ones later included in *Suzanne et Louise* were first exhibited in Paris in October 1979. The work was published in 1980, with a print-run of around 6,000 and was, until very recently, almost *introuvable*. The only copy I was able to locate while undertaking initial research for this chapter was the one held in the Bibliothèque Nationale. However, a number of the photographs were subsequently reprinted, first in *Le Seul visage* and then in *Photographies*. Thus the textual body of a work which is concerned above all with the ageing process has itself grown and aged, developing from three distinct *avant-textes*, reaching maturity in the published volume and subsequently experiencing decline and dismemberment. And the aunts will go on to make brief guest appearances in a number of other works by Guibert, including *Mes Parents*, *Les Gangsters* and *A l'ami qui ne m'a pas sauvé la vie*. In October 2005, just as work on the present study was nearing completion, the anomalous position of this second of Guibert's published works was resolved when *Suzanne et Louise* was republished by Gallimard in a facsimile edition, differing only from the 1980 first edition by incorporating a number of corrections, said to be 'corrections d'auteur' in a short prefatory note.[9]

In view of the rarity of the work, a very brief overview of its contents does not seem out of place here. It consists of some ninety-seven unpaginated pages and some forty-four photographs. The text is in Guibert's own manuscript, complete (in the first edition at least) with the odd slip of the pen, adding a sense of intimacy as though this were an ordinary family album. The work is arranged under a series of headings: sometimes these are little more than captions for the facing or following photographs; on other occasions they serve to introduce a longer narrative fragment. The most significant of these fragments are concerned with the history of the project; Louise's time as a Carmelite nun; Louise's hair; the death of their dog and its replacement;

---

[8] Guibert, *La Mort propagande* (Paris: Régine Desforges, 1977). Note that, by contrast with *Suzanne et Louise*, this early text was quickly republished once Guibert had become established as a writer of stature: *La Mort propagande et autres textes de jeunesse* (Paris: Régine Desforges, 1991).

[9] Guibert, *Suzanne et Louise* (Paris: Gallimard, 2005). This second edition is also unpaginated.

Guibert's dreams of Suzanne's death; his love-letter to Suzanne; a sequence of cadaverous photographs entitled 'Le simulacre' and a discussion of what will happen to Suzanne's body when it arrives at the medical school after her death.[10] Even from this briefest outline of the text's principal episodes it will be apparent that many of the thematic concerns of Guibert's later works are already present in *Suzanne et Louise*: in particular, the erotic fascination with death, the dramatization of bodily weakness and the experimentation with transgressive desire, in this case of an incestuous kind.

Suzanne et Louise: ethics and aesthetics

As a text about old age by a younger photographer-author, what can be said of the ethical status of *Suzanne et Louise*? To what extent does it constitute an act of intergenerational empathy of the kind called for by Beauvoir? Guibert notes in one of the sections concerned with the history of the project that: 'Les images qu'elles possédaient d'elles-même [sic] s'arrêtaient à trente ans: "on est beaucoup photographié dans sa jeunesse, puis on vieillit et on devient laid, la vieillesse n'est pas montrable", c'est l'idée commune'.[11] The comment, part his and part attributed to one of the great-aunts, prefigures his own analysis of the limitations of the family photograph in *L'Image fantôme*:

> La photo marque la vie à la naissance, puis au mariage, ce sont les deux points forts. Entre-temps, comme la craie sur la toise, comme ces petites ciselures de croissance qu'on peut remarquer sur un os, à chaque anniversaire elle suit la poussée du corps, puis elle l'oublie, elle le dénie. Le

---

[10] Not only is the book unpaginated but it also lacks a table of contents. It might be helpful to give a full list of the captions/section headings here: 'Prologue', 'La Pièce', 'Les jambes de Suzanne', 'La photo', 'Le Carmel', 'Le rachat', 'La pose', 'Une transformation', 'Tonton-clown', 'La mort du chien', 'Amok', 'Le rêve', 'Le songe', 'La lettre', 'La transfiguration', 'Les cheveux de Louise', 'L'odeur préféré de Suzanne est celle de l'eau-de-vie de cerise et des bonbons anglais', 'Le Paradis', 'L'odeur préféré de Louise est celle de l'éther', 'Un simulacre', 'Le cadavre', 'A la fin ils reviennent pour saluer...', 'La mise-en-scène', 'Le vernissage', 'Le scénario'.
[11] Guibert, *Suzanne et Louise*, 'La Pose'.

corps adulte, le corps qui n'est plus vierge, le corps vieillissant tombe dans une trappe noire: il n'est plus photogénique.[12]

The family photograph, Guibert suggests, is bound up with procreative heterosexuality and its repressive idealization of The Child. This particular fixation on the figure of the child, a phantasmatic creation produced to further a range of repressive social purposes, has been analysed trenchantly and provocatively by Lee Edelman, who terms it 'reproductive futurism'.[13] *Suzanne et Louise* might be seen as Guibert's alternative family album, the album of his preferred 'alternative family', a project which bears implicitly, obliquely, on queerness in trying to loosen the hold of procreative heterosexuality over the medium and practice of photography. For, as Guibert must have known, foremost among the earliest popular uses of photography in the nineteenth century was the memorializing of the family and photography has remained ever since a powerful expression of 'family values'. As Susan Sontag puts it, 'Cameras go with family life'.[14]

What Guibert does in *Suzanne et Louise* is to attempt to free photography of its fixation with the life of the child by taking the ageing body as its central subject. Thus the link between photographic reproduction and reproductive futurism is weakened. Here too, his photographic practice in this earlier text can be illuminated by reference to *L'Image fantôme*: the section which lends its title to the work as a whole frames a photographic aesthetic in which photography comes to stand in an essential relation to the ageing body. Guibert describes how he tried to take his mother's picture in 1973, how this involved his first washing and styling her hair, dressing her, applying make-up and how, in the end, the photograph failed to come out. There is much that could be and has been said about this section but what I would emphasise here is the essential relationship between photography and the decline of the ageing body. Guibert remarks of his mother's age (she is forty-five) that it is 'un âge où elle était encore très belle, mais un âge désespéré, où je la

---

[12] Guibert, *L'Image fantôme*, 'Exemple de photo de famille', p. 30.
[13] Lee Edelman, *No Future: Queer Theory and the Death Drive* (London: Duke University Press, 2004), p. 2.
[14] Susan Sontag, *On Photography* (London: Allen Lane, 1978), p. 8.

sentais à l'extrême limite du vieillissement, de la tristesse'.[15] When he
has taken the photograph, or at least thinks he has:

> une fois la photo prise, l'image fixée, le processus du vieillissement pouvait
> bien reprendre, et cette fois à une vitesse vertigineuse; à cet âge, entre
> quarante-cinq et cinquante ans, où il surprend si brutalement les femmes; et
> je savais qu'une fois le ressort détendu elle laisserait faire avec un
> détachement, une sérénité, une résignation absolue, et qu'elle continuerait à
> vivre avec cette image dégradée sans tenter de la récupérer[...].[16]

The photographer suspends the work of the ageing process, if only for
a moment. The relationship between photography and ageing
suggested by this passage is essential and double-edged: photography
is capable of arresting the work of the ageing process for a moment,
yet the price of this brief suspension is hastened decline thereafter.
This exchange recalls the similar bargains which feature so often in
the fairy-tales analysed by Propp: the price of a moment's reprieve
from the ravages of time is much accelerated ageing thereafter, as
though the subsequent acceleration were the price exacted for the
hubris of this human contrivance.[17]

Thus the leading section of *L'Image fantôme* points to an
essential relationship between photography and the ageing body.
There are two senses in which Guibert is here revisiting well-trodden
ground in photographic theory. Fox Talbot, writing in the late 1830s,
had noted the medium's special aptitude for recording 'the injuries of
time'.[18] Christian Metz has called photography the 'mirror of our
ageing'[19] and Sontag has argued that: 'To take a photograph is to
participate in another person's (or thing's) mortality, vulnerability,
mutability. Precisely by slicing out this moment and freezing it, all
photographs testify to time's relentless melt'.[20] The second way in
which Guibert is revisiting well-trodden ground is in his
foregrounding of the banality of his subjects. The 'Prologue'

---

[15] Guibert, *L'Image fantôme*, p. 11.
[16] Ibid., p. 14.
[17] See Vladimir Propp, *Morphology of the Folktale*, tr. by Laurence Scott (London: University of Texas Press, 1968).
[18] See Sontag, *On Photography*, p. 69.
[19] Christian Metz, 'Photography and Fetish', reprinted in *The Photography Reader*, ed. by Liz Wells (London: Routledge, 2003), p. 140.
[20] Sontag, *On Photography*, p. 15.

introduces them as follows: 'Louise et Suzanne, deux vieilles femmes
seules, recluses, deux soeurs. Petites, grises et courbées pour celui qui
les croise dans la rue, banales'.[21] The medium of photography is
inherently open (in principle, any thing or event can be photographed
and anyone can take pictures) and this openness, together with the
ubiquity of photographic images, has often been felt to imply a risk of
banality, both in the practice of photography itself and in writing
about it:

> Taking photographs [...] levels the meaning of all events.
> (Sontag, *On Photography*[22])

> Mes photos participaient toujours, jusqu'au bout, du "quelque chose
> quelconque" [Lyotard, *La Phénoménologie*, p. 11]: n'est-ce pas l'infirmité
> même de la Photographie, que cette difficulté à exister, qu'on appelle la
> banalité?
> (Barthes, *La Chambre claire*[23])

For Guibert, I would argue, banality is a risk to be acknowledged but
ultimately, and by the prowess of the artist, to be circumvented.
Guibert, in his choice of subject in *Suzanne et Louise*, is quite openly
flirting with banality in a manner reminiscent of the Modernist cult of
the 'nominal subject' as exemplified in Edward Steichen's austerely
beautiful photograph of a milkbottle on a New York fire escape. In
literary terms, the parallel with Baudelaire is striking: in his poem
'Les Petites Vieilles', a distinction is also implied between the narrow
perspective of the ordinary passer-by and the artist's enhanced vision
of these elderly women.[24] Whereas the passer-by sees only a
procession of 'ombres ratatinées' (1.69), the poet sees the palimpsest
of their present and past existence. In both 'Les Petites Vieilles' and
Suzanne et Louise, as in the photograph of the milkbottle, there is a
sense that such superficially unpromising, elderly, subjects allow for a
more compelling demonstration of artistic prowess.

The prologue also establishes Guibert in a privilged position
in relation to his subjects: he is, he says, their only visitor:

[21] Guibert, *Suzanne et Louise*, 'Prologue'.
[22] Sontag, *On Photography*, p. 11.
[23] Barthes, *La Chambre claire*, pp. 40-1.
[24] Baudelaire, *Les Fleurs du Mal*, ed. by Antoine Adam (Paris: Garnier, 1994), pp. 99-102.

> Elles ne se parlent pas, sauf quand il vient les voir, chaque dimanche. Elles
> ne lui posent pas de question sur sa vie ou son travail, mais font passer leur
> parole à travers lui. Elles se jouent, pour lui, la comédie de leurs rapports.
> Elles le séduisent, elles sont jalouses. Il se tait et les écoute.[25]

Perhaps we wonder how he can be so sure that they don't speak when
he's not around: even if he means not that they literally do not speak
but that they do not communicate in any meaningful sense, the
question still arises. The 'Prologue' also points forward to the longest
single sequence of photographs in the work, entitled 'Une
transformation', the subject of which is Louise's hair:

> Louise n'a jamais coupé ses cheveux depuis sa sortie du Carmel, en 1945.
> Ses longs cheveux gris et épais tombent jusqu'au bas de son dos. Elle en est
> fière. Elle les peigne interminablement puis les natte autour de sa tête. Elle
> les rince au vinaigre, ses beaux cheveux gris. Obscènes pour une femme de
> son âge.[26]

The first picture in the sequence entitled 'Une transformation' shows
Louise with her hair up, secured in an austere plait; in the pictures
which follow she is then shown gradually untying her hair until it is
completely free, rinsing it, before letting it fall.[27] According to
Guibert, she has been rejuvenated and appears with 'le visage
détendu, extraordinairement belle, et ayant perdu son âge'.[28]

The sequence entitled 'Une transformation' shares many
features with the eponymous section of *L'Image fantôme* to which I
have already referred. Both the treatment of the mother's hair in that
work and this sequence from *Suzanne et Louise* are sexually charged
and recall a common nineteenth-century erotic trope.[29] But how to
interpret the judgement that Louise's 'beaux cheveux gris' are
'obscènes pour une femme de son âge'? It suggests that Guibert
recognizes the erotic significance of her hair and the rituals of care

---

[25] Guibert, *Suzanne et Louise*, 'Prologue'.

[26] Ibid., 'Prologue'.

[27] Two photographs from this sequence are reproduced in the posthumous collection,
Photographies (Paris: Gallimard, 1993). Both bear the caption: 'Louise 1979-80'.
This collection is also unpaginated.

[28] Guibert, *Suzanne et Louise*, 'Une transformation'.

[29] As exemplified in Baudelaire's 'La Chevelure', *Les Fleurs du Mal*, pp. 29-30.

associated with it, even if, by speaking of obscenity, he seems to rearticulate the societal assumption that the elderly are not sexual beings. Yet these rituals are usually performed by Louise in private; ordinarily, her hair in public is carefully and austerely plaited. It is Guibert who orchestrates the erotic display, he who asks her to perform a show of seduction. This photographic *mise-en-scène* of incestuous desire (which will be echoed, this time in writing, in a later love-letter to Suzanne), is of course a passing insult to Guibert's hated genre of the 'straight' family photograph. But more importantly here, it is as though he wants to sexualize or resexualize her, to place her on display as a sexual being, an old woman whose body, the 'Prologue' noted, 'n'a jamais été touché'. He wants to give her what he thinks she desires: youth and sexuality.

How then should we assess the ethical significance of Guibert's attempt to rejuvenate and (re)sexualize his great-aunts? As is true of the mother in *L'Image fantôme*, the attention which Louise lavishes on her hair stands as a fragile exception to a patriarchal rule. For Guibert's father forbids his wife to use cosmetics and dye her hair and, in Louise's case, her ritual of brushing, washing and plaiting runs counter to the absolute prohibition, from her convent days, on touching, and indeed even looking at, the body:

> on n'avait pas le droit de toucher son corps, pas le droit même d'y porter son regard [...] pas de miroir au Carmel, et même pas le droit de surprendre son reflet dans une vitre, ou dans l'eau de la cuvette, pendant la toilette du matin. Pendant huit ans je ne me suis pas vue. Mais je ne regrette rien.[30] ('Le Carmel')

Thus their hair has become a site of exception to patriarchal prohibition for both Louise and the mother. Louise's Piaf-like 'je ne regrette rien' is rather too off-hand and indeed too much of a cliché to be entirely convincing. Her hair has become a locus of tension, for although she remains attached to and nostalgic about the rigours of convent living and the values associated with it (we see a photograph of her next to a crucifix holding a painting of Christ[31] and the text, 'Le Carmel', speaks of this continuing attachment), she nonetheless left in 1945 and appears to have done little thereafter other than keep house

---

[30] Guibert, *Suzanne et Louise*, 'Le Carmel'.
[31] This is also reproduced in *Photographies*, also with the caption 'Louise 1979-80'.

for her sister. For both women, hair is one small space for
inventiveness, is (somewhat unusually, it might be added) one of the
interstices in patriarchal power and Guibert's intrusion here seems
unwarranted and presumptuous. In the case of the mother, what he
seems to think of as the transgressive quality of his incestuous desire
is, I would suggest, tame and inconsequential. The case of Louise is
more interesting by far. Guibert recounts how, after he shows her the
photographs of her hair down, she cuts it for the first time since 1945.
She doesn't recognize herself in the rejuvenated and resexualized
images he has orchestrated of her: '"Ce n'est pas moi"', she says. And
when she cuts her hair, it is the narrator's turn not to recognize her: 'je
ne la reconnais plus; je ne vois plus, cruellement, qu'une petite vieille
femme sans beauté, sans dimension'.[32] She cuts short not only her hair
but also his enthusiasm: she thereby refuses to be a docile body and to
further the fantasy of his power to rejuvenate and resexualize. This is,
then, an act of symbolic castration in which her cutting her hair
castrates him by denying his power over her, frustrating his
confidence in his own artistic prowess and curtailing his fantasy. He,
in turn, repudiates her as a boring old hag. She is now held to be 'sans
dimension': the suggestion is that she has elected to return to banality,
in spite of all his best efforts to rescue her from this state.

Although it will by now be clear that the sense in which
Suzanne et Louise answers Beauvoir's call for intergenerational
empathy is rather limited, the interest of this work is not exhausted
there. This text also provides ample material for a critical discussion
of Guibert's photographic aesthetic and a comparison between it and
Barthes's writing on the medium, a discussion I shall outline but not
pursue at length here.

Guibert's stated view of photography, like that of Barthes, is
rigorously anti-intentionalist. In a fragment from *Suzanne et Louise*
entitled 'La Photo', Guibert writes:

> Je crois que ce sont d'autres choses, que des objectifs, qui font les "bonnes
> photos", des choses immatérielles, de l'ordre de l'amour, ou de l'âme, des
> forces qui passent là et qui s'inscrivent, funestes, comme le texte qui se fait
> malgré soi, dicté par une voix supérieure...[33]

---

[32] Guibert, *Suzanne et Louise*, 'Les cheveux de Louise'.
[33] Ibid., 'La Photo'.

Thus he suggests that the source of aesthetic value in photography lies in the extent to which the photograph surpasses, or remains independent of, the intention of the photographer, 'comme le texte qui se fait malgré soi'. There is a pun on 'objectifs' (lenses / aims or intentions): good photos are neither exactly a matter of lenses or intentions.

In this avowed anti-intentionalism, Guibert remains entirely faithful to Barthes, whose profoundly anti-intentionalist stance is one of the few features common to both his early and late texts on photography. Commenting in *Mythologies* on an exhibition of 'Photos-chocs' at the Galérie d'Orsay, Barthes writes of the photographer in question that: 'il a presque toujours *surconstruit* l'horreur qu'il nous propose, ajoutant au fait, par des contrastes ou des rapprochements, le langage intentionnel de l'horreur'.[34] He adds that the 'Photos-chocs' are 'trop intentionnelles pour de la photographie'.[35] In *La Chambre claire*, he writes of what he calls the 'studium', the poor relation in the photographic pair studium/punctum:

> Reconnaître le *studium*, c'est fatalement rencontrer les intentions du photographe, entrer en harmonie avec elles, les approuver, les désapprouver, mais toujours les comprendre, les discuter en soi-même, car la culture (dont relève le *studium*) est un contrat passé entre les créateurs et les consommateurs.[36]

Thus Barthes (both early and late) and Guibert share a stated aversion to intentionalism in photography. Yet notwithstanding Guibert's express view of the nature of photography, it is hard to imagine a more strongly intentionalist practice of photography than Guibert's in *Suzanne et Louise* and indeed in his other work. His portraits are so strongly stylized, so posed and calculated. See the particularly forceful examples of the photograph of Louise's feet next to the gnawed bone, which seems to strive so hard for an arresting juxtaposition and the sheer staginess of the pictures of Louise wearing the dog-muzzle and those of her lying in the bath in the funereal sequence 'Le

---

[34] Barthes, 'Photos-chocs', *Mythologies* (Paris: Seuil, 1957), p. 105.
[35] Barthes, ibid., p. 107.
[36] Barthes, *La Chambre claire*, pp. 50-1.

Simulacre'.[37] In their wilful search for arresting contrasts and the theatricality of their posed look, these and the vast majority of Guibert's other photographs seem about as far removed from Barthes's anti-intentionalism and Guibert's stated view of photography as they could possibly be. The consistently intentionalist and wilfully aesthetic character of Guibert's photographic output brings to mind the rhetorical question posed by writer and photographer Wright Morris: 'In the photographer's aspiration to be an "artist" does he enlarge his own image at the expense of the photograph?'[38]

It could be said in response that, for Guibert, this may be a case of *qui perd gagne,* in the sense that precisely by confounding his stated anti-intentionalism, that is, his anti-intentionalist intention, the photographs confirm it. For the reader to decide whether s/he is persuaded by this all too easy resolution of what seems to be an inherent conflict between Guibert's stated convictions about photography and his practice of it.

*

The sense in which *Suzanne et Louise* can be said to constitute an act of intergenerational empathy of the kind envisaged by Beauvoir must be carefully spelled out. It does indeed challenge the genre of the family photograph and what in historical and commercial terms have been the 'family values' of photography as a medium: it places the ageing body at the very centre of its photographic aesthetic, thereby distancing the practice of photography from the cult of youth and 'reproductive futurism'. So far so good. If the attempt to rejuvenate and resexualize the subjects is rather presumptuous, as I argued above, the text at least allows us to read the story of the failure of this attempt, the story of Louise's resistance and her refusal to be a docile subject.

---

[37] The picture of Louise with the muzzle is reproduced in *Photographies*, again with the title 'Louise 1979-80', and one of the pictures of Louise in the bath from 'Le Simulacre' is reproduced in Guibert, *Le Seul visage* (Paris: Minuit, 1984), p. 29.
[38] Wright Morris, 'In Our Image', reprinted in *The Photography Reader*, ed. by Wells, pp. 67-75, p. 70.

The interest of *Suzanne et Louise* is not limited, however, to its ethics of biography. A substantial body of photographs, it offers an important insight into Guibert's photographic aesthetic. His photographs in this volume and elsewhere can be criticized for their profoundly intentionalist approach. In this respect they are different from both Barthes's idea of what photography should be and Guibert's own professed views on the matter. I have tried to show in this chapter that, in their combination of a thoroughly intentionalist approach and their particular choice of subject, they are entirely in keeping with a Baudelairean, Modernist, tradition which flirts with banality in order better to show off the artistry of the artist.

There is a sense in which this Modernist-intentionalist approach inevitably draws attention away from the ostensible subjects and back to the photographer. What then can be said of the autobiographical remainder in this supposedly biographical project? Even to the extent that Guibert's text reaches out to the elderly other, his concern may also be a distraction from the prospect of his own ageing. For in the company of Suzanne and Louise, there is no doubt that he remains 'le petit-neveu', a decidedly young man. In other words, the contrast between him and his great aunts is so great (and the difference of generation is compounded by differences of sex and sexuality) that he emerges rejuvenated, younger than ever. The empathy which Guibert's text undoubtedly evinces does not prevent its also using Suzanne and Louise to ward off the prospect of its author's becoming old.

Conclusion

In each of the texts examined, the representation of ageing and old age is marked by ambiguity and the reaction of the human subject is, correspondingly, characterized by ambivalence. In *La Vieillesse,* Beauvoir's attitude to the various cultural stereotypes of old age which she examines is itself highly ambivalent, particularly by contrast with her approach to the stereotypes of femininity analysed in *Le Deuxième Sexe*. Beauvoir's political determination to improve the lot of the elderly in society, an ambition shared by gerontologists, is tempered by her refusal to deny – as they invariably do – that growing older is a process of decline and diminution. Beauvoir exhorts her younger readers to empathise with the elderly people that they will become, yet also recognizes that there is something alien about old age that means that such attempts at intergenerational understanding will be tinged with failure. I placed particular emphasis on Chapter Five of *La Vieillesse*, where she characterizes the experience of growing older in terms of a pattern of schizoid alternation, 'une contradiction indépassable', between the subject's inner sense of self-sameness and the reality of their outer appearance: in its self-divided, ambivalent, attitude to old age, *La Vieillesse* embodies or acts out this particular characterization.

Like *La Vieillesse*, Gide's *Journal* (as Beauvoir herself indicates) is marked by ambivalence in its representation of the ageing process. While Gide affirms that 'la constatation de la progressive déchéance de l'âge' is the highest task of any *journal intime*, his *Journal* is remarkable for its evasiveness in this matter: there is a sense of profound moral danger for the diarist in admitting that he is in the grip of an uncontrollable process of decline. Gide's ambivalence takes the form of a textual practice of equivocation: typically, a particular failing is discussed, attributed at first to his being old before being redescribed as merely the result of some transitory affliction. Gide, like Beauvoir in *La Vieillesse* and *La Force des choses*, seems to share Montaigne's reluctance to accept the sublimatory consolations of culture for the visceral losses of age:

> Il est possible qu'à ceux qui emploient bien le temps, la science et
> l'expérience croissent avec la vie; mais la vivacité, la promptitude, la
> fermeté, et autres parties bien plus nôtres, plus importantes et essentielles,
> se fanent et s'alanguissent.[1]

However, like Montaigne and Beauvoir, Gide remained committed to
his own cultural projects, of self-writing and self-fashioning, well into
old age.

The forms of ambivalence with respect to the representation
of ageing in Violette Leduc's work were found to be different again.
Rather than schizoid alternation (as in *La Vieillesse*), or equivocation
(as in Gide's *Journal*), Leduc's autobiography is divided between
passages which offer a full representation of 'le temps sensible' and
others which altogether deny the reality of the ageing process by
performing the abiding presence of childhood suffering in adult
experience and thereby effacing the years that have elapsed. This
representational ambivalence is doubled by one of attitude: when
granted access to representation, Leduc's own ageing is alternately
welcomed and feared. She is alone in exhibiting, in addition, this
second form of ambivalence: none of the other writers whose work I
have discussed ever looks forward with anticipation to old age as
Leduc sometimes does. Not that this is exactly joyous anticipation:
part of the reason Leduc wishes to be old is because she feels it could
hardly make her more ugly yet it is likely to disfigure her
contemporaries, allowing her to make up some of the distance.

Disfigurement or mutilation proved to be central to
Beauvoir's view of her own ageing in *La Force des choses*. I argued
that there is an uncomfortably close connection between torture and
ageing in that work and that this view of ageing – as violence inflicted
on the self by otherness – was a precursor of the view of ageing as
othering expounded in Chapter Five of *La Vieillesse*. Yet Beauvoir's
two biographical texts and the nature of her participation in
PROMENADE suggest that, for all that old age brings alienation, its
being a time when the self is essentially in the hands of others can
allow for extreme manifestations of solidarity and mutual assistance.
Thus if old age is, for the self, an experience of tragic loss and

---

[1] Montaigne, *Essais*, I, ch. 57, 'De l'âge' (Paris: Garnier-Flammarion, 1969), pp. 387-89.

disfigurement, of increased dependency and occasionally of helplessness, this may all be seen as inviting the other's care. The ambiguity of old age for Beauvoir as a biographer and autobiographer is thus both existential and ethical: damage inflicted on the self invites the care of others; correspondingly, the ageing self's experience of suffering alienation may encourage that self to care for others.

Care for the ageing other also proved to be one facet of Guibert's relationship with his two great aunts in *Suzanne et Louise*, where he strives to dramatize lives that are thought by him, somewhat presumptuously, to be inherently banal. While this text bears witness to a real concern for the ageing other – one in whom the otherness of age is redoubled by that of sexuality and gender – it must also be seen as an attempt by the photographer to demonstrate his prowess by making something of superficially very unpromising subjects. Moreover, while the young photographer-author is undoubtedly reaching across the generations in a gesture of empathy with two old women, this act also reinforces a certain image of himself: in their company, there can be no doubt of his youth. In looking at Guibert's project in this way, my aim has not been to moralize: rather, I would suggest that only by recognizing the extent of the ambivalence in this work can we avoid forming an overly idealistic misconception of it and come more fully to appreciate the rich complexities of such intergenerational relationships.

The emphasis on ambivalence and ambiguity in my findings coheres with one of the major themes of twentieth-century literary criticism: ambiguity has long been recognized as one of the defining features of literary discouse.[2] It is by virtue of this inherent potential, or even predilection, for ambiguity that literary discouse has continued to contribute meaningfully to discussion of the ageing process in a century in which gerontology and the social sciences in general have sought to claim this ground for themselves. Social-scientific discourse, by contrast, is ill-equipped to tolerate the ambiguity which these texts suggest is central to the meaning of the human ageing process. Nor are ambiguity and ambivalence about old age restricted to these particular texts. As Thomas Cole has remarked:

---

[2] Most famously perhaps in William Empson, *Seven Types of Ambiguity* (London: Chatto & Windus, 1947).

> Aging, like illness and death, reveals the most fundamental conflict of the
> human condition: the tension between infinite ambitions, dreams, and
> desires on the one hand, and vulnerable, limited, decaying physical
> existence on the other – the tragic and ineradicable conflict [...]. This
> paradox cannot be eradicated by the wonders of modern medicine or by
> positive attitudes towards growing old.[3]

My work suggests that literary discourse is particularly well suited to
engage with the conflict and ambiguity held by Cole and others to be
essential features of the human ageing process and to reflect the
ambivalence which consequently marks subjective responses to that
process. Ageing reflects the ultimately tragic character of even the
most privileged forms of life: even if political and material conditions
were ideal, human existence would remain essentially ambiguous.
Vladimir Jankélévitch, in his chapter on ageing in *La Mort*, pinpoints
the internal contradiction in the human lifestory that renders it
ambiguous. He writes that the human lifecourse is both 'un avènement
continué à l'être, et *du même coup* (non par surcroît, mais du même
coup) [...] un acheminement continué vers le non-être [...] Ni progrès
simple ni simple régression'.[4] For Jankélévitch, the ageing process is
the gradual unfolding of this kernel of contradiction:

> La vie a bien un sens, mais ce sens est contrarié par un non-sens, qui
> pourtant la conditionne; à mesure que le temps passe, le contresens du
> vieillissement impliqué dans le sens affleure avec plus d'insistance à la
> surface du devenir; et de même que l'organisme vieilli répare des pertes de
> plus en plus mal, compense de plus en plus lentement les effets des
> traumatismes, de même l'espérance optimiste, luttant pied à pied contre les
> démentis sans cesse renouvelés de l'échec et de la déception, se fait de jour
> en jour moins convaincue, chaque année un peu plus difficile à soutenir;
> oui, chaque jour il devient un peu plus malaisé de dire pourquoi on vit, et en
> vue de quoi, et à quoi rime tout cela.[5]

The wisdom gained with age, in Jankélévitch's view, would thus
amount to a lucid realization of the ultimately self-cancelling,
ungrounded and arbitrary character of this and every human life.
Although Jankélévitch's tone is rather more resigned in the above

---

[3] Thomas Cole, *The Journey of Life* (Cambridge: Cambridge University Press, 1992),
p. 239.
[4] Vladimir Jankélévitch, *La Mort* (Paris: Flammarion, 1966), Part I, Ch. IV, 'Le
Vieillissement', pp. 168-96, p.168.
[5] Ibid., pp. 169-70.

passage, the impulse to strive for post-religious lucidity about the human condition is very much one he shares with the Beauvoir of *La Vieillesse* and *La Force des choses*. Though Beauvoir is far more overtly interested in the material welfare and practical freedom of her fellow beings, this interest is not allowed to eclipse but rather stands alongside a bleak sense of the inherently self-cancelling character of the human lifestory. I would suggest then that one of Beauvoir's most neglected aesthetic and philosophical achievements is her tragic vision, a vision which turns the bare life-story of human senescence into a post-religious passion. The *hubris* of forward-looking human aspiration, in Beauvoir's tragedy of the ordinary life, is ground down with age: the ageing self is doomed to continue to hope, plan and fear, even as the time remaining to it draws ever nearer to a close. Of course this would not be tragedy – merely decline – without the obligation of the self's conscious participation in this very process: 'L'animal décline, mais il n'assiste pas à son déclin; l'homme décline et en même temps assiste à son propre déclin'.[6] Much has been said about, indeed against, the alleged 'humanism' of Beauvoir and others of her generation. I would argue, however, that Beauvoir's engagement with the ageing process should be seen as a determined attempt, in a post-religious context, to think fully the essentially tragic encroachment of non-meaning, of death, into the being of the human subject. Even as we continue to be absorbed in the busy profusion of our daily projects, death makes its quiet progress within. In this respect, Beauvoir's tragic dramatization of ordinary ageing is akin to Deleuze's restaging of Freud's death drive in the radically anti-humanist notion of the 'fêlure'. We are accustomed to the noise of busy, project-orientated, instinct-driven, living and seldom attend to the background silence of death's gradual progress.[7]

Yet Beauvoir's vision of the tragedy of ageing, in *La Vieillesse* and *La Force des choses*, for all that it frames the process in terms of *othering*, takes little account of the concrete other, the other

---

[6] Jankélévitch, *La Mort*, p. 191.

[7] 'Ce que la fêlure désigne, ou plutôt ce qu'elle est, ce vide, c'est la Mort, l'Instinct de mort. Les instincts ont beau parler, faire du bruit, grouiller, ils ne peuvent pas recouvrir ce silence plus profond, ni cacher ce dont ils sortent et dans quoi ils rentrent: l'instinct de la mort, *qui n'est pas un instinct parmi les autres*, mais la fêlure en personne, autour de laquelle tous les instincts fourmillent.' Deleuze, *La Logique du sens* (Paris: Minuit, 1969), Appendix 3, 'Zola et la fêlure', pp. 373-86, p. 378.

person. The tragic vision is essentially one of an isolated self absorbed in its own anguish; it is a form of negative narcissism. This brings me to the second strand of my argument: the relation between self and other. In Beauvoir's case, her two biographical texts and *PROMENADE*, redress this imbalance by addressing the intersubjective reality of ageing and extreme old age. Thus the tragedy of the individual self's decline – in both its bodily and mental aspects – and growing dependency are, at the same time, an ethical opportunity for the other. Beauvoir as a biographer lends her strength to her two fading subjects, writing and thinking for them, in their place, when they can no longer do so for themselves. This does not involve great acts or miracle cures: all that the narratives can really do for their subjects is to bear witness to their decline, to write their last painful chapter, to offer their respective life-stories completion. There seems to me to be a continuity between this biographical expression of care and the nursing of a patient into extreme old age, to death. This could not be further than writing for writing's sake: this is writing as an ethical act, an act of care.

The range of Beauvoir's biographical engagement with ageing – Françoise, Sartre and the cast of *PROMENADE* – brings to the fore both the democratic inevitability of the process as such and, at the same time, the ways in which class differences condition the nature of the experience. Even great thinkers can suffer from incontinence, even they age and die; yet the privileged material circumstances of Françoise's and Sartre's later years contrast markedly with the impoverishment of the hospices and the mining town in *PROMENADE*. For all that Beauvoir is undoubtedly interested in the experience of ageing as a story of the self's tragic decline, I would not wish to underplay her political emphasis on the concrete, practical, realities (and inequalities) of the elderly other in society. I have shown that *PROMENADE* in particular manages to combine these two perspectives: we see both the universal tragedy of the ageing self, which affects Beauvoir no less than the residents of Ivry and Chancueil, yet we also see foregrounded a political and ethical imperative to improve the lot of the elderly poor. Thus in Beauvoir's engagement with old age, the ageing self is the locus of splitting and alienation; the ageing other calls for political and ethical care.

An ethics of care for the ageing other is also implicit in Guibert's *Suzanne et Louise*, though this text lacks the balancing political element present in Beauvoir's work. Yet this care on the part of the younger photographer-author is, as I have suggested, overdetermined: his interest in Suzanne and Louise is informed by his desire to establish a theoretical position on the nature of photography and by the urge to show his mastery of this art by transforming such superficially unpromising material. Yet above all, his engagement with the ageing other allows him to forge a negative self-definition: in relation to them, he is most certainly not old. His message could almost be the biblical, 'While you grow older, I live'. Guibert's position in relation to old age, as I have analyzed it, may be related to Heidegger's reflections on death: thinking about another person's death is an inauthentic concern and a means of avoiding what is, according to Heidegger, the only authentic meditation on death, namely that which bears upon my own death. Thus interest in the other's death (or, as in Guibert's case, ageing), however well-intentioned, is always also a screen and an evasion. In the photographic context of Guibert's work, this metaphor of the screen seems particularly appropriate. By contrast, the Heideggerian paradigm does not fit Beauvoir's case: her interest in the ageing other is closely intertwined with her thoughts on her own senescent decline. Thus the ageing other may be an object of care, ethical and political, or else a screen hiding the subject's reluctance to reflect on their own senescence.

Gide, while still young, often reflected on his own ageing. Initially in the *Journal*, ageing is intermittently construed as part of his broader project of self-fashioning or, as I have called it, 'autopedagogy'. Yet we should perhaps hesitate to qualify this as an authentic meditation on ageing, in the Heideggerian sense, on account of the practice of equivocation I have identified in the relevant passages of his diary: for when Gide is not toying with various models of how he plans to age, he is busy presiding over a cult of youth. Yet by contrast with Guibert, to the extent that the younger Gide avoids confronting the possibility of his own senescence, his strategy for so doing does not involve using ageing others as 'screens'. His youthful textual games of equivocation do not use ageing others as counters. Yet these games do, on occasions, use younger others in this way: pederastic pedagogy, in addition to fulfilling a range of other needs, allows the ageing Gide to retain his attachment to youth by living vicariously through the younger partner.

Leduc's treatment of the ageing other – her mother, that is – proved to be different again. Violette tends to disavow her mother's old age, seeking thereby to return to the suffering of her own childhood: the age of this older person to whom she remains profoundly attached is denied and this denial reflects back on herself. Yet this is only one side of Leduc's Janus-faced autobiographical text: elsewhere, where she alone is concerned, she looks forward to being old with expectation. The tendency towards *radotage* in Leduc's work is one which goes hand in hand with the gradual isolation of the speaking subject. The ageing self, for Leduc, is one which becomes increasingly detached from the social world, from others. If Beauvoir's biographical texts suggest that the ageing other is owed a duty of ethical and political care, the reclusive ageing self in Leduc's work seems intent on refusing such gestures.

Thus a diverse overall picture emerges. The ageing other is owed a duty of ethical and political care (Beauvoir); it constitutes both an object of care (Guibert) and also a 'screen', allowing the subject to avoid authentic meditation on the reality of his own ageing. Or else the ageing other is absent (Gide) and the emphasis falls on the ageing self and its possible uses for the *younger* other. Leduc's autobiography seeks to deny the reality of the (m)other's old age yet relishes and indeed performs the prospect of her own. Common to all the texts, however, is a sense of the close interdependence of self and other in the writing of old age: talk about the age of the other seems always to reflect back on the self and vice versa.

What, finally, of senescent textuality? I used this term to refer to the reflexive phenomenon of texts which talk about old age while also performing some or all of the characteristics which they identify with that phase in life. The notion of senescent textuality is, I would argue, a usefully flexible way of connecting thematically what might otherwise appear to be isolated incidents of textual performativity. I suggested that the works examined in the first three chaptcrs by Beauvoir (*La Vieillesse*), Gide (his *Journal* and *Ainsi soit-il*) and Leduc (the autobiographical trilogy and *L'Affamée*) all exhibited slightly different forms of senescent textuality. These were, respectively, repetition and self-contestation, *ressassement* and *radotage*.

What are the advantages of the approach I have taken to senescent textuality? First, it allows a view to be taken of an author's engagement with the ageing process which emphasises the text while parenthesising the awkward, ultimately unanswerable and uninteresting questions (typical of the 'late style' approach) about the correlation between particular textual features and the age of the writer concerned. Moreover, when a text has been written and edited or rewritten over many years (as is the case, for example, with Gide's *Journal*), such questions are not merely unanswerable but meaningless. The concept of senescent textuality provides a loose framework for the study of ageing and old age in literature that places the emphasis firmly on the processes at work in the text in question without these necessarily needing to be related to the age of the author at the time of writing. This is an advantage even in the case of autobiographical writing: while the experiences related must of course refer to the writer, the way in which these are narrated, their textual form, cannot simply be reduced to a function of the author's age, even when the experiences in question are of senescence.

The study of senescent textuality implies a commitment to look at a text's engagement with ageing in terms not just of what it says but also of how it says this: the focus falls on form in addition to, and in relation to, content. I shall now briefly compare each of the three examples of senescent textuality given above. *La Vieillesse* performs its own description of the ageing process by becoming progressively more self-divided, torn between two discursive traditions and two competing aims, political and philosophical: to improve the lot of the elderly in society and to analyze the tragedy of decline that is an ordinary life-story. It also performs its description of the ageing process by way of repetition and, moreover, repetition which appears to be unwitting: it exhibits, in several ways, the automatism that Beauvoir claims is one characteristic of old age. In his *Journal*, Gide displays a horror of *ressassement*, both in life and writing; in *Ainsi soit-il*, by contrast, he has embraced *ressassement* in both, seeing this as the only way to stave off impending desirelessness. Gide indulges his urge to repeat anecdotes and rehearse grievances, over and again. Compared with the rigour of the diary, Gide celebrates the 'licence' of his textual form in *Ainsi soit-il* 'pour reparler', to return to ground already covered, out of pure indulgence.

Gidean *ressassement*, like Beauvoir's repetitive automatism, stages the gradual eclipse of the speaking subject: anecdotes move indifferently from one speaker to the next, self-perpetuating linguistic entitites with lives of their own that eclipse that of the individual through whom they happen to be passing. Similarly, Beauvoir's practice of repetition in *La Vieillesse* seems to replace the strong, forward-looking, humanist subject with a nexus of aptitudes and discursive possibilities. Their staging of the gradual eclipse of the subject is thus one way in which these particular texts by Gide and Beauvoir reflect the ageing process on a formal level.

Rather than eclipse, Leduc's practice of senescent textuality, *radotage*, heralds withdrawal, a gradual removal of the speaking subject from the world of mutual human understanding. Her obsessive re-orchestration of childhood memories in accordance with the logic of the signifier, in sound and graphic patterning, helps to consolidate the subject as an impoverished and isolated totality. *Radotage* is undoubtedly, in its connotations, the most pejorative of all of the three principal modes of senescent textuality I have examined: the self-absorbed subject is isolated from others by their ridicule or indeed their uncomprehending indulgence. However, the performance of eclipse in Gide's and Beauvoir's senescent textuality is hardly celebratory either: though art is often used as a way of forgetting the vicissitudes of human life, of which ageing is one, it does not always bring the hoped-for comfort. If in search of positive reinforcement, turn instead to the anti-ageist pamplets of gerontologists and advertisers.

That these conclusions are bleak perhaps throws some light on the phenomenon of widespread neglect, to which I have already alluded on a number of occasions. Neglect and evasion have characterized the reception of so many of these texts. Leduc's work in general, apart from *La Bâtarde*, has yet to attract the extent of critical attention I believe it deserves. The prominence of ageing in this work is perhaps one, though by no means the only, reason for this neglect: Leduc's writing can be formidably dense, is thematically unattractive to more conservative readers, and challenges interpreters in ways that have nothing to do with its engagement with ageing and old age.

La Vieillesse is an extreme example of unjust neglect: this substantial work by a major writer, clearly considered by its author to be no less significant than *Le Deuxième Sexe*, has seldom attracted more than passing references from Beauvoir scholars and specialists in old age alike. The edulcorating American mistranslation of the title as *The Coming of Age* is further indication of precisely the sort of avoidance Beauvoir herself denounces in the work. *PROMENADE AU PAYS DE LA VIEILLESSE* and *Suzanne et Louise* also offer striking examples of critical and cultural reluctance to explore the landscape of old age. These texts had each, in their own way, been forgotten, not having been shown again or, for many years, republished, despite being works of quality and significance by two major figures. Similarly, the suppression of ageing from psychoanalytic accounts of human development presents a no less flagrant, theoretical, example of avoidance and one that is intimately related to the reluctance to dwell on ageing in those other cultural discourses over which it exerts such influence.

The urge to put aside such questions is eminently understandable: who would want to think (much) about human decline? What end does such thinking ultimately serve other than depressive introspection? If we are born to love and die, live and age, then reading the ageing process will always be an attempt to confront with lucidity one facet of the inherent ambiguity of the human condition. This is not inherently self-indulgent and does not preclude reaching out to help others affected by old age, as all who persist eventually are, nor should it be thought to devalue other struggles against other forms of real oppression.

Appendix 1

Interview with Marianne Ahrne, director of *PROMENADE AU PAYS DE LA VIEILLESSE* (12 May 2001, Stockholm)

O.D. - Where did the idea for a film about old age come from?

M.A. - I wasn't at all interested in old age at the time. I was thirty-four. But I was interested in Simone de Beauvoir. She had been a great literary encounter for me when I was in my twenties. I always felt very connected to her – I was always moved by her books, by the despair and pain that was at the bottom of her novels – *Le Sang des autres*, *L'Invitée*. I was hoping that one day I might be able to make a film based on *L'Invitée*. I was more interested in fiction than documentaries – yet, documentaries is how I started out, and in the long run it was a good thing to do. Working with documentaries is a fascinating way to learn about the world and listen to other people. As a young director, that´s exactly what I needed.

One of my earliest films, after film school, was about abortion in France. I wasn't especially interested in abortion either, but at that time I was trying to make a start in film-making and I adopted the principle of the dragon in the fairy-tale – when you cut off one head, he grows three new ones – so each time I got refused, I had three new proposals. One of these came from a friend of mine, who was French, a man, who was interested in making a film about abortion, because, at that time, it was illegal in France. 343 women, among them Simone de Beauvoir, had signed a petition, saying that they had had an abortion – and they did this because they thought that the state wouldn't dare put them on trial. They were right, they won in the end. I don't really think that Simone de Beauvoir ever had an abortion, because she recounted everything and she never talks about that. So I think she signed out of loyalty. Anyway, she was one of the women to be interviewed for that film. But when I came to Paris for the shooting, she was in Rome, with Sartre. She agreed to do the interview, but I didn't have the money to go to Rome. So the foreign correspondent of Swedish Television, in Rome, did the interview with her. He was a formal old man, and she resented him, so she's terrible in the interview – very harsh and aggressive. She was like that when she didn't like somebody: it showed. She was so antipathetic in that interview that I just used only a little bit of it. Anyway, we started to write to one another. I still wanted to make a film of *L'Invitée*, but then I read *La Vieillesse* – and what she said there was interesting to me. She said that old people were "entourés d'une conspiration de silence" and the last sentence [on the inner leaf] is "C'est pourquoi il faut briser la conspiration du silence : je demande à mes lecteurs de m'y aider". *This* was the spark for me. Together with Bertrand Hurault, who was a friend of mine and with whom I wrote other scripts, we contacted Simone de Beauvoir, and told her that we wanted to make a film *with* her about old age. She was very nice to us for, at that moment, she had an American producer who wanted to make a film on the same subject. He had infinitely more money than we, but she thought our project was more faithful to her book and closer to what she wanted, so she threw him out and went along with our project.

O.D. - This was a project for a film about old age?

M.A. - Yes, this was the project for the film you have seen. Then we simply got started. I had a budget of 180,000 Swedish kronor, something like £12,000 pounds, from Swedish Television.

O.D. - When did you start working on the film?

M.A. - I shot the film in the autumn of 1974. I had six weeks of preparation in total, during which we went to see lots of old people. Bertrand Hurault and I did most of the writing, but Pepo Angel is also credited as a writer, because he did the research with me and came up with some ideas. You can't really separate these things in a documentary. Then we checked everything with Simone de Beauvoir, so she was also involved in that process.

O.D. - How did you find the old people in the film?

M.A. - One thing led to another. First we went to the big institutions: Ivry, Nanterre. There we heard about individual trajectories. And we went to an organization called the Petits Frères [as featured in the film] and found lots of individuals who were interesting, and so on. Also, something happened to me while preparing the film – I could sit at a table in a café and if there were old people around, I would probably look at them in a certain way. On several occasions, they came over to my table and started to tell their stories. They felt my interest and came. We used some of these people too.

O.D. - In *La Force des choses*, Beauvoir talks about her dislike of public exposure. I wondered how you overcame that. Some of the scenes in her flat are really very intimate, more so indeed than in any other film she featured in. Did she suggest filming in her flat?

M.A. - I don't remember it being any problem – I don't remember any discussion about it at all. I think we had quite a good relationship. Through the years we really became friends. Some years later I worked on a scenario for *L'Invitée* together with her. I lived in Paris for a year and I saw her every week or every two weeks. I was there when Sartre died. Our friendship grew gradually, but the connection was there from the beginning... I wasn't afraid of her, and I think she liked that. She could be intimidating. I remember when she took me out to lunch for the first time, in connection with this film. She was always very efficient, frighteningly efficient, in a way. She invited me to a nice place and she said: "Et votre enfance, et votre adolescence, comment c'était?". I had a feeling that I had to spit out my childhood and my adolescence *very* quickly. She had no patience with anything slow. So I did, in full speed, with all the complications – and there were quite a lot of them - in French. I thought: this is really impossible, it won´t make sense. Afterwards, she didn't hestitate for two seconds before spitting out an analysis of what I had said. The strange thing was that it was very, very, accurate. She had nailed me like a butterfly with amazing speed. We never returned to that subject again.

Later, when I talked to her about what I thought about her personally, she listened very attentively with something childish and open in her eyes, as if she was – well – without defence. I remember that expression, because it touched me. But there is also a comment on the back of the English edition of *L'Invitée* [*She Came to Stay*] about her: an author whose tears freeze as they fall. That is extremely accurate! She had such a quick intellect that no sooner had the tear formed than that was it: she had already found the words to express it, and the words were crystal clear. Yet, she was a person of enormous feeling and pain. The pain that is in *L'Invitée*... I think it's one of the most painful novels I've ever read. I talked to her about this volcano of feelings inside her that she is able to formulate immediately. She listened very carefully and agreed.

I also remember when Sartre died: she told me about everything that had happened and then she cried – but she was totally unsentimental at the same time, totally. She said "I can think about this and it doesn't make me cry. I can remember it and it doesn't make me cry. It's the words that do it, that create the feeling – *c'est les mots qui font naître l'émotion*". Her words, her formulating the thing, made the pain come.

O.D. - That's very interesting.

M.A. - That's very interesting and I recognize something of myself in that. I'm rather certain that she had a personality that very much veered towards Asperger's Syndome – high-functioning Asperger's. Not that she had the Syndrome but a personality with some of those characteristics. Contrary to the narcissistic writer, who thinks 'I am great, I am special, I have to talk about *me* because I am interesting', the writer with Asperger's thinks 'I have no imagination, so I have to talk about me – it doesn't matter because I am not important, but at least I can analyse my life and perhaps this will serve some purpose for other people.' I think that's her. She's *sans égards* towards herself when she writes – and she can be that towards others too – but it doesn't exclude love, as when she writes about Sartre in his old age. Some people see her as cruel in *La Cérémonie des adieux*, but I see that work as the end of a great love story – there is still love, but clear-sighted love. Totally unsentimental and clear-sighted.

O.D. – How did you view the relationship between *La Vieillesse* and the film?

M.A. – We used almost nothing from the part where she talks about the old age of famous people. We – Simone de Beauvoir included - wanted to do something that was a commentary in the present. With her agreement, we had great freedom regarding the book: we could pick up any phrases we wanted from it. She herself was going to be the 'red thread' – the intellectual red thread, tying these images from real life together with her commentaries – and whatever we found in real life, we filmed it the way it was, not according to the book. But she had been to certain places [while researching the book] and we revisited them. There were some places she did not go, however, but we did. She had *not* been able to get into Nanterre, for example. She hadn't even been to Ivry, and we were surprised that she had been to so few places. We started right away by going everywhere we could. We were shocked: I and my team, all in our early thirties – we were really shocked. We took Simone de Beauvoir to Ivry, one day. The first person she met was an old lady, in one of these big rooms where there were thirty-eight people, many of them tied to their beds and not even untied to go to the toilet. Just indescribable. She talked to one of those ladies, who clearly had dementia and kept saying that her mother would come to visit her.

When Simone de Beauvoir came outside, I was amazed to hear her say that it's not so bad for everybody because this woman's mother would come to visit her. I just looked at her – one of the most intelligent writers in French literature – and the woman she had spoken to in there was about a hundred years old... Then, when I was going to interview her in front of the camera, it was useless. Inside, I had seen her emotion, but outside, the tear had frozen. She appeared so cold that I couldn't use that interview at all.

Simone de Beauvoir was not a visual person, and in two ways. Although she liked the cinema very much and could analyze it perfectly, her creativity was with words, not images. She had very little imagination, in terms of images. The second difficulty was that she was not easy to film, just because she was so intellectual and so quick to formulate her views. It would have come out nicely in writing, but on screen, it's often more interesting to see the emotion than to hear a perfect thesis.

O.D. – I was interested particularly in the scene where she interviews a nurse who works at Chancueil. As Beauvoir becomes more and more irritated, the expression on the nurse's face becomes increasingly nonplussed...

M.A. – The nurse was funny because she wasn't impressed by Simone de Beauvoir. She hardly knew who she was and she didn't give a shit. Many people have strong feelings about that scene: some because they think that Beauvoir just runs over the nurse like a steamroller. Others just think it's funny... Simone de Beauvoir herself was very matter-of-fact about it: she thought she was like that and that was that. But what happened during the interview was funny. We had picked this nurse because she talked to us the way she talks in the interview. She was fed up with old people, liked only the ones who stayed in bed and never said a word... She was not at all politically correct.

We shot the scene with two cameras, and when we changed rolls, I told Pépo to take the nurse aside and tell her that she had to resist more, and I took Simone de Beauvoir aside and told her that she had to listen more and get the nurse to talk. "Oui, oui, oui, oui, oui!", she said. But she didn't change at all. As soon as she was on, she reacted as violently as before. She got more and more irritated, and the two of them ended up shouting and interrupting each other.

O.D. – How many of the scenes did you stage?

M.A. – I staged a very small number of the scenes (which weren't very good, in fact, because these people were no actors). I staged the scene with the two people crossing the street: a truck comes past and the driver shouts "Au cimetière, les vieux cons!" The scene when the old woman sees the sea for the first time was based on a true story, but we took another woman to the coast, as the first one had already died. She was a wonderful little lady though – walked along the coast talking to herself, saying whatever came into her mind – we didn't ask her to do that, but it worked out very nicely.

O.D. – In terms of the relationship between the film and the book, what about the scene in the second minute, when a man says "On n'est vieux que pour les autres!" – that's a quotation from the book, I think, and in a way it encapsulates Beauvoir's thesis in the second half.

M.A. – Absolutely. And that was a scene we staged – the man is a retired actor. We wanted to have a montage at the beginning which more or less corresponded to the book.

O.D. – The reviewer in *Le Monde* implies that there was an element of deception involved in your gaining entry to the hospice at Nanterre, that you said the film was only for Swedish television...

M.A. – Probably. We had great difficulty getting in there. It's run by the police and we had to have an interview with the director. We had had trouble at Ivry because we filmed that scene with the *infirmier* who talks about old people going to the morgue – in front of them - and who wasn't entirely sober when we filmed. And in Nanterre, we filmed much more than they would have wanted us to film. In the beginning, we had no idea that the film would be shown anywhere else than in Sweden. It was only later that MK2 wanted to show it in the cinema in France. But we had a long talk with the director [of the Nanterre hospice] – and I had a very distinguished script-girl, very bourgeois, who worked wonders with the director – she spoke to him much better than I could have done... without lying, but somehow without telling the whole truth.

O.D. – I thought it was interesting that you were allowed to film people taking baths, for example, given attitudes to the elderly body prevalent in France.

M.A. – For the whole morning when we were filming, for three hours, that man was sitting in his own excrement trying to get out of a bath-tub without water. That too was indescribable. He was there asking for help, and no-one cared. I'm sure they wouldn't have wanted us to film that. But once we were in, they didn't control us. That's the advantage of being a small team...

O.D. – And of not being French?

M.A. – Yes, absolutely.

O.D. – Was Beauvoir with you when you filmed in Nanterre?

M.A. – No, she saw it on film. She saw the rushes. But mainly she saw the film after it had been edited.

O.D. – Was she involved in the editing?

M.A. – No. But we had a script that we followed to about 80 percent. In a documentary, there's always a certain freedom – a necessary margin for improvisation. We had a script, a basic structure we all agreed on and she was involved in producing that. She was a great help all along, we had no problems of collaboration.

O.D. – I'd like to ask you about the scene when Beauvoir is in her tidy and generously-furnished flat – and she puts on a record. That scene is intercut with a scene featuring a bed-bound old woman in a small, dirty, two-room flat. Beauvoir says things like "J'ai toujours envie de voyager" and the old woman in the bed complains that she can't get up the stairs. Was there a critical or self-critical intention in the cutting between those scenes?

M.A. – Yes, exactly – and with Simone de Beauvoir's consent. She was very aware that she was more privileged than many other people because she had the desire and the money to travel, she had the desire to create and the means to do so. She was very aware of that and her attitude was, "Use me!". The first thing she said when she saw the film was "I think I have been very well used", "Vous m'avez très bien utilisée". She set no conditions on how she would look, in the moral or any other sense.

O.D. – Why wasn't the film shown on French television?

M.A. – The first reason was that we had promised the three old ladies who talked about their sexuality that we wouldn't show it on T.V. in France as long as they lived, and that was a promise that was more important than the promise to the director of Nanterre, because you could destroy somebody's life if you did not keep it. Especially with the sixty-two year-old lady who had discovered physical love with her Robert – she hadn't told her children. She said it wouldn't matter if the film were shown in the cinema because her children didn't go to the cinema. They were very open, those ladies.

Bibliography

Althusser, Louis, *L'Avenir dure longtemps* (Paris: Stock/IMEC, 1994)

Améry, Jean, *Du Vieillissement. Révolte et résignation* (Paris: Payot, 1991) translated by Annick Yaiche (*Über das Altern*, Stuttgart: Klett, 1968)

Appignanesi, Lisa & Forrester, John, *Freud's Women* (London: Penguin, Second Edition 2000)

Arber, Sara & Ginn, Jay (eds.), *Connecting Gender and Ageing: a Sociological Approach*, (Buckingham and Philadelphia: Open University Press, 1995)

Bagnell, P. & Spencer Soper, P. (eds.), *Perceptions of Aging in Literature: A Cross-Cultural Study* (New York: Greenwood Press, 1989)

Bair, Deirdre, *Simone de Beauvoir: A Biography* (London: Vintage, 1990)

Baisnée, Valérie, *Gendered Resistance, The Autobiographies of Simone de Beauvoir, Maya Angelou, Janet Frame and Marguerite Duras* (Amsterdam & Altanta: Rodopi, 1997)

Barthes, Roland, *La Chambre claire. Note sur la photographie* (Paris: Gallimard/Seuil, 1980)

Baudelaire, Charles, *Les Fleurs du Mal*, ed. by Adam (Paris: Garnier, 1994)

Beauvoir, Simone de, *Le Deuxième Sexe* (Paris: Gallimard, 1949), vols. I & II

— , *Mémoires d'une jeune fille rangée* (Paris: Gallimard, 1958)

— , *La Force de l'âge* (Paris: Gallimard, 1960)

— , *La Force des choses* (Paris: Gallimard, 1963), vols. I & II

— , *Une Mort très douce* (Paris: Gallimard, 1964)

— , *La Vieillesse* (Paris: Gallimard, 1970)

— , *Tout Compte fait* (Paris: Gallimard, 1972)

— , *La Cérémonie des adieux* (Paris: Gallimard, 1981)

Berezin, M., 'Normal Psychology of the Aging Process, Revisited, II: The Fate of Narcissism in Old Age: Clinical Case Reports', *Journal of Geriatric Psychiatry*, vol. 10 (1977), 9-26

Bertin, Evelyne, *Gérontologie, Psychanalyse et déshumanisation: silence vieillesse* (Paris: L'Harmattan, 1999)

Bianchi, Henri, *Le Moi et le Temps: psychanalyse du temps et du vieillissement* (Paris: Dunod, 1987)

— (ed.), *La Question du vieillissement. Perspectives psychanalytiques* (Paris: Dunod, 1989)

Bieber, Konrad, *Simone de Beauvoir* (Boston: Twayne, 1979)

Biggs, Simon, *Understanding Ageing. Images, Attitudes and Professional Practice* (Buckingham: Open University Press, 1993)

— (ed.), *Journal of Social Work Practice*, Special issue: *Counselling and psychotherapy with older people*, vol. 12, no. 2 (November 1998)

Booth, Wayne (ed.), *The Art of Growing Older: Writers on Living and Aging* (Poseidon Press, 1992)

Boulé, Jean-Pierre, *Hervé Guibert: Voices of the Self* (Liverpool: Liverpool University Press, 1999)

Bowie, Malcolm, *Lacan* (London: Fontana, 1991)

Brady, J. (ed.), *Biological Timekeeping* (Cambridge: Cambridge University Press, 1982)

Brewi, Janice & Brennan, Anne, *Passion for Life: Lifelong Psychological and Spiritual Growth* (New York: Continuum, 1999)

Buisine, Alan, 'Le photographique plutôt que la photographie', *Nottingham French Studies*, vol. 34 (Spring 1995)

Buot, François, *Hervé Guibert. Le jeune homme et la mort* (Paris: Grasset, 1999)

Butler, Robert, 'Ageism: another form of bigotry', *Gerontologist* 9:243 (1969)

— , *Why Survive? Being Old in America* (New York: Harper & Row, 1975)

— , 'The Life Review: An Interpretation of Reminiscence in the Aged', in *Readings in Adult Psychology. Contemporary Perspectives*, ed. by Allman & Jaffe (New York: Harper & Row, 1982)

de Ceccatty, René, *Violette Leduc, Eloge de la Bâtarde* (Paris: Stock, 1994)

Charcot, J.-M., *Leçons sur les maladies des vieillards et les maladies chroniques* (Paris: Delahaye, 1868)

Cohler, Bertram, 'Adult Developmental Psychology and Reconstruction in Psychoanalysis', in *Adulthood and the Aging Process*, ed. by Greenspan & Pollock (Washington: NIMH, 1980), 459-85

Cole, T. & Gadow, S. (eds.), *What Does it Mean to Grow Old? Reflections from the Humanities*, (Durham: Duke University Press, 1986)

Cole, T.,Van Tassel, D. & Kastenbaum, R. (eds.), *Handbook of the Humanities and Aging*, (New York: Springer Publishing, 1992)

Cole, T., *The Journey of Life. A Cultural History of Aging in America* (Cambridge: Cambridge University Press, 1992)

Cole, T. (ed.), *Voices and Visions of Aging* (New York: Springer, 1993)

Cole, T. & Winkler, M., *The Oxford Book of Aging* (Oxford: OUP, 1994)

Comfort, Alex, *A Good Age* (New York: Crown, 1976)

de Courtivron, Isabelle, *Violette Leduc* (Boston: Twayne Publishers, 1985)

Dacher, Michèle & Weinstein, Micheline, *Histoire de Louise: des vieillards en hospice* (Paris: Seuil, 1979)

Daniels, Norman, *Am I My Parents' Keeper? An Essay on Justice Between the Young and the Old* (Oxford: Oxford University Press, 1988)

Danon-Boileau, Henri, *De la vieillesse à la mort: point de vue d'un usager* (Paris: Hachette, 2002)

Davis, Colin, *Ethical Issues in Twentieth-Century French Fiction: Killing the Other* (Basingstoke: Macmillan, 2000)

Davis, Oliver, 'The Ageing Process in *A la recherche du temps perdu*' (unpublished master's thesis, University of Oxford, no. K2832, 2001)

Dayan, Josée & Ribowska, Malka, *Simone de Beauvoir* [published film script] (Paris: Gallimard, 1979)

Deleuze, Gilles, *La Logique du sens* (Paris: Minuit, 1969)

Deutscher, Penelope, 'Bodies, Lost and Found: Simone de Beauvoir from *The Second Sex* to *Old Age*', *Radical Philosophy* 96: 6-16

— , 'Three touches to the skin and one look. Sartre and Beauvoir on desire and embodiment', in *Thinking Through the Skin*, ed. by Ahmed & Stacey (London: Routledge, 2001), pp. 143-159

— , 'Beauvoir's *Old Age*', in *The Cambridge Companion to Simone de Beauvoir*, ed. by Claudia Card (Cambridge: Cambridge University Press, 2003), ch. 14, pp. 286-304

Empson, William, *Seven Types of Ambiguity* (London: Chatto & Windus, 1947)

Erikson, E., *Childhood and Society* (New York: Norton, 1950)

— , *Identity and the Life Cycle* (New York: International University Press, 1959)

— , *The Life Cycle Completed: A Review* (New York: Norton, 1982)

Esposito, Joseph L., *The Obsolete Self. Philosophical Dimensions of Aging* (Berkeley: University of California Press, 1987)

Evans, Ruth (ed.), *Simone de Beauvoir's The Second Sex. New Interdisciplinary Essays*, (Manchester: Manchester University Press, 1998)

Fallaize, Elizabeth, *Simone de Beauvoir: a Critical Reader*, (London: Routledge, 1998)

Featherstone, Mike & Wernick, Andrew, *Images of Aging. Cultural Representations of Later Life* (London: Routledge, 1995)

Freeman, J.T., *Aging, its History and Literature* (New York: Humane Sciences Press, 1979)

Freud, Sigmund, 'Thoughts For The Times on War and Death' (1915), Standard Edition, vol. XIV, 273-302

—, 'Remembering, Repeating and Working-Through' (1914), S.E., 12, 145-156

—, 'Beyond the Pleasure Principle' (1920), Penguin Freud Library, vol. 11, *On Metapsychology* (London: Penguin, 1991), 269-338

—, 'On Psychotherapy' (1905), S.E. 7, 255-68

Furlong, Monica, *The End of Our Exploring* (London: Hodder & Stoughton, 1973)

Gannon, Linda R., *Women and Ageing. Transcending the Myths* (London: Routledge, 1999)

Gide, André, *Ainsi soit-il ou Les Jeux sont faits* (Paris: Gallimard, 1952)

— , *Journal* (Paris: Gallimard/Pléiade, 1996), vol. I, ed. by Eric Marty

— , *Journal* (Paris: Gallimard/Pléiade, 1997), vol. II, ed. by Martine Sagaert

Gilmore, Leigh, *Autobiographies. A Feminist Theory of Women's Self-Representation*, (Ithaca & London: Cornell University Press, 1994)

Girard, Pièr, *Oedipe masqué. Une lecture psychanalytique de L'Affamée de Violette Leduc* (Paris: des femmes, 1986)

Gorsuch, N., 'Time's Winged Chariot: Short-Term Psychotherapy in Later Life', *Psychodynamic Counselling*, vol. 4 (1998), 191-202

Gorz, André, 'Le Vieillissement', *Les Temps Modernes*, no.187, Dec. 1961 (Part I) and no. 188, Jan. 1962 (Part II)

Goudeket, Maurice, *La Douceur de vieillir* (Paris: Flammarion, 1965)

Green, André, *Narcissisme de vie et narcissisme de mort* (Paris: Minuit, 1983)

Grosclaude, Michèle, 'Mémoire, Souvenir, Savoir, Démence', in *Temps, vieillissement, société* (Paris: SOPEDIM, 1982), 117-36

Grotjahn, M., 'Psychoanalytic Investigation of a Seventy-one-year-old Man with Senile Dementia', *Psychoanalytic Quarterly*, vol. IX (1940), 80-97.

— , 'Some Analytic Observations About the Process of Growing Old', *Psychoanalysis and the Social Sciences*, vol. 3, 301-12.

— , 'Analytic Psychotherapy With the Elderly', *Psycho-Analytic Review*, 42, 419-27.

Guibert, Hervé, *La Mort propagande* (Paris: Desforges, 1977)

— , *Suzanne et Louise* (Paris: Editions Libres/Hallier, First Edition 1980; Second Edition Gallimard 2005)

— , *L'Image fantôme* (Paris: Minuit, 1981)

Guillain, Georges, *J.-M. Charcot. His Life, His Work*, translated by P. Bailey (London: Pitman, 1959)

Herfray, Charlotte, *La Vieillesse en analyse* (Paris: Desclée de Brouwer, 1988)

Holmes, Diana, 'Colette, Beauvoir and the Change of Life', *French Studies* LIII:4 (October 1999), 430-443

Howells, Christina, *Sartre: The Necessity of Freedom* (Cambridge: Cambridge University Press, 1988)

Hughes, Alex, *Violette Leduc: Mothers, Lovers, and Language* (London: Modern Humanities Research Association, 1994)

— , *Heterographies: Sexual Difference in French Autobiography*, (Oxford: Berg, 1999)

— , 'Reading Guibert's *L'Image fantôme*', *Modern and Contemporary France*, vol. 6, no. 2 (1998), 203-14

Idt, Geneviève, 'Simone de Beauvoir's *Adieux*: a funeral rite and a literary challenge', in Aronson & van den Hoven (eds.), *Sartre Alive*, (Detroit: Wayne State University Press, 1991)

Jaques, Elliott, 'Death and the mid-life crisis', *International Journal of Psycho-Analysis*, 46, 502-14. Reprinted in *Melanie Klein Today: Developments in Theory and Practice*, vol. 2: *Mainly Practice*, ed. by Elizabeth Bott Spillius (London: Routledge, 1988), 226-248. All page references are to reprint.

Jankélévitch, Vladimir, *La Mort* (Paris: Flammarion, 1966)

Jansiti, Carlo, *Violette Leduc* (Paris: Grasset, 1999)

Jeanson, Francis, *Simone de Beauvoir ou l'entreprise de vivre* (Paris: Seuil, 1966)

Jones, Ernest, *Papers on Psycho-Analysis* (London: Baillière, Tindall & Cox, 4th ed. 1938)

Jouhandeau, Marcel, *Réflexions sur la vieillesse et la mort* (Paris: Grasset, 1956)

Jung, 'The Stages of Life', in *Modern Man in Search of a Soul* (London: Routledge, 2001 edition), 97-116

Kadish, Doris Y., 'Simone de Beauvoir's *Une Mort très douce*: Existential and Feminist Perspectives on Old Age', *The French Review*, vol. 62, No. 4, March 1989, 631-639

King, Pearl, 'Notes on the Psychoanalysis of Older Patients. Reappraisal of the Potentialities for Change During the Second Half of Life', *Journal of Analytical Psychology* 19:1 (1974), 22-37

Reprinted in a revised version as 'In My End is My Beginning' in *Psychoanalysis and Culture: A Kleinian Perspective*, ed. by David Bell (London: Duckworth, 1999), 170-188

— , *International Journal of Psycho-Analysis* 61 (1980), 153-60

Kristeva, Julia, *La Révolution du langage poétique* (Paris: Seuil, 1974)

— , *Soleil noir. Dépression et mélancolie* (Paris: Gallimard, 1987)

Lacan, Jacques, *Ecrits* (Paris: Seuil, 1966)

— , *Encore* (Paris: Seuil, 1975)

Ladimer, Bethany, *Colette, Beauvoir, and Duras. Age and Women Writers*, (University Press of Florida, 1999)

Lawton, M. Powell & Salthouse, Timothy A. (eds.), *Essential Papers on the Psychology of Aging* (New York: New York University Press, 1998)

Leduc, Violette, *L'Asphyxie* (Paris: Gallimard, 1946)

— , *L'Affameé* (Paris: Gallimard, 1948)

— , *La Bâtarde* (Paris: Gallimard, 1964)

— , *La Folie en tête* (Paris: Gallimard, 1970)

— , *La Chasse à l'amour* (Paris: Gallimard, 1973)

Lehman, *Age and Achievement* (Princeton: Princeton University Press, 1953)

Lejeune, Philippe, *Le Pacte autobiographique* (Paris: Seuil, 1975)

Marks, Elaine, *Simone de Beauvoir. Encounters with Death*, (New Brunswick: Rutgers University Press, 1973)

—, 'Transgressing the (In)cont(in)ent Boundaries: The Body in Decline', in *Simone de Beauvoir: Witness to a Century* (*Yale French Studies*, no. 72), ed. by Wenzel (New Haven and London: Yale University Press, 1986), 180-200

Mannoni, Octave, 'Relation d'un sujet à sa propre vie', *Les Temps Modernes*, no. 528 (July 1990), pp. 55-77

Marson, Susan, *Le Temps de l'autobiographie: Violette Leduc ou la mort avant la lettre*, (Paris: Presses Universitaires de Vincennes, 1998)

—, 'The Beginning of the End: Time and Identity in the Autobiography of Violette Leduc', *Sites* 2:1 (1998), 69-87

Messy, Jack, *La Personne âgée n'existe pas: une approche psychanalytique de la vieillesse* (Paris: Payot & Rivages, 1994, repr. 2002). References are to 2002 edition

Micale, Mark, 'The Saplêtrière in the Age of Charcot: An Institutional Perspective on Medical History in the Late Nineteenth Century', *Journal of Contemporary History*, vol. 20 (1985), 703-31

Minois, Georges, *Histoire de la vieillesse en Occident de l'Antiquité à la Renaissance* (Paris: Fayard, 1987)

Mitchell, Juliet, *Mad Men and Medusas. Reclaiming Hysteria and the Effect of Sibling Relationships on the Human Condition* (London: Allen Lane/Penguin, 2000)

Moi, Toril, *Simone de Beauvoir: the Making of an Intellectual Woman* (Oxford: Blackwell, 1994)

Montaigne, *Essais* (Paris: Garnier-Flammarion, 1969)

Montandon, Alain (ed.), *Ecrire le vieillir* (Clermont-Ferrand: Presses Universitaires Blaise Pascal, 2005)

Nemiroff, Robert & Colarusso, Calvin (eds.), *The Race Against Time: Psychotherapy and Psychoanalysis in the Second Half of Life* (New York: Plenum, 1985)

Neuman, S. (ed.), *Autobiography and Questions of Gender*, (London: Cassell, 1991)

Okely, Judith, *Simone de Beauvoir, a Re-reading*, (London: Virago, 1986)

Péquignot, Henri, *Vieillesses de demain. Vieillir et être vieux* (Paris: Vrin, 1986)

Philibert, Michel, *Les Echelles d'âge dans la philosophie, la science et la société. De leur renversement et des conditions de leur redressement* (Paris: Seuil, 1968)

Porter & Porter, *Aging in Literature*, (Troy, Michigan: International Book Publishers, 1984)

Procès-verbal de la Fête de la vieillesse. 5ème Arrondissement (Paris: Lemaire, An 6)

Renard, Paul & Jansiti, Carlo, *Violette Leduc*, special edition of *nord' Revue de critique et de création littéraire du nord/pas-de-calais*, no. 23 (June 1994), (Lille: Centre National des Lettres)

Rétif, F., 'Simone de Beauvoir et l'autre', *Les Temps Modernes,* no.538 (1991)

— , *Simone de Beauvoir. L'autre en miroir*, (Paris: L'Harmattan, 1998)

Rodgers, Catherine, *Le Deuxième Sexe de Simone de Beauvoir. Un héritage admiré et contesté* (Paris: L'Harmattan, 1998)

Sandblom, Philip, *Creativity and Disease: How Illness Affects Literature, Art, and Music* (New York: Boyars, 1995)

Schilder, Paul, *The Image and Appearance of the Human Body. Studies in the Constructive Energies of the Psyche* (New York: Wiley, 1950)

Schneider, Monique, *Généalogie du masculin* (Paris: Aubier, 2000)

Schur, Max, *Freud: Living and Dying* (London: Hogarth/Institute of Psycho-Analysis, 1972)

Schwartz, Murray & Woodward, Kathleen (eds.), *Memory and Desire* (Bloomington: Indiana University Press, 1986)

Sears, Elizabeth, *The Ages of Man* (Princeton: Princeton University Press, 1986)

Segal, Hanna, 'Fear of Death: Notes on the Analysis of an Old Man', *International Journal of Psycho-Analysis*, vol. 39 (1958), 178-81.

Segal, Naomi, *André Gide: Pederasty and Pedagogy* (Oxford: Oxford University Press, 1998)

Settlage, Calvin, 'Transcending Old Age: Creativity, Development and Psychoanalysis in the Life of a Centenarian', *International Journal of Psycho-Analysis* 77 (1996), 549-564

Sheridan, Alan, *André Gide: A Life in the Present* (London: Hamish Hamilton, 1998)

Shildrick, Margrit, *Leaky Bodies and Boundaries: Feminism, Postmodernism and (Bio)ethics*, (London: Routledge, 1997)

— & Price, Janet (eds.), *Vital Signs: Feminist Reconfigurations of the Bio/logical Body* (Edinburgh: Edinburgh University Press, 1998)

Simons, Margaret, *Feminist Interpretations of Simone de Beauvoir*, (Pennsylvania: Pennsylvania State University Press, 1995)

Sokoloff, Janice, *The Margin that Remains: A Study of Aging in Literature* (New York: Peter Lang, 1987)

Song, Ryan, 'Comparative Figures of Ageing in the Memoirs of Colette and Beauvoir: Corporeality, Infirmity, Identity', in *Corporeal Practices. (Re)figuring the Body in French Studies*, ed. by Prest & Thompson (Bern: Lang, 2000), pp.78-89

Sontag, Susan, *On Photography* (London: Allen Lane, 1978)

— , 'The Double Standard of Aging', in *Readings in Adult Psychology. Contemporary Perspectives*, ed. by Allman & Jaffe (New York: Harper & Row, 1982), pp. 324-333

Stearns, P., *Old Age and European Society: The Case of France* (London: Croom Helm, 1977)

Stanley, L., *The Autobiographical I: the Theory and Practice of Feminist Autobiography*, (Manchester: Manchester University Press, 1992)

Stuart-Hamilton, Ian, *The Psychology of Ageing: An Introduction*, 3rd Edition (London: Kingsley, 2000)

Svevo, Italo, *As A Man Grows Older*, tr. by Beryl de Zoete (London: Putnam, 2nd Edition 1949)

Tidd, Ursula, *Simone de Beauvoir: Gender and Testimony*, (Cambridge: Cambridge University Press, 1999)

Tinker, Anthea, *Elderly People in Modern Society* (London: Longman, 3rd Edition 1992)

Veysset, Bernadette, *Dépendance et vieillissement* (Paris: L'Harmattan, 1989)

Waller, Margaret, *The Male Malady: Fictions of Impotence in the French Romantic Novel* (New Brunswick: Rutgers University Press, 1993)

Weatherill, Rob (ed.), *The Death Drive: New Life for a Dead Subject?* (London: Rebus, 1999)

Wenzel, Hélène, *Simone de Beauvoir: Witness to a Century*, Yale *French Studies*, no. 72 (New Haven and London: Yale University Press, 1986)

Woodward, Kathleen & Schwartz, Murray (eds.), *Memory and Desire: Aging, Literature, Psychoanalysis* (Bloomington: Indiana University Press, 1986)

Woodward, Kathleen, 'Simone de Beauvoir: Aging and its Discontents', in *The Private Self. Theory and Practice of Women's Autobiographical Writings*, ed. by Benstock (London: Routledge, 1988), 90-113

— , *Aging and its Discontents: Freud and other Fictions* (Bloomington: Indiana University Press, 1991)

Wyatt-Brown & Rossen, Janice (eds.), *Aging and Gender in Literature*, (Charlottesville: University Press of Virginia, 1993)

Yahnke, Robert & Eastman, Richard, *Literature and Gerontology: A Research Guide* (London: Greenwood Press, 1995)

Zarit, Steven, *Readings in Aging and Death* (New York: Harper & Row, 1977)

Zerilli, Linda, '"I am a woman": female voice and ambiguity in *The Second Sex*', *Women in Politics*, 11:1 (1991), 93-108

— 'A process without a subject', *Signs*, 18:1 (1992)

Index